THE
EVERYTHING® JEWISH WEDDING BOOK

Dear Reader,

I am an Orthodox rabbi who has performed a wide variety of Jewish weddings. I have found Jewish wedding books that are accessible but not fully traditional and Jewish wedding books that are very traditional but not accessible to most readers. It is my hope that this book will fill the gap. It is written in accord with Jewish legal tradition; at the same time, it is meant to be fully accessible and useful to both the learned and the unversed.

Weddings among the Jewish people today are extremely varied depending on the couple's rabbi and denomination; how religious, learned, or observant the couple is; and myriad other factors. I believe that Jewish law and tradition have much to teach us, even if we do not observe it all or do not think it fully relevant. My hope is that you will take the information and ideas I have included and use them to weave your wedding into a tapestry that is deeply Jewish, personally meaningful, and inspiringly spiritual. May the One who spends eternity matchmaking bless you with a meaningful wedding and loving life together, and may you build a *bayit neeman b'yisrael*—a trustworthy house among the Jewish People.

Rabbi Hyim Shafner

Welcome to the EVERYTHING® Series!

These handy, accessible books give you all you need to tackle a difficult project, gain a new hobby, comprehend a fascinating topic, prepare for an exam, or even brush up on something you learned back in school but have since forgotten.

You can choose to read an *Everything*® book from cover to cover or just pick out the information you want from our four useful boxes: e-questions, e-facts, e-alerts, and e-essentials. We give you everything you need to know on the subject, but throw in a lot of fun stuff along the way, too.

We now have more than 400 *Everything*® books in print, spanning such wide-ranging categories as weddings, pregnancy, cooking, music instruction, foreign language, crafts, pets, New Age, and so much more. When you're done reading them all, you can finally say you know *Everything*®!

Answers to common questions

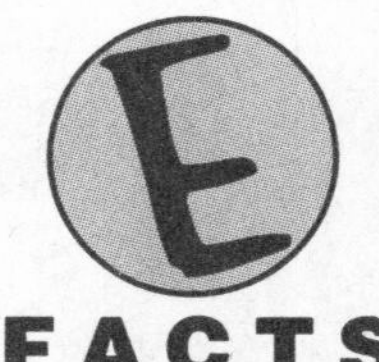

Important snippets of information

Urgent warnings

Quick handy tips

PUBLISHER Karen Cooper

DIRECTOR OF ACQUISITIONS AND INNOVATION Paula Munier

MANAGING EDITOR, EVERYTHING SERIES Lisa Laing

COPY CHIEF Casey Ebert

ACQUISITIONS EDITOR Katie McDonough

ASSOCIATE DEVELOPMENT EDITOR Elizabeth Kassab

EDITORIAL ASSISTANT Hillary Thompson

THE EVERYTHING® JEWISH WEDDING BOOK

2nd Edition

Mazel tov! From the chuppah to the hora, all you need for your big day

Rabbi Hyim Shafner

adamsmedia
Avon, Massachusetts

To my parents, who made the dough; my brothers, family, and teachers, who kneaded it; my ezer kinegdi, *sugar and spice; and our children, new loaves from ancient yeast.*

An Everything® Series Book.
Everything® and everything.com® are registered trademarks of F+W Media, Inc.

Published by Adams Media, an F+W Media Company
57 Littlefield Street, Avon, MA 02322 U.S.A.
www.adamsmedia.com

ISBN 10: 1-59869-548-7
ISBN 13: 978-1-59869-548-9

Printed in the United States of America.

J I H G F E D C B A

Library of Congress Cataloging-in-Publication Data
is available from the publisher.

Contents

Acknowledgments

My biggest thanks go to my wife Sara, whose trust, love, and teaching have enabled us to have a wonderful marriage and life together. She gave up nights out and time together so I could write this book and still offered support and encouragement, constantly reassuring me that my efforts were good for the Jewish people. Hopefully when our children's weddings come we will once again be able to stand talking about weddings. Thank you to Lee, who convinced me the book was needed. To my parents, whom I can never even begin to thank for their example of a good and loving marriage, for their love and sacrifices in giving me a Jewish education and teaching us a toraht chesed—that the Torah must inspire all people and make God's world better—and for teaching me that the Jewish people can be one and that the universe was made by *Hashem* and so must be of value. Thank you to my children, Benny, Yonah, and Hava, for putting up with my time spent writing even while asking me how I could still be doing it—"It must be a million pages!"

Thank you to those in my community who put so much effort into reading chapters and drafts and offering advice and insight; I beg forgiveness if I have left anyone out. To my dedicated professional reader and advisor Dalia Oppenheimer. To Jen Lottsoff, Rabbi Hershey and Chana Novack, Sharon and Russel Roberts, Suzanne Pritzker, Andy Love, Shane Graber, Heather and Jonathan Douek, Eva Gardner, Keren Douek, Phyllis Shapiro, Ben Alpert, Judy Winkelman Seplow, Dick Seplow, and Jeff Glogower, who all spent time reading and giving me much valued input. My thanks to our humble loving teacher, Rabbi Abraham Magence, *zt"l*, who entrusted me with his holy and supportive community. My thanks to the Infinite Creator who gave me years in this universe, so strange and beautiful, and the special learning opportunities, resources, family, and *mazal* that I have had. May I merit using it all to serve the Jewish people and to help make God's world a place of great *tikun*, love, and many happy and peaceful marriages.

Top Ten Unforgettable Jewish Wedding Moments

1. Eruptions of "Mazel tov!" with the breaking of the glass.
2. The groom seeing the bride at the *bedekin* for the first time after days apart.
3. Making a l'chaim at the *tish* with very old scotch.
4. Eating for the first time all day, and for the first time as husband and wife, in the *yichud* room together.
5. The mothers of the bride and groom trying their darndest to break the too-thick plate.
6. Seeing your best friend in a gorilla suit doing wedding shtick, dancing and jumping rope in the middle of the dance floor.
7. Lifting the bride and groom up on chairs at the dancing while they hold on for dear life.
8. A relieved groom not being able to get more than a few words of Torah out before the crowd erupts in loud song.
9. Dancing so wild that everyone, including the bride, is sweating profusely.
10. The bride and groom, even at the biggest moment of their lives, thinking about and praying for others in need.

Introduction

▶ IN A JEWISH life there are many special moments, a bris (circumcision celebration) or baby naming when one is born, a bar or bat mitzvah when one matures, and numerous other holidays, parties, achievements, and milestones. A wedding is perhaps the most momentous occasion of them all. It is one that will define the rest of an individual's life because the person you marry strongly influences how you will live your life. Who you marry will, over time, color your view of the world, your opinions on raising children, your perception of what is valuable, and the meaning of your individual life.

The formal idea of marriage in Judaism goes back to the Torah, the Bible, given to the Jewish people more than 3,500 years ago. However, the concept of two people, a man and woman, being alone and then finding each other, becoming bound to each other forever, and raising a family together, goes back all the way to Adam and Eve. Thus, in Judaism, weddings are seen as one of the foundational concepts upon which the world is built.

Your wedding is, of course, going to be a special day to you, one into which you will put much preparation, anxiety, and forethought. From a larger Jewish perspective, though, your wedding is much more. It is a moment within which all of history is encapsulated, upon which everything hinges. Your wedding moment harkens back to the first moments of the universe—the wedding of Eve and Adam—and your wedding day is the foundation upon which the rest of the future of the humanity and your people is to be built. The Talmud in the book of Sanhedrin teaches that just as in the Torah all of humanity blossomed from one man and women, so too, "each person is equivalent to an entire universe."

Jewish people are all very different but hopefully this book will help you, wherever you stand within Judaism, to guide you in planning your wedding, to give you a sense of the different Jewish practices associated with weddings and their beauty, and to help you shape your own wedding into one that is meaningful and spiritually inspiring. This may not be the only wedding book you will use; if your wedding is one that is more to the creative side or one that is more on the traditional side, additional books and websites will help you to fill out the complete picture of your wedding day. Some of these references can be found in Appendix D.

There will be times in the process of planning your wedding that will be anxious, other times that will be reflective, and still others that will be fun. Use this book to learn about the potential that each part of a Jewish wedding holds and to help navigate some of the more complex situations that planning a wedding can inevitably bring.

This book includes Jewish historical and theological perspectives along with, obviously, a lot of practical advice. A well-planned wedding is a good balance of all of these—practical and well choreographed, but also infused with Jewish meaning, spirituality, and history.

This book will be useful in learning the traditional Jewish perspective and practices and some ways that they can be adjusted. Depending on whom your rabbi or wedding officiate is going to be and on what part of the Jewish community you and your family identify with, you may decide to do things in the way that they are described in this book or perhaps very differently. As you read, know that you can take the basics of the tradition and tailor them to fit you and make your wedding meaningful. No matter how your Jewish wedding will look, crafting your wedding from a place of knowledge of Jewish history and tradition will be a positive approach. Best wishes for a great and inspiring Jewish wedding!

CHAPTER 1

Love and Partnership, Jewish Style

In Jewish thought, marriage—and the love that should be part of it—is not only realistic and practical but also, at the same time, unifying and profound. A marriage relationship, since both partners become a greater whole through it, is perhaps the most important and powerful one in life. Jewish mysticism even teaches that in order to understand our relationship to God, we must first know a relationship of love with another human that is so encompassing we become one on an emotional, physical, and spiritual level.

Jewish Views of Love

Judaism's most ancient and basic book, the Torah, depicts several examples of love relationships. A close look at the first one of these can reveal a great deal about Judaism's insights into love, relationships, and marriage.

Adam and Eve: The First Love

The first couple in the Torah is Eve and Adam. There are actually two versions of the story of the creation of and the relationship between Adam and Eve. In the first chapter of the Torah, Adam and Eve are created at the same time in the image of God and are then sent off together into the world. In the second chapter of the Torah, Adam is created first and is all alone in the world in the Garden of Eden. God looks at Adam and declares, "It is not good for the Man to be alone; I must make for him an *ezer kinegdo.*" The words *ezer kinegdo* mean a helper opposite him, or more literally translated, "a supporter against him." In an attempt to find Adam a mate, an *ezer kinegdo*, God creates all the animals and brings them to Adam.

What had God been doing since he created the world?
This is the Talmud's question and the answer it gives is that God is busy making marriage matches, and, says the Talmud, it is as hard as splitting the Red Sea!

In the biblical story, Adam gets to know and names each one of the animals but can not find among them an *ezer kinegdo*, a proper mate. God puts Adam to sleep and makes Eve from his rib. When Adam wakes he suddenly realizes that the woman standing before him is the right mate for him. According to Jewish tradition they were married by God in the Garden of Eden (with no caterer!) on the sixth day of creation just before the first Shabbat, the first Sabbath.

True Love Is Supportive and Challenging

The name the Torah uses for mate is both very strange and very telling. Adam's mate must be a "helper against him." Though these terms seem contradictory, Eve and Adam must be to each other mutual helpers and supporters, but they must also challenge each other.

The Torah here is teaching a profound idea. A true love relationship is one in which there is so much trust, concern, and deep understanding that the two partners support and love each other, and because of this support and trust they can also challenge each other to become better people than they are now. Though it takes work, a couple can help each other grow as individuals. Their relationship will grow and deepen in turn.

FACT

There is a concept in Judaism called a *bashert*, (as in, "He is my *bashert*!") a soul mate that you are destined to marry. Though some Jewish sources believe that there is one *bashert* for each person; others feel we often have many potential mates, and the one we commit to and make a great relationship with over time becomes our bashert.

Soul Mates

When asked to describe what they love about each other, many couples say they have similar values and goals in life and support each other, but that they also appreciate having very different, often opposite, personalities. They almost always describe balancing each other, completing each other, or challenging each other just by being so different from one another. Just like Adam and Eve, in great relationships partners support each other but also confront each other and thus nurture one another to grow personally, emotionally, and spiritually.

According to the Midrash, an ancient Jewish commentary on the Torah, both stories of the creation of Adam and Eve can be read as one story. According to this reading, Adam and Eve were first created as one person with two faces, back to back, and then divided into two independent beings.

Thus their ultimate marriage is a linking of true soul mates, two people who once shared one body and soul and are now reunited. This becomes forever a paradigm of human relationships. When we find our soul mate or grow our relationship with our spouse, we often feel completed, as if we have found our other half.

FACT

> The story is told of the renowned Rabbi Aaron Kotler who was being driven to a big lecture he was going to give. Just after getting in the car the Rabbi excused himself and went back into his house to wish his wife a good day, thus reflecting the Talmud's dictum that a married couple are truly one and that a man should honor his spouse more than himself.

In this scenario, Adam and Eve must first be separated from each other before finding each other as soul mates and coming together again. This teaches us that independence, becoming ourselves as unique individuals and truly knowing ourselves, is a necessary prerequisite for a healthy relationship with another person. If a couple has not come to comfortably be themselves first and know themselves well, if they are too emotionally needy and unable to be emotionally present for each other, a deep love relationship of support and challenge cannot fully come to be. These are the foundations for true and long lasting *ezer kinegdo* love.

Some questions to ask ourselves in measuring whether a relationship has the potential to become a lasting marriage are: Do I feel I can be myself with this person? Do we trust each other? Do I feel better or worse about myself when I am with them? Do we value similar things in life?

Jewish Views of Marriage

There are several instances of people courting, meeting, and marrying each other in the Torah. Two of the earliest ones in the family of the Jewish people are exceptional and quite different from each other: that of Rebecca and Isaac and that of Rachel and Jacob. We will look at both as a way to see that just as people are diverse, so too are their relationships. The resulting engagement and wedding processes are also different. There are profound lessons to be learned from these paradigmatic relationships, and they have many things in common with many of our own engagements and marriages.

Isaac and Rebecca

In the Bible, Abraham and Sara, the first Jewish couple, have a son named Isaac. When they decide it is time for Isaac to marry, Abraham sends his servant Eliezar to Abraham's own extended family, who live in his hometown of Padan Aram in Mesopotamia, to find a wife for Isaac. Eliezer does not know who the woman should be, so he makes a deal with God. Eliezer says that when he first gets to the city and goes to the water well, whichever woman greets him, offers him water, and offers to get water for his camels will be the woman for Isaac to marry.

FACT

In many traditional societies, people are married without knowing or seeing each other first. The Talmud, Judaism's most basic book of law and tradition, forbids this. If a couple gets married without knowing each other and finds they do not like each other this would be a violation of the biblical command to "love your neighbor as yourself."

At first glance, looking for a woman or man who draws water for a stranger's camels does not necessarily seem like a good way to find a spouse. Perhaps Eliezer should have asked about her interests, her goals in life, or her philosophy about raising children to be sure she would be a good fit for Isaac. The Torah here is really teaching us a profound marriage lesson: The most important criterion in finding a mate, the most important factor in making a relationship work, is the personal character of the two partners. No doubt similar values are important, but two people need not have the same desires, likes and dislikes, or even life experiences to make a deep and lasting relationship. Being able to be present and emotionally available and having some similar values are important, but the Torah places each others' character above everything else. Both parties must be able to see beyond themselves to be kind and giving to each other.

Marriage Before Love?

When Eliezer brings Rebecca back to see Isaac, she sees Isaac from afar praying in a field and she asks Eliezer if that is Isaac. Eliezer says yes, and Rebecca proceeds to cover her face with a veil. Rebecca and Isaac meet and immediately get married. After they marry and move into the same tent together the Torah tells us that Isaac loved Rebecca.

Not every story of love and marriage is the same in the Torah or in our lives, but it is important to realize that love can grow over time. Sometimes we expect love to be much more like a movie with fireworks and love at first sight, or at least for it to be so by the time we stand under the chuppah together. However, it is often the case that two mature and giving people will nurture their love slowly into a deep bond. As long as the right ingredients and values are present, you can ignore your normal wedding day jitters and rest assured that, with the right work and attention, your relationship will grow even deeper over time.

Not All Marriages Are the Same

Isaac and Rebecca's son Jacob is very different from his parents and so meets and marries his spouse in a very different manner.

Jacob and Rachel

Rachel and Jacob meet in a very different way than Jacob's parents Isaac and Rebecca. Jacob is running away from his brother Esah, who is trying to kill him, and Rebecca tells Jacob to run to his Uncle Laban's home. When he is near his destination he sees some shepherds near a water well about to give water to their flocks of sheep. He asks them if they know his Uncle Laban and they say yes. "And look," they say, "here comes his daughter Rachel with Laban's flocks of sheep." Jacob then asks them why they are standing around the well and they reply that they have to remove the heavy rock from the top of the well to give their sheep water.

Jacob looks over at Rachel, who is approaching with her families' sheep, and single-handedly lifts the rock off of the well. He then gives water to the

Rachel's sheep, kisses Rachel, and weeps. Jacob tells Rachel who he is and she runs to tell her family.

Though Jacob and Rachel's story involves both a well and and one future spouse is helping and giving water to the other, Jacob's love for Rachel and the way he expresses it is clearly very different from that of his father and mother, Isaac and Rebecca. While Rebecca and Isaac's love for each other needs time to grow, Jacob is deeply moved by his love for Rachel even at first sight. However, he will have to work for fourteen years for his uncle Laban to finally marry Rachel, and he does the work willingly since he loves her so much.

Learning from Our Ancestors

Though the relationship that Jacob and Rachel have is so different from the one Isaac and Rebecca nurture, there is much to learn from both. Whether it is love at first sight or love that grows over time and even after marriage, the important aspects of keeping a relationship going are both partners' ability to give to one another deep loyalty like Jacob's for Rachel—even over the course of many years—and a vision of their future together. Judaism teaches that like the love of our ancestors, every relationship plays an important part in a much bigger picture of our world and the future that will emerge from the relationship. If you and your fiancé have similar values and you fit into a bigger meaningful worldview beyond your love for each other, you will always feel joined as one.

How to Know if He or She Is the One

We all know that some of the signs of a good relationship—feelings of joy when you are around the other person, feeling excitement at seeing them, feeling that you can "be yourself" with them, and feeling trust between you. When we realize that the other person appreciates who we are and they will not leave the relationship without first coming to a decision about the relationship together, this is a sign of trust.

Real Life, Real Relationships

We sometimes think our relationships should be like those we see in the movies. Boy and girl meet, fall in love, there's background music, and they ride off into the sunset together. It's great for a two-hour movie, but we must be careful not to think that it's a reflection of real life or a true possibility in a real human relationship. In real relationships, couples wake up the next day and need to negotiate who will do the laundry.

Similar levels of education can be important in a marriage. Ideally, spouses should be able to discover the world, life, and each other together. In a good relationship they should be able to discuss ideas and their life's goals, direction, hopes, and dreams together. These are important parts of any good relationship.

Of course, real life does not have to take away from great relationships. In great relationships the trust and love is strong and people can learn how to negotiate without threatening to end the relationship. They can appreciate their spouse's great qualities while knowing that they, like all of us, might not be good at everything.

Sometimes men think that even if they have trouble being emotionally present they can overcome the gap between them and their partner by buying material things. Gifts in a marriage are only meaningful if they reflect a deeper relationship in which one loves and respects the other and is willing to engage in conversation, support, and a sharing of lives.

In Jewish thought, marriage is not just the official seal on a good relationship or even a sanctified ceremony. It reflects a genuine desire to give to the other person. If both people feel they have a duty to give to and support the other, if both partners feel they are doing more than their share, the marriage will work. While having our needs met is important, one should always ask not what their spouse can do for them but what they can do for their spouse.

Respect

In good relationships, spouses have a deep sense of respect for one another. While knowing their partner's challenges, they usually see their partner's strengths more clearly. This does not mean they think their partner is better than them. Instead, they appreciate that their partner is different and that as a couple they can cover a lot of bases together.

People are much more flexible than we realize, and they often change over time. It is not uncommon for couples who have been married for many years to be surprised by their spouses. The things they thought their spouse liked when they married may not be the same now. Seeing our marriages not only as perfect or made in heaven, but as an ongoing work of art makes for patient and understanding spouses.

Overcoming Marriage Anxiety

Almost everyone is anxious at times about their approaching wedding and marriage. They might be nervous about the doors they are closing to other relationships and to other life opportunities or the compromises they will have to make in their career. A certain degree of anxiety is normal, but some anxiety can be a warning signal that something is not right in the relationship and should be looked at more carefully before the couple commits to a lifetime together.

Normal Anxiety Versus Red Flags

One good way to put your anxiety into perspective is to remember a time when you were embarking on something new. Think about your first day at a new school or job, or remember your last big purchase. Were you this anxious then? Have you felt this anxiety in serious relationships before? Does this anxiety feel similar or very different? Do you feel you can share this anxiety with your future spouse? If you can, that is a sign of a good relationship. You are feeling the effects of the standard pre-engagement or pre-wedding anxiety. If you cannot put your finger on the feeling, or if the anxiety expresses itself in your mind by becoming critical of your future husband or wife, this may be cause for some further exploration of the relationship with a counselor or rabbi.

There is a great story about two friends, Bob and Bill. Bob fixes Bill up with one woman after another, and when Bob asks about them Bill complains that one was too short, another was not funny enough, and another was too heavy. Finally, exasperated, Bob says, "Hey Bill, lighten up, it's not like you're buying a new car or something!" The lesson is a good one. Each individual person is complex. No one will ever fit a laundry list of what you want, but that is part of the beauty of marrying a real person. They are not perfect; they are just themselves. This is what makes life exciting and helps each spouse in a relationship grow over time.

How would you feel if your fiancé was not there any more? This can be an important question to ask yourself when you feel pre-marriage anxiety. It might help you ascertain if it is regular nervousness or some bigger issue in the relationship or in how you see each other.

Talking to other people who know you both can also be helpful. What do your close friends and relatives sense about your relationship? Does it seem healthy, mutual, and mature from the outside? How did they feel when they were getting engaged? This may help you get some perspective and find out if your own level of anxiety is typical. If your fiancé is feeling anxious, talking to others may help you remember that your fiancé's anxiety may be very normal and is not an implicit criticism of you.

Trying to Change Your Fiancé

If you find yourself hoping that after you get married your spouse will change, this is a cause for concern. Going into a marriage wanting to change someone is not healthy and puts an undue burden on any relationship. While people do change, one must go into a marriage with the expectation that what you have experienced with your future life partner and how you see them is what you will be getting.

If you are stuck between the two poles of "am I just blowing some issues out of proportion?" and "what if these issues continue to bother me forever in this marriage?" it might be good to seek the counseling of a professional to help sort it out.

CHAPTER 2

Getting Engaged

Impending wedding plans. Telling your friends and family. Hoping for everyone's approval and blessings. While becoming engaged can be a stressful time, it should also be a time of great joy and anticipation. There are many Jewish customs associated with engagement announcements, parties, and traditions, some of which are more essential than others. These customs will help you to make this meaningful and joyous step in the marriage process one to share with those you love and with the new relatives who will soon enter your family.

When Is It Time to Make It Official?

There is no hard and fast rule as to how long to date before becoming engaged, and many factors may enter into the couple's decision. In some Jewish communities there is strong emphasis on getting engaged quickly, after five to ten dates, while among others a couple might date for several months or years before deciding to become engaged. In any case, care should be taken to be sure the couple knows each other well enough and has gotten to know each other's families since they will be part of the couple's life for many years to come.

Enclosed Orthodox Communities

In Jewish communities that are insular and homogeneous, people tend to only see each other or date a few times before becoming engaged. In these Jewish communities the couple's families will often know each other already, and the man and woman who are becoming engaged will have grown up in very similar, quite traditionally observant Jewish backgrounds. Even before dating, the families or a *shadchan*, a matchmaker, will have "checked out" the man and woman, receiving confidential reports from their friends and families to be sure the two are compatible before they ever meet.

FACT

In more traditional Jewish circles people often meet though *shadchanim*. When the couple actually does get engaged or married there is usually a customary matchmaker's fee to be paid to the *shadchan*.

Couples such as these usually have the same religious values, the same goals, and the same picture of what they want their future family to look like. For couples from such well-defined and close-knit religious communities, though the dating period is very short, the prospects for a marriage that works well are promising. Indeed, for these couples, much of their dating process and getting to know each other revolves around thinking about and comparing notes on how they see the building of a Jewish family together.

Traditional Communities and Open Orthodox Communities

Observant or traditional Jews who are from more heterogeneous communities may need to take more time to get to know each other to be sure the proposed relationship is one that will work. More modern observant Jews are usually knowledgeable about the world and well educated in the secular realm, often attending universities and other institutions of higher general learning. Though their religious practices will be similar, couples who are not from an insular Jewish community and have spent time in the world outside a Jewish community will need more time to get to know each other to be sure that the person they are dating has similar values, goals, and outlooks. The amount of time spent together before becoming engaged in these communities will often range from several months to a year or two.

The dating process for more modern Orthodox Jews may be longer than that of their more insular orthodox brethren, but at the same time they will feel bound by traditional Jewish law, not having sex or touching intimately before marriage. This can result in some difficult tension for the couple between their Jewish commitment and their prolonged desire for each other.

Liberal Jewish Denominations

More liberal Jewish denominations have fewer rules about the process and timeline of engagement. Conservative Jews believe in conforming to Jewish law and limiting their sexual activity to marriage, perhaps encouraging a slightly faster engagement than other more liberal denominations who may or may not discourage premarital sex. In the end, though, the time spent dating before an engagement is announced is for the most part up to the couple and their family and is quite flexible among more liberal Jewish communities and denominations.

If the bride and groom hail from different Jewish communities or backgrounds altogether, the process of being sure he or she is the one may be particularly challenging. When done with forethought, care, and a willingness to learn from each other's differences, couples can build a trusting and long-lasting relationship and marriage. Some questions to ask yourselves and each other are: What religious traditions are must-haves for each of you? Which are compulsory right now and which can be grown into? Do you both have an attitude of religious growth? Can you compromise?

Sometimes understanding each other's religious life well is more important than changing your practices to be the same. In any case, couples who have different Jewish backgrounds often find that making time for Jewish study together can help each partner develop a clear view of the other's religious life and Jewish practice in general.

Engagement Customs

There are many ways for a couple to become officially engaged. Though traditionally we imagine the man on one knee asking for a woman's hand in marriage, some couples become engaged after talking about it together and deciding that it's time—without a ring, a bended knee, or a billboard in Times Square. Though in many instances it is expected that the man will propose to the woman, for some couples it's quite appropriate and flattering for a woman to propose, or to decide together.

Proposing

If you are going to propose, give it some thought. The process of proposing should reflect your personalities. Just because one friend rented a camel and dressed up as a sheik with an entourage to propose and another had an engagement ring baked into his girlfriend's dessert (risking serious dental mishaps), you do not have to follow their examples. When it comes to proposing, be sure that it's real, that it is a moment to remember, and that you are both involved in the intimacy of it instead of putting on a show for the neighborhood or trying to live out one partner's dramatic fantasies.

Men can set a good foundation for marriage by realizing that most women appreciate forethought and planning but do not expect you to be someone you are not.

Think about the person you are proposing to. What would make him happy? Is he shy by nature, in which case he might not want a large audience at the proposal? You might propose over a quiet dinner rather than asking the band to sing it for you. On the other hand, perhaps she appreciates drama and would love you to go to lots of trouble to set up something larger than life. In such a case you can rent out a digital billboard in Times Square with the words "Marry Me!" blinking in big lights as you turn the most populous corner in the world at 42nd Street and Broadway.

FACT

In the Talmud (Kiddushin 12b), a marriage proposal is known as *shidduchin* and is seen as a step in forming the legal bond that will become a full-fledged marriage. To marry without first proposing formally was considered immoral.

The Ring

In many instances the groom gives the bride a diamond engagement ring, but this is by no means always the case, nor is it required. You might decide together to get a simpler ring and save the money for a down payment on a future home or for the wedding or honeymoon. If the groom does decide to buy a ring, there are many ways he can do so. The couple can go together to choose one the bride likes and the groom can afford, or they can ask their families about heirloom diamonds and use one in its current setting or have the diamond reset to fit the bride's finger and personality.

The custom of a groom giving the bride a gift of jewelry goes back thousands of years in Jewish tradition. This piece of jewelry sometimes had a stone in it to set it apart from a wedding ring, which has no stone. Of course, the stone in an engagement ring need not necessarily be a diamond.

Breaking the News

Though you may want to shout out your news to the entire world immediately, there are more effective, calm, and mannered ways to announce your engagement. First, the bride and groom should talk together about whom to inform and in what order and manner. Will a cousin feel slighted if he finds out after one of your friends? Whose parents should you tell first? What about a friend who may be resentful or sad in response to your news?

When it comes to announcing your engagement, the order and method you will utilize depends on your life and family situation. If either the bride or groom has children, they should be told first and carefully. Parents, siblings, and close friends will be told next. After you have shared the news with these close relations, many couples opt to place an announcement in the newspaper declaring their engagement.

Telling Your Children

If you have children, you should make time for younger children to get to know your prospective spouse, preferably under circumstances that appeal to the children. This will encourage them to see this potential stepparent as someone fun and not threatening. Often, children will fear that their parent's new "friend" will try and take over the role of their other biological parent.

Obviously there are many factors involved in such a complex relationship, and the process of introducing children to a parent's prospective mate will be different for everyone. It should be done with forethought and sensitivity. Often, parents of younger children find it helpful to enlist a counselor or therapist for advice. How children see this potential member of the family at the beginning is important in setting a healthy foundation for the relationship to come. Slowly, after getting to know their father or mother's potential spouse, children can begin to see this person as part of their family.

Younger children often fear that their parent will have less love for them with another person in the picture. They should be reassured that just as they love their parents and siblings, and just as a parent loves more than one child, love is not in short supply. Different people are loved in slightly different ways and there is enough to go around. If children are willing and excited about the upcoming marriage, they should be included in the planning process and ceremony wherever possible. They can serve as ringbearers, walk down the aisle, or stand next to the couple as they receive a blessing from a grandparent.

Grown children often have different concerns. They may wonder if their parent's prospective spouse will become a burden either physically or finically. Older children will often insist on a prenuptial agreement before their parent's wedding. This is often a wise choice because finances can be complex and grown children's interests on both sides should be considered equally.

The remarriage of a parent can bring up many underlying anxieties, even for grown children. It is important to remember the Talmud teaches that the biblical commandment to honor one's parents, number five of the ten famous commandments, includes stepparents.

Telling Parents, Siblings, and Friends

After telling children, each partner's parents should be told. If you live far from your parents and your parents do not know your fiancé well, you may want to arrange a time for both of you to spend a day or two with each set of parents and receive their blessing.

Common manners have traditionally dictated that after both sets of parents have been told, the groom's parents should invite the bride's parents to get together and meet each other. Once the couple is married, the bride's parents and groom's parents will be known as *mechutonim*, the Hebrew word for in-laws, and will share a special relationship.

In Judaism it is customary to meet with both sets of parents and receive their blessing before becoming engaged, but occasionally a parent will not give their blessing or does not want the couple to marry. The couple can go ahead with their marriage without violating the commandment to honor one's parents since marrying and having children is just as much of a mitzvah as honoring parents.

In these early days of engagement and parties, couples must sometimes mediate between their parents. Different families inevitably have different sensibilities and customs and may have different expectations. Whether in regard to the initial meeting, engagement parties, wedding arrangements, or payment, the bride and groom must often alert their parents as to the other's family's expectations.

FACT

In Jewish communities of yore, the first time the prospective groom met the bride's parents his knowledge of Talmud and Jewish tradition would be subtly (or not so subtly) tested by his prospective father-in-law. This was sometimes done by putting a wide variety of foods before the groom and seeing if he knew the correct blessings to make and in what order to make them.

Siblings and close friends should be told next. Sometimes a friend or sibling of the bride or groom who has faced relationship difficulties may seem hurt when they hear the news of an engagement. Think about these situations in advance and break the news personally and gently, stressing how important their support and your connection with them is to you.

Newspaper Announcements

There are lots of options for phrasing newspaper engagement announcements. Pieces of information such as the bride and groom's schools attended, religious affiliations, and a photo of the couple are often included. Many communities have a Jewish newspaper that accepts engagement announcements, and this is a most appropriate place to share your joyful news with the greater Jewish community.

It is not difficult to prepare a newspaper engagement announcement. Check with your local newspaper to see if they have a form to fill out. Usually this includes the paragraph you will write and how they want your photograph submitted. Today, many newspapers have online forms and prefer that a photo be sent in digitally. Some newspapers also charge a small fee for submission.

Before submitting an announcement, look through your local paper at some of the engagement announcements to decide what style appeals to you. Then call the newspaper's lifestyle editor to check on the preferred method of submitting your announcement and whether the newspaper will publish engagement photographs or only a wedding picture. When you submit your announcement, be sure to include your contact information and the date you would like the announcement to appear. Submit all the required information directly to the editor and be sure to write your contact information on the back of the photo you submit, though you should realize that it may not be returned to you.

Jewish Engagement Parties

Engagements are a great celebration in Jewish life and there are actually several traditional types of Jewish events marking and celebrating an engagement. You might limit your engagement parties to traditional Jewish types, or you may opt for a women's only shower or a shower for men and women in addition to your engagement party.

The L'chaim and Vort

The Hebrew word *L'chaim* literally means "to life." It is the phrase Jewish people say when drinking a toast. Often just a few days after a couple gets engaged they will have a *L'chaim*, an informal get-together for family and close friends, to announce and celebrate the engagement and share their immediate joy with others. This can be a great opportunity for the bride and groom's families to spend some time with each other, get to know each other, and celebrate the engagement and their new connection together.

In Yiddish, the language of Eastern European Jewry, the word *vort* literally means "a word" and refers to a larger engagement party that is usually held several weeks or months after the *L'chaim*. The *vort* gets its title from either the fact that the bride and groom are giving their word to marry each other, or that this is a meal at which words of Torah and mazel tov, good wishes, are spoken on behalf of the new couple.

The *L'chaim* and *vort* are optional parties of recent vintage and are not demanded by Jewish law. Many couples have engagement parties at which family and friends get together, people bring gifts, and the couple's engagement is celebrated. Titling the celebration with its more traditional Hebrew or Yiddish name is not essential but can serve to connect the celebration to Jewish tradition and set a more meaningful and historic tone. If you do use either name, make sure to make a note on the invitation explaining the meaning of the party's title. People who are unfamiliar with such Jewish nomenclature and practices will be intrigued and interested.

While several people may want to make toasts, be sure to appoint a friend or family member to prepare in advance a meaningful *L'chaim* or *vort* that contains some Jewish thought and connects to the occasion. This will help to lend the whole party extra spiritual meaning.

Tanaim: To Sign or Not To Sign?

In Judaism, weddings are a unique balance between holy, spiritual, and emotional moments on the one hand and business transactions on the other. One ancient businesslike custom is to sign a document called the *tanaim*. The *tanaim*, which literally means "conditions," is a contract the two families enter into, essentially agreeing to go through with the wedding on the appointed wedding date.

Though in the past *tanaim* were usually signed at such a party often many months prior to the wedding, in recent times most couples who sign *tanaim* do so at the wedding itself. This is due to the fact that *tanaim* are indeed binding contractual agreements and to break them would be a violation of one's solemn word. So as not to risk violating such a contract and still keep older traditions alive, the *tanaim* are often signed just before the wedding ceremony when the danger of reneging is almost nil.

Nevertheless, in some Jewish communities, *tanaim* are indeed still signed at an engagement party a long time before the wedding. Even in communities where this is not true, the bride and groom can elect to sign *tanaim* at their engagement party. Though it comes with the risk of binding oneself in a powerful way (and may contain a specific monetary penalty for not going though with the wedding), signing *tanaim* at the engagement party does imbue the party with a much more profound significance and a heightened sense of commitment and trust.

Another option might be to create your own *tanaim* and sign them at the engagement party, something in your own language as a personal commitment, followed by a poetic reading of it. You could even follow this with a traditional breaking of the plate by the mothers, friends, or family and distribute the pieces as a memento of the occasion.

When Couples Need Counseling

Just because there are issues over which a couple argues or has difficulty negotiating before marriage does not mean their relationship is not workable. In fact, the ability to work through disagreements and communicate well can help to lay a strong foundation for a real, honest, and flexible relationship.

Getting Help

If a couple faces many issues of difficulty or they find that they have divergent values in life, love alone may not always be enough to make a relationship work. Often, though, the relationship is a good one. In such cases, a third party such as a couples counselor can help you negotiate your differences and figure out if the relationship is essentially a good one.

Professional psychotherapy or counseling is often a good choice for relationship and commitment issues. Even before marriage, engaged couples will sometimes enter short-term couples counseling to talk about and work through issues they are facing. Whether these issues concern religious differences, family conflicts, or differences in expectations, therapy can be a great help, even if it just provides a safe space in which each person can feel free to express their feelings without being criticized.

Fear of Commitment

Sometimes the issues that arise within a relationship emerge from one or both partners' fears of commitment. Such fears usually manifest themselves in other parts of a person's life also. It is not uncommon for someone to be overly indecisive about a course of study or career for fear it will lock out other options. Fear of commitment may be even more heightened when it comes to choosing a lifelong mate who will help to determine the course of—and many aspects of—one's life.

Ours is a time in which people have myriad options. Sometimes our desire to leave options open and not miss anything can be detrimental to sustaining long-term relationships. One of the great realities of life is that true depth, fulfillment, and meaning come only through limitation. With relationships, when we leave all of our options open, nothing can become deep. When we choose one relationship to be our primary one, closing the doors to others, only then can we focus deeply and nurture that one relationship into a lifelong partnership in which we become, like the Bible says, "as one person."

Determining the Type and Severity of Marriage Anxiety

There are at least three kinds of engagement and pre-marriage anxiety. The first is the general anxiety of embarking on a new path, which usually passes with time, the support of close friends and relatives, and discussion with one's future spouse. The second is a more objective anxiety about aspects of your future spouse, her job, her family, or her character traits. You must examine these and decide whether you can live with the issues at hand without trying to change the person. The third type is a more extreme personal fear of committing to a marriage and long-term relationship. You can deal with this type of anxiety with the help of individual professional therapy or counseling focused on the sources of your fears and techniques to overcome those fears.

Testing for Jewish Hereditary Disorders

Many populations have genetic disorders because their gene pool is limited. Certain hereditary diseases and conditions are more prevalent among Jewish people. While anyone can be a carrier of Tay-Sachs disease, a recessive hereditary disease of the nervous system that is nearly always fatal, the incidence of the disease is significantly higher among people of Eastern European (Ashkenazi) Jewish descent, which comprises 90 percent of the American Jewish population. Approximately one in every twenty-seven Jews in the United States is a carrier of the Tay-Sachs gene.

Jewish Hereditary Diseases

There are several other genetically inherited diseases that are more common among the Jewish population than the general population. These include familial dysautonomia, cystic fibrosis, canavan disease, glycogen storage disease, fanconi anemia, Bloom syndrome, Niemann-Pick disease, mucolipidosis, and Gaucher's disease. Couples may choose to test themselves only for diseases that might result in a child's death or debilitation. For instance, Gaucher's disease, which is caused by the lack of a certain enzyme, can now be treated. The missing enzyme can be produced artificially to treat patients.

FACT

According to the National Human Genome Research Institute, about one in 250 people in the general population are carriers of the recessive gene that causes Tay-Sachs disease. In addition to people of Ashkenazi descent, non-Jewish French Canadians living near the St. Lawrence River and in the Cajun community of Louisiana have a higher incidence of Tay-Sachs.

Most of these diseases are carried by recessive genes, which means the disease can only manifest itself if a child receives the recessive gene from both parents. If the child receives one recessive gene and one dominant gene, he will be a carrier of the disorder but will have no symptoms of the disease. If a carrier marries someone who is not a carrier, there is no chance that they will have a child with the disease. If two carriers have a child there is a one in four chance that they will have a child with the disease and a one in two chance that they will have a child who will be a carrier.

Since it takes two parents who are both carriers of a recessive gene to have a child with the disease, if only one parent is tested and found not to be a carrier, this is enough to guarantee that the couple will not have a child with the disease.

The Screening Process

There are several ways to check to see if either you or your fiancé is a carrier of a hereditary disease. Either or both partners can go to their doctor to be tested for any of the genes. There are also Jewish organizations such as Dor Yisharim that conduct easy, anonymous testing. They often will test both potential partners early in the dating process and notify them of whether the match is recommended or not. The information of who is a carrier stays confidential.

If two Tay-Sachs carriers marry, in-vitro fertilization shows promise. Fertilized ova can be screened to see if they have both Tay-Sachs alleles. Only those ova without the disease are implanted in the woman's uterus. Obviously, couples should speak with their doctors or health professionals about genetic history or other health issues that may arise in their upcoming marriage.

CHAPTER 3

The Planning Process

3

Careful and detailed planning is obviously an important factor in any wedding. The more planning you do early on in the process, the less unnecessary stress you will endure as the date gets closer. Since people will inevitably have differing preferences that may trigger conflicts, it is important to remember that a wedding—while auspicious, incredible, and important—is only one day.

Modern or Traditional?

Traditionally, the bride and her mother, with limited input from the groom's side, planned the wedding. Today, many couples get married later in life and the couple themselves may find that they are doing much of the wedding planning as a team.

Wedding planning can be a very stressful process. Bride and groom meet each other and want to get married and be together forever, a seemingly simple and beautiful proposition. However, even though you love each other and get along, you may be coming from very different families that sometimes have very different ideas about how a wedding should look and feel.

If your wedding is to be large, consider hiring a wedding planner to help deal with many of the details and relieve some of the pressure on you and your families. The presence of a professional third party can also help you avoid some of the potential conflicts that can erupt between family members with regard to wedding details, preferences, and traditions.

There are many style and detail decisions to be made in planning your wedding. How formal or informal it will be, how large or small, where and when it will be, who will perform it and how—the decisions can go on and on. You will have to decide to what extent you want your wedding to reflect the more traditional aspects of a Jewish wedding. So many of the Jewish traditions associated with weddings hold great religious and mystical depth and will serve to make your wedding day—and the relationship it symbolizes—powerful, meaningful, and sacred. At the same time, there are many traditions that are less essential and more flexible.

For instance, traditionally many of the ceremonial parts of a Jewish wedding were performed by men. However, even within traditional Jewish law, many of these blessings, readings, and rights may be facilitated by women. Indeed, many aspects of a Jewish wedding may be easily altered to retain their traditional Jewish flavor and allegiance to Jewish law, while including modern ideas and ritual aspects such as gender inclusivity and friends or relatives who may not be Jewish.

Toward the beginning of the wedding planning process, after reading about and becoming familiar with the various aspects of a Jewish wedding, it is wise for the couple and their families to think through and discuss the various aspects and stages of the wedding. This should then be discussed with the rabbi since different rabbis, synagogues, and temples may have varied requirements with regard to Jewish law and tradition.

Who Pays for What?

Wedding costs can easily take on a life of their own, quickly multiplying beyond your means. Before the wedding planning begins, create a ballpark budget, with the parties who are contributing money for the wedding. This will help determine many of the broader aspects of your wedding, such as size, location, and menu.

Options

Jewish law does not speak much to the question of how wedding costs should be split. Traditionally in the United States, the bride's family paid for the reception, photographer, flowers, and invitations. The groom's family paid for the rings, the rabbi, music, liquor, and the honeymoon.

Sometimes families have different expectations of who will pay for engagement parties, pre-wedding meals, and various parts of the wedding itself. If the wedding will include a weekend and Shabbat and the bride's parents are paying for the wedding, it would be appropriate for the groom's parents to offer to pay for Shabbat meals for both families and their guests.

While even today the bride's family often assumes the cost of the wedding, many brides and grooms get married later in life and may be financially established enough to pay for large parts of the wedding themselves. Additionally, depending on their financial situations, the two families may decide to split the cost of the wedding. In Israel today this is almost always done.

If one set of parents is paying for the wedding, there is an inherent danger that the other family may feel left out of the planning process. It is the bride and groom's responsibility to be a liaison and make sure both families feel their concerns are being addressed. You might involve the parents who are not paying by sending each other pictures, going dress or tux shopping with them, calling them periodically with updates, asking their opinions, and, of course, telling them how excited you are to meet their relatives.

FACT

In Israel the parents of the bride and groom usually pay not only for the wedding but also for the home the bride and groom will live in after they are married. This may be one of the reasons why Israeli weddings tend to be much more informal and less costly than their diaspora counterparts.

If the family paying for the wedding is much more financially wealthy than the other, they should nevertheless take care not to plan such a lavish wedding that the other family might be embarrassed. This is especially true if the groom's family is paying for the wedding since today many people still assume the bride's family foots the bill.

Balancing Needs and Wants

While a wedding is only one day in your life, it is an important one for most couples. What aspects are more or less important to the bride and groom will be an important factor in deciding how to budget. For instance, you might feel that you can save money on the menu by having fish instead of meat or by passing hors d'oeuvres instead of serving a smorgasbord. You might use the money you saved to have a videographer in addition to still photos.

Here are some questions to consider when determining your wedding budget:

- How many people do we want to have?
- Who will be paying for the wedding?
- Do we want a more formal or more informal wedding?

- What would we do with the money saved?
- What do we envision when we think about our forthcoming wedding?
- Would we be comfortable taking a loan to pay for the wedding?

The Guest List

Frequently, up to four lists will comprise the master wedding guest list—the bride's list, groom's list, and lists from both sets of parents. The guest list is usually an important aspect of the wedding for both sets of parents to talk about.

Dividing It Up

If the wedding is to take place in the hometown of either one of the sets of parents, they may require more spaces; the family that lives farther away may need fewer since inevitably some people may not be able to travel. If the family that is not paying for the wedding truly needs more spaces at the wedding they could offer to contribute toward these extra meals. Of course, diplomacy will be very important in any negotiations between the two families. Remember that the wedding is just one day, but the two families will be connected forever.

At some less formal traditional Jewish weddings, guests who are part of the couple's or family's community but are not close enough to make the guest list are instead invited to the ceremony and for the first set of Jewish dancing. These guests are not given a place card or a seat and they are expected to leave after the first set of dancing and hors d'oeuvres. This way the wedding has lots of people and energy and more friends feel included, but costs are kept within reason.

Inviting Children

Deciding which children to invite can be especially thorny. In large families, inviting all the children can make wedding costs prohibitive. The general rule is to be consistent. When it comes to inviting children, draw clear lines between immediate and non-immediate relatives and between children above and below certain ages. This kind of consistency will help you avoid hurt feelings.

In any case, care should be taken not to hurt the feelings of anyone who is not invited. The Talmud writes that one must even be careful not to invite someone who is only being invited because you know she cannot come. In Jewish law, such scheming is considered misleading and is a form of lying. Of course, if you truly want a guest at the wedding but know he will not be able to attend, it is fine to invite him since you are not creating any false pretenses.

Parental Roles and Responsibilities

Parents of the bride and groom were traditionally involved a great deal in planning and paying for the wedding. For many couples this is still the case, but others may be more financially independent and may involve their parents less. It all depends on the individual's family situations and the parents' and the couple's desires. Sometimes the bride and groom might pay for much of the wedding, but the bride's mother will plan the wedding with her to support her and bond over a momentous event. Other times, parents will have a great deal of influence in the planning process.

FACT

At a lesser-known Jewish European wedding custom known as the *muzinka* dance, parents who are marrying off their last child are seated in the center of the dance floor and presented with wreaths. Guests then dance in a circle around them to the tune of the Yiddish song "*Die Mezinke Oysgegeben*" ("The Youngest Daughter Is Given").

A Jewish wedding is not just the marriage of bride and groom, but a merging of two families. These families hopefully will be *mechutonim* for many years to come, so it is important that both sets of parents and their families feel that they are involved and honored equally. Sometimes one family may be less familiar with Jewish wedding ceremonies or Judaism in general, and the rabbi should be asked to work with those parents in familiarizing them with the Jewish wedding process and finding ways to involve them even with a limited knowledge of Judaism or Hebrew.

Within a Jewish wedding ceremony there are several places in which the parents of bride and groom should consider playing a significant role. In any wedding the parents of bride and groom may make a toast to thank relatives and friends and wish mazel tov to the bride and groom. At a Jewish wedding, parents traditionally play several other roles at the *tish*, *kabalat panim*, ceremony, and reception. There are fewer roles for siblings and extended family, but these family members might be given honors such as reciting some of the *sheva berachot* under the chuppah or the seven blessings after the grace after meals, or the making of the *hamotzie* blessing on the bread.

The following are the traditional parental roles at a Jewish wedding:

- Bride's mother and groom's mother sit next to the bride at the *kabalat panim* (pre-wedding reception)
- Groom's father and bride's father sit next to the groom at the *tish*
- Groom's father and bride's father enter into the tanaim agreement together at the *tish*
- Bride's mother and groom's mother break a plate together at the *tish*
- Mother of the bride and mother of the groom walk behind the bride and help with her train during the seven circles under the chuppah
- Mother of the bride helps lift her veil and drink from the cup of wine under the chuppah

Of course, beyond the specific ceremonial roles that parents and family may play at the wedding, they must also fulfull the general responsibility of being supportive and encouraging at this momentous time in the couple's life.

Steering Clear of Potential Conflicts

Weddings are wonderful for many reasons, among them that they are a time for two completely different families to plan a large party for everyone they know. Therein lies the potential for many conflicts. Expectations and traditions may differ between the families and among individuals. Both the bride and her mother often feel quite invested in the wedding planning process, but generational and individual differences may be the source of disagreement.

Making It a Good Experience

Wedding planning is notorious for setting off arguments between parent and child. Sometimes the stress causes old arguments that have nothing to do with the wedding to flare up again. In the best of situations, the wedding planning process serves as an exciting bonding experience for parent and child, bride and groom, and the two new families of *mechutonim*.

It is important to realize that weddings are turning points not only for the bride and groom, but also for parents, who may consciously or unconsciously see this as a joyous but possibly difficult turning point in their own lives. For some parents the marriage of their child signifies the end of one life stage—that of being solely responsible for a child. They may feel on some level that they are losing a child, or they may feel anxiety over seeing the birth of a new generation that will ultimately take over their own role as parents in the world.

Though the rabbi may not always know the family of the bride or groom well, it is often important to ask the rabbi to meet with one or both families to help them feel included in the process and to explain aspects of the wedding traditions. Do not hesitate to ask for this; it is by no means beyond a rabbi's responsibility.

It is important to have open and supportive conversation with those involved in the planning process. Be honest about feelings and generous with thanks and praise. If things get very heated sometimes the rabbi or a trusted friend of the family may be able to step in for an informal counseling session.

Pick Your Battles

It is wise for the bride and groom to decide in advance as a couple and as individuals what aspects of the wedding and its planning may ignite conflicts and to pick their battles. Though you may have lots of opinions, if you are not the main person planning the wedding, decide carefully when to express yourself.

For example, if you care a great deal about the type of music that will be played but not much about the food or who the rabbi will be, choose carefully when to put your foot down. There are almost always several people involved in the process of planning a wedding, each with different expectations and desires. If everyone is clear about their needs and preferences and even clearer about what they are willing to compromise on, the planning process will go much more smoothly. What is most important to each of you and what you can and cannot compromise on should be one of the first things you discuss when you begin to plan your wedding.

Making Decisions Together

Planning a wedding, a giant party given by two very different families for all of their friends and relatives, can be difficult. Though the stress of wedding planning can bring back past hurts and create the potential for explosive arguments, with some care and a team approach, the process of planning a wedding can be a joyous one.

Getting Started

Begin by making a list of all the things that will need to be arranged and the decisions that will need to be made; divide and conquer, reporting back to each other as things fall into place. Elicit input from each other and offer your opinions and preferences if you feel strongly about a particular item or arrangement.

Though this is sometimes a difficult beginning to a relationship, it can be a good proving ground, allowing you the experience of making decisions in times of difficulty as a couple. Use this as a learning process, not an opportunity to take your fiancé to task. Approach it with open eyes to realize how different the two of you are and how you make decisions differently.

Sharing the Load

Whether the wedding planning team is the bride and her mother or involves the groom and others, you should see yourselves as a team. Giving constructive input when it is needed is always good. A bride and groom and often one or both sets of parents can be very invested in the wedding. If the two families are from different cultures or traditions they may have very different images of how the wedding should go. Nonetheless, it is important to remember that a wedding is one day, but your relationship with each other needs to last a lifetime.

There will be things about your wedding that you will both disagree about and that your families will want to weigh in on. Be careful not to let family issues or family members pit you and your fiancé against each other by asking you to take sides. You as a couple must first come to agreement and then present a united front.

Jewish weddings are not a show but a holy event between the couple, between the two families, and between the community and God. If you keep your eyes on that bigger perspective, on what is truly valuable about a wedding, many of the potential conflicts can be averted.

A Special Gift: Hachnasat Kallah

Hachnasat kallah, attending to the bride or assisting her in entering her wedding, is a great Jewish mitzvah. There are many aspects to *hachnasat kallah*, ranging from actually leading her to the wedding ceremony with dancing and music to attending to the things she needs on her wedding day. In some situations, anonymous charitable donations are given to the bride and groom by their community to help a needy couple defray modest wedding costs. Many Jewish communities have assistance even for brides who are not very needy. One example is a wedding dress *gemach*, a bank of wedding dresses that can be borrowed at no cost and returned after the wedding is over.

In Judaism, in many ways it is the bride who is considered the star of the wedding day. The Talmud tells us that the mitzvah of *hachnasat kallah* is one for which a person is rewarded in this world as well as in the next (Babylonian Talmud, Shabbat 127a), and it takes precedence over many other holy acts. Though it is less true today, in more ancient times it was not the groom who was led singing and dancing to see his bride, but the bride who was led with great fanfare to her chuppah.

FACT

The Talmud tells of such great joy that accompanied the dancing before the bride that one of the rabbis of the Talmud actually carried the bride on his shoulders dancing.

Often the mitzvah of *hachnasat kallah* takes the form of helping a needy bride and her family to pay for the costs of the wedding. Jewish law relates that *hachnasat kallah* is perhaps the greatest form of charity that there is since it not only saves a bride from embarrassment on her big day but actually facilitates the development of the world, since the first commandment in the bible is to marry and have children.

CHAPTER 4

Registering

Soon after you become engaged you can, believe it or not, go to stores you like and register for the gifts you would like to receive for your new home. Registration is the process of walking through a store with your fiancé and picking out what you want. Usually these are items that will fill your new home—dishes to eat off of, linens to sleep on, and art to hang on the walls. Your registration should also include Jewish items that you will need in your new home for Jewish rituals and celebrations.

Why Register?

Though some of our parents and grandparents who were born in previous generations consider registering a bit gauche, registering is highly acceptable today. Registering not only makes your life easier in that you will for the most part receive exactly what you need, want, and admire, but it also makes the lives of those who wish to buy gifts for you so much simpler. No longer do brides and grooms receive five of the same toaster and four blenders only to have to waste time returning things. Now everyone is able to choose exactly what you desire.

Friends and relatives can shop for gifts to buy you from your registry just by logging onto the website of the store or stores at which you are registered. This makes their lives easier and makes shopping for your gift an easy and pleasurable experience. Registering is usually a win-win situation for all parties involved.

The Process

Several weeks after your engagement you will both need to go to a store or stores, walk though, and write down what items you will register for. You may not have a home that you are sharing yet, so you will need to use your imagination together. Take some time to walk around the store and get a sense of each other's tastes. Bride and groom will both have to live with these choices for a long time, so teach each other what you like and practice the art of compromise.

The actual registration process depends on the store at which you are interested in registering. Larger department stores may have a special guide or person to help you operate the machine that scans each item you wish to register for and set up your registry information on the store's website. If you are registering in a smaller outlet or Jewish store the regular sales person will probably give you paper and pen and a registry page to fill out.

You should try to register as early as possible so that people can buy you things off of your registry for an engagement party if they want to. You can let people know where you are registered by word of mouth, on your wedding information website, or even as a card sent with the wedding invitation or wedding festivities information.

Differing Tastes

What are future life partners to do if their tastes differ? As time goes on and your relationship progresses, many couples find that some of their taste preferences begin to merge or reach a shared medium just from living together and becoming one unit. This is probably not true at the time of your wedding gift registration, though. Registering together is a good practice for a lifetime of negotiation and of making decisions together, some of which are much bigger than what dishes to buy.

Judaism teaches that peace between wife and husband is one of the most important things there is. Use your registry decision-making process as a practice ground and training camp for equitable and peaceful decision making together.

Disagreeing and Compromise

Like any other time you disagree, be sure to hear each others' points of view before expressing your own. Realize that when you feel you are giving more than you should, in reality you are both probably in an equal compromise. In registry conflict, as in life, you won't have an opinion on everything. Be sure to pick your battles. If you don't really care about what pattern the dishes are but you dearly want to register for that "History of Beers of the World" book, be supportive of your partner's dish choices and learn from them what they appreciate.

Sometimes one partner is more interested in the design and look of dishes and home décor than the other. Register together but realize one of you might be more excited by colors and patterns than the other. If so, let that person do most of the choosing; the other partner can just say yes or no. Unless one partner hates it, the partner most excited by the process will get to live out this once-in-a-lifetime fantasy of compiling a dream list of dishes, silverware, and home décor and not having to spend a dime on it. Sometimes one future spouse is interested in the decorative side and the other is more interested in the small appliance side. You can split up in the store and do your research with different salespeople, coming together after an hour or two for each other's final approvals.

Judaism teaches that the home is a reflection of the ancient Jewish Holy Temple in Jerusalem. Our tables are like an altar, and the bread we consume is sprinkled first with salt just as it was in the temple. Even the wine we drink on holiday occasions is modeled on the wine that was poured in service to God in the Jerusalem temple, the most holy Jewish spot on earth. Eating food and preparing it can be such a holy act in Judaism that each food actually has its own blessing before it is eaten. As you register, think about the bigger picture, the way in which your dishes and home items will be used for you and your family to eat off of and how holy this is considered. Perhaps like our first Jewish ancestors Sara and Abraham, you will experience the very holy act of welcoming guests into your home with these dishes that you now register for.

Gear for a Jewish Home

A Jewish wedding is the beginning of the process of building a Jewish home and family. While many religions center themselves on a place of worship, Judaism views the home as the paramount place of sanctity. Registering at a Jewish bookstore or online (see Appendix D for a few websites) for Judaica for your home can be a very educational and exciting experience. Find a Jewish bookstore in your area and take some time as a couple to go there and look at the books and Judaic supplies. The experience of shaping your home into an inspiring Jewish space will help you to focus on a shared Jewish life path together.

Everyday Judaica

A Jewish home can be recognized by the many Jewish symbols, books, and objects a Jewish family uses throughout the year. Judaism is primarily composed of *mitzvoth*, holy actions, and so there are many tools that can be helpful not only on the Sabbath or holidays but every day in building a Jewish home and life together.

Mezuzahs

The first moment one enters a Jewish home, a symbol of its holy space, a *mezuzah*, is seen right on the front doorway. A *mezuzah* is one of the most basic marks of a Jewish home. The Torah states "you shall write them on the doorposts of your home and on your gates," referring to the words of Judaism's most holy and ancient prayer, the *shema*. The *mezuzah*, which many Jews affix to every doorway in their house, is a rolled-up piece of parchment upon which has been handwritten the words of the *shemah* by a special scribe called a *sofer.* Since Jewish law states that each doorway should have a *mezuzah*, the average home may need twenty or so *mezuzahs*. Registering for the parchment scrolls and decorative covers can be a great way to give people the option of buying you a Jewish gift that you will use and look at several times a day, every day.

If you are not careful to register for your *mizuzot* locally or online with a trusted *mezuzah* source you can easily end up with *mezuzahs* that are not kosher because they have not been properly written and prepared. There are many *mizuzot* on the market masquerading as kosher for which you can pay a high price but which are only machine copies or have nothing at all in their cases.

The parchment *mezuzah* scroll should have a decorative box to hold it and affix it to the doorpost. While the outer box is only a cover and the true *mezuzah* is what is written inside the decorative box, its cover is important in protecting and honoring the *mezuzah* itself. You can spend a little on a basic Lucite case or many hundreds of dollars on one of metal or clay handcrafted by an artist. Many people choose a more expensive *mezuzah* cover for their front door and less expensive covers for inside doors. There are also many *mezuzah* covers in the middle price range that are reasonable but beautiful.

A *Tzedakah* (Charity) Box

No Jewish home is complete without a charity box (sometimes called a *tzedakah* box in Hebrew or *pushka* in Yiddish). *Tzedakah*, giving charity, whether to the needy, to a community institution, or to Israel, is one of the foundational aspects of a Jewish home. From a young age many Jewish children are trained to put a few coins each week before the Sabbath in a charity box, a practice that teaches the basic Jewish tradition of giving to those in need.

You can register for *tzedakah* boxes in many different versions and designs. Some are basic, just a tin box or can with a slot in the top for coins. Others are very elaborately decorated or made by artists out of clay or metal. They serve not only as a repository for charitable giving but as an *objet d'art*, beautifying your home.

Jewish Artwork

From the decorative to the abstract, a growing world of Jewish artwork has emerged on the scene over the past few decades. Having Jewish art on your walls makes the statement that your home is a Jewish one, and it gives those who dwell in the home a Jewish feeling of beauty. The Talmud says that a beautiful (though not ostentatious) Jewish home serves to widen our vision and put the mind at ease. Jewish art today runs the gamut from inexpensive crafts, challah (Shabbat bread) covers, and wall hangings to very expensive one-of-a-kind pieces that can be purchased from galleries. Choosing inspiring Jewish art for your registry will bring some Jewish light into the everyday workings of your household.

Jewish Books for Your Registry

It is no coincidence that the Jewish people are sometimes referred to as "People of the Book." Judaism is a long-lasting and deep tradition so there are many Jewish books in English and other languages about every aspect of Jewish practice, Jewish thought, and Jewish life.

No Jewish home is complete without a Jewish Bible. One choice is the Chumash, the Five Books of Moses (Genesis through Deuteronomy). Another is the Tanach, a book containing the Five Books of Moses, the books of the Jewish prophets, and additional ancient holy writings such as the Book of Psalms by King David and the Megilah, the Book of Esther, which is read on the holiday of Purim.

Since prayer is such an important part of Jewish life and tradition, most Jewish homes also have a prayer book, a *siddur.* Many versions of both the Bible and the prayer book are available today in both Hebrew and English, and you can register for them at any Jewish bookstore either in person or online.

Traditionally time is taken for Jewish prayer three times a day—morning, afternoon, and night—thus feeding the soul as we feed our bodies. Many Jews pray in community in a synagogue, but prayer can also be said in the home. Therefore, having a prayer book and a Bible containing the psalms that are often prayed at any time is essential.

As you peruse the Jewish bookstore to register, you will no doubt come across many books about Jewish traditions, Jewish history, Jewish mysticism, Jewish stories, children's books, and ancient Jewish texts with modern English translations. Pick a few that appeal to you to keep on your bookshelf. A book that covers the Jewish lifecycle or Jewish Sabbath and holidays throughout the year will come in very handy as you celebrate the holidays in your new home together and begin having children of your own. Reading about the holidays and their significance can make those celebrations, especially in your first year of building a Jewish home together, that much more meaningful. See Appendix D for some suggestions of basic books about these topics.

Shabbat and Holiday Items

Some of the most beautiful and memorable times in a Jewish home and marriage are the Jewish Sabbath and the Jewish holidays, of which there are several throughout the year. Each Jewish holiday celebrates a different moment in Jewish history and embodies a different idea and spiritual pathway. Thus the tools, symbols, and ritual objects for each one will differ.

Shabbat Items for Your Registry

When the sun sets on Friday evening, the Jewish Sabbath, or Shabbat, begins. This auspicious moment is usually marked with the lighting of two candles. If you don't already have your own heirloom or personal Shabbat candlesticks, you should register for some. Though simple or crafty Shabbat candlesticks are popular, Shabbat candlesticks are often made in sterling and can be quite expensive. If the price is high, several of your relatives or friends can opt to buy them for you together. Each week you will remember them as they share in your mitzvah, your holy act of ushering in the Shabbat though the lighting of the candles.

Here's a list of Sabbath and holiday items for which to consider registering:

- Shabbat candlesticks
- *Challah* board and knife
- *Kiddush* cups
- Havdalah (end of Shabbat ritual) set
- Rosh Hashanah honey bowl
- Matzah cover
- Hanukah menorah
- Prefabricated *sukkah*
- Decorative Omer counter
- Passover Seder plate

Each Friday night the Sabbath is honored when families gather for the recitation of *kiddush*, a blessing that is said as part of the festive Shabbat meal over a cup of wine or grape juice. Typically a *kiddush* cup is made out of silver, so many couples register for a *kiddush* cup or are given one as a wedding gift to use on Friday nights and Sabbath days.

Each Saturday night the end of the Sabbath is marked in a similar way to the *kiddush*. This ritual is called *havdalah*, which means separation. It marks the separation of the Shabbat from the weekday that is about to begin. The *havdalah* ceremony utilizes several ritual objects that can be placed on your Jewish registry: the cup for *havdalah* (which is similar to the *kiddush* cup), the spice box that will hold sweet spices to be smelled as part of the *havdalah* ceremony, and a *havdalah* candle and candle holder. Together these items comprise the *havdalah* set. They can be made out of anything but are often crafted of metal, glass, or clay.

Holiday Items for Your Registry

The first holiday of the Jewish year is Rosh Hashanah, the New Year celebration. Besides hearing the blowing of the shofar, the ram's horn, one of the customs on Rosh Hashanah is to eat an apple dipped in honey as a symbol of hope for a sweet year. Many Judaica stores carry special decorative honey bowls, often made of ceramic by specific artists for the holiday.

The next festival in the yearly cycle is *sukkot*, the seven-day celebration commemorating God's protection of the Jewish people as they traveled from Egypt through the desert for forty years to the land of Israel. During this week the Torah says the Jewish people should dwell in *sukkot*, eating meals and even sometimes sleeping in the *sukkah*.

The *sukkah* is a hut with strong walls and a natural roof, usually made of branches, bamboo, or unfinished wood. Many Judacica stores sell prefabricated *sukkah* walls that go up quickly and can be assembled by one or two people for the holiday celebration. Though a prefabricated *sukkah* is a bit more expensive, you may want to consider this as part of your Jewish registry.

You can make the walls of a *sukkah* out of almost anything. If you wish to save some money, use wood or canvas from a home supply store for walls. As long as they are strong enough to withstand the wind and don't flap, you are okay. Use bamboo or tree branches and leaves for the *schach* (the natural roof).

Hanukah is next. Hanukah is an eight-day celebration that begins on the twenty-fifth day of the Hebrew month of Kislev. It usually falls sometime in December. Special eight-branched candelabras called menorahs are lit each night of the holiday, and the number of candles increases each night from one on the first night until all eight are lit on the last night. The lighting of the menorah commemorates the Jewish people's victory against the Greeks, who had tried to coerce the Jews to convert to their pagan ways and had violated the Jewish people's Holy Temple in Jerusalem.

The Jewish people, led by the Maccabees, triumphed over the Greeks. After the war was over, the Jews entered their Temple to rededicate it (the word Hanukah means dedication). They could only find one jar of oil—enough to light the seven-branched candelabra that began the service in the temple each day. They lit this, and the oil miraculously lasted for eight days until they were able to procure new olive oil for the lighting. In commemoration of this miracle, the Jewish people light a Hanukah menorah each night of Hanukah.

FACT

Though this fifty-day Count of the Omer is a happy and anticipatory one, the first thirty-three days are days of mourning during which no weddings are held. During one Omer in the second century, 24,000 students of the great Rabbi Akiva were killed by a plague. The plague lifted on the thirty-third day, Lag Ba'Omer.

A Hanukah menorah can be one that holds candles or one that holds olive oil. An olive oil menorah, since it is the original type, is considered a better quality menorah than one that holds candles, though a candle menorah is certainly fine. Menorahs can be made out of any nonflammable material. You can register for one for the whole family or one for him and one for her. They are most often made of silver, glass, or clay.

The next big festival is Passover, on which most Jews have a Seder meal, reenacting and remembering the exodus from Egypt and the birth of the Jewish nation 3,500 years ago. Seder plates are great for a registry item and can be made out of silver, glass, or ceramic.

All Seder plates have room for at least five symbols of the Passover seder—an egg, bitter herbs, a green vegetable, a shank bone, and often either salt water or romaine lettuce. Some Seder plates are made with a built-in matzah holder for the three pieces of unleavened bread that will be used at the Seder. You may also wish to register for a decorative matzah cover that is placed over the matzah at various points in the Seder meal.

On the second day of Passover, the Counting of the Omer begins. The Omer is the fifty-day span between Passover and the next holiday on the Jewish calendar, the holiday of Shavuot. Each night one counts both the days and the weeks that have passed in anticipation for the coming holiday of Shavuot, the day that has no symbols but marks the giving of the Torah to the Jewish people at Mount Sinai fifty days after their departure from Egypt.

Many Judaica shops sell special Omer counters, often made of wood with a scroll of paper inside on which is written the correct count for each of the fifty days. Each day after counting the Omer, the day number is changed in preparation for the next day. A counter such as this is very helpful as a reminder each evening for the family to count the day. Having an Omer counter provides a focal point around which to gather with each other and declare this sacred count together.

Registering for Kosher and Passover Kitchen Items

If you are planning to have a kosher kitchen or a kosher for Passover kitchen during the holiday of Passover, these will be important considerations to keep in mind as you and your fiancé register for dishes and kitchenware.

FACT

Though fish are animals, they are considered pareve—something that is neither meat nor dairy. Thus fish can be cooked in either a meat or dairy pot and eaten with either type of utensils and dishes.

Kosher Kitchen Considerations

In a kosher kitchen, kosher ingredients are used for cooking. In addition, any foods that contain products that come from an animal (other than milk or fish) are not cooked or mixed with dairy products.

Many Jewish people keep a kosher kitchen, though not all do so at the same level of care and strictness. Some might buy kosher meat but may not necessarily check their other food products to be sure they were produced under kosher supervision. Others might not buy kosher meat but will take care to separate milk and meat foods in their kitchen.

Whatever your current level of kashrut observance, you will want to think about your registry in light of this so that you register for the proper amount of items you will require and won't have to buy them later.

The Bible dictates that one should not cook a baby goat in its mother's milk. Though this verse refers only to not cooking meat and milk together, the Talmud and Judaism's oral tradition make clear that the separation of meat and dairy means that the two cannot be cooked in the same pots—even at different times—or eaten with the same utensils.

When you register for separate meat and dairy dishes and utensils, be sure that the patterns are different enough to avoid confusion and mix-ups. Though for most utensils there is a fairly easy process by which to remedy any mixups and re-kosher the item, for some utensils undoing kosher problems can be a bit more difficult.

Couples that celebrate the Shabbat each week usually register for a set of Shabbat dishes and silverware that is fancier than their everyday set. You may also want to consider registering for other accoutrements to honor the occasion. A tablecloth and a vase for fresh flowers are a nice touch.

Some things in a kosher kitchen can be used for both meat and dairy; for instance, drinking glasses are usually used for both meat and dairy, and a clean microwave oven can be used to heat both covered meat and covered dairy foods—though not at the same time. Most kosher kitchens have one stove and oven that are used for both meat and dairy with a few cautious parameters. (For more detailed books and websites on this subject, see Appendix D or speak to a local rabbi.)

Small Appliances for Your Kosher Kitchen

Toaster ovens in most kosher kitchens, due to their small size, are usually designated either meat or dairy. If you have a double sink you can designate one side for meat and one for dairy; if you have only one sink, usually a rack or insert of some kind is used for meat and a separate one for dairy. Bread machines are usually designated pareve and no milk products are used in them so the bread may be eaten with meat or dairy. Often two dish racks are used, one for meat and one for dairy, as well as separate sets of knives.

Many Judaica stores also sell stick-on labels that read "meat" and "dairy." Labeling confusing utensils or drawers and cabinets with these can save you from misplacing your utensils and using them for the wrong foods. Having a carefully labeled kosher kitchen will also prevent relatives and friends who are cooking in your kitchen from becoming too confused.

Many people use disposable paper plates and utensils on Passover for either meat or dairy. That way they need only buy one set of dishes for Passover, though they will need some separate pots and pans for meat Passover cooking and dairy Passover cooking. It is important to remember, of course, that while Passover is an auspicious holiday it only lasts for one week.

Passover Dishes

The Bible (Exodus 12) commands that on the holiday of Passover no *chometz* (leavened bread or grain product) should be eaten or owned by a Jewish person. Just as with the general laws of kosher, this means you must refrain from eating bread or other risen grain products. In addition, the dishes or vessels you used to cook these products must not be used to cook Passover food.

If your kitchen will be generally kosher the rest of the year and strictly kosher during Passover, you will require a second two sets of dishes and utensils for Passover. With a bit of pre-holiday cleaning and effort, though, most kitchen appliances can be made kosher for the Passover holiday.

Be sure to register for Passover dishes that will store easily since fifty-one weeks a year they will be in your basement, garage, or storage closet. In addition, think through how much pre-Passover work you will be willing to do. With minimal effort, silverware you use the rest of the year can be made kosher for Passover each year in the days prior to the holiday.

Your Trousseau

The idea of a trousseau comes historically from the bride's dowry. In many parts of the world, both husband and wife brought certain items into the marriage as part of their new home. The groom was expected to pay for the new home and its furnishings, and the bride brought more personal items, such as her clothing and linens that the couple would use. The bride's contribution was called the dowry, or a trousseau in old French.

Though quite uncommon in the United States today, a trousseau usually consists of linens, heirlooms, and other special things she has bought or collected that she wishes to save for use in the home she and her husband will start together. In some countries today, such as India, the trousseau is alive and well and refers to the clothing that a bride assembles for her wedding, for pre- and post-wedding parties, and for her honeymoon.

In Jewish history, brides and grooms did indeed enter a wedding with a dowry or trousseau for her and a dower given to the couple by the groom's family. These are alluded to in traditional documents that many couples sign, the *tanaim* and the *ketubah*, which will be explained later in this book. Today, few Jewish couples bring into the marriage the dowry and dower amounts mentioned in these documents. Rather, like most couples, they bring what they have and share all of it. Often, if couples are younger, parents will give them a "dowry" and "dower" to assist them in their new transition.

In earlier times, Jewish weddings began a year before the wedding ceremony with the signing of contracts that guaranteed each side would go though with the wedding. The contracts often outlined the bride's trousseau and what the groom would bring into the marriage. The process of gathering the trousseau and building a home for the couple began a year before the actual ceremony because it would take this long to prepare it all.

CHAPTER 5

Choosing a Wedding Date and Location

Choosing a date and location are important decisions since they will determine the look and feel of your wedding day, which family and friends will be able to make it your wedding, how long you will have to plan your wedding, and how many people you can invite. There are many different kinds of special days in the Jewish year, and you should consider taking into account Jewish traditions. Many days are appropriate for your wedding, but it is against Jewish law and tradition to hold a wedding on certain days.

The Jewish Calendar

The Jewish calendar may be an important factor in scheduling your wedding. The Jewish year contains days when traditionally no weddings are held, but there are many other days to choose from. It can be a bit confusing if you are not familiar with this system, so here are some guidelines.

How the Jewish Calendar Works

The Jewish calendar is a lunar calendar, which means that each cycle of the moon equals one Jewish month. Every Jewish month begins on the new moon and ends just before the next new moon. Originally, the Jewish people did not decide when each month would begin based on a set calendar system. Instead, in ancient Jerusalem, two witnesses would come to the court and say they saw the new moon and the court would then declare that day the first day of the new month. Each new month was communicated to areas outside of Israel though a series of bonfires on hilltops signaling the beginning of the new month.

FACT

Today outside of Israel, most holidays except Rosh Hashanah are one day longer than inside Israel. The reason for this dates back about 2,000 years to the Roman occupation of Israel. The Romans often messed up the new moon bonfire communication process by lighting hilltop fires on the wrong days. As a result, everyone outside of Israel had to remember both possible days on which a new month and any subsequent holiday could begin.

From day one of each month, all the Jewish people would count the required number of days until each holiday to begin their celebrations. For instance, Passover begins on the fifteenth day of the Hebrew month of Nisan, so everyone would count fifteen days from the start of the new month (when they saw the bonfire), and all the Jews would celebrate the first day of Passover together on the fifteenth day.

Since a lunar month has only twenty-nine days and the Jewish holidays have to be in certain seasons—for instance, the Bible specifies that Passover is a spring season holiday—we add a leap year every three or four years. This ensures that the Jewish and regular (solar) calendars remain in close proximity to each other and the holidays will fall in their proper seasons. As a result of the difference in calendars, the Jewish holidays and days on which weddings are not held will be on a slightly different secular calendar date each year. There are many Jewish calendars available online (see Appendix D for some helpful websites). The months are counted from Nisan, the month in which Passover falls, although the New Year does not start until the month of Tishrey.

The following are the months in the Jewish calendar:

1. Nisan
2. Iyar
3. Sivan
4. Tamuz
5. Av
6. Elul
7. Tishrey (New Year)
8. Cheshvan
9. Kislev
10. Tevet
11. Shevat
12. Adar
13. Adar II (in a leap year only)

Holidays, Holy Days, and Commemorations

The Jewish year contains three main festivals of biblical origin on which no weddings are held. Passover, which is the festival celebrating the Jewish people's redemption from Egyptian bondage, is an eight-day celebration that begins on the fifteenth of the Hebrew month of Nisan. Shavuot, the festival commemorating the giving of the Torah at Mount Sinai, falls exactly fifty days after the second day of Passover and lasts for two days. Sukkot, the Festival of Booths, begins on the fifteenth day of the Hebrew month of Tishrey and continues for eight days.

In addition to the festivals, there are the biblical High Holidays, or Days of Awe: Rosh Hashanah, which is two days; and Yom Kippur, the

Day of Atonement, which lasts one day. Because each of these holidays is so important in its own right, Jewish weddings are not held during any of them. Jewish weddings should not take place on the Jewish Sabbath, which begins each week on Friday night at sundown and ends on Saturday night. Jewish weddings can be held on a Saturday if they do not begin until after dark.

The holidays of Passover and Sukkot, each of which is seven days long in Israel and eight days long in the diaspora, are composed of one or two days at the beginning and one or two at the end that are true holidays. The four or five interim days are called *Chol Hamoed*, or the weekday of the holiday. These days are like half-holidays, and weddings should not be held on them.

Several rabbinic holidays also fall throughout each calendar year. These rabbinic holidays were instituted after the Jewish people came to the land of Israel in the year 1273 B.C.E. They are not biblical in origin, but they are still very important.

The most famous of the rabbinic holidays are Hanukah and Purim. Hanukah falls on the twenty-fifth day of the Hebrew month of Kislev. It is a celebration of the Jewish victory over Greek oppression. Purim, which falls on the fourteenth of the Hebrew month of Adar, celebrates the defeat of the wicked Haman, who tried to destroy the Jewish people in the period of the Persian Empire. Weddings are permitted during Hanukah, but they are discouraged during Purim except in situations of great need. Weddings are also discouraged on the eve of any major holiday.

Days of Sadness, Days of Joy

In addition to the festivals, there are two main times in the Jewish year that are not appropriate for weddings. These days commemorate sad events in Jewish history. The first sad period is called the Three Weeks and the second is called the Omer.

The Three Weeks

This three-week period falls during the summer and begins with a fast day known as Shivah Asar B'tamuz, the seventeenth day of the Hebrew month of Tamuz. This day commemorates the siege of Jerusalem in the year 70 C.E. These three weeks are a time in which weddings are not held. The period ends with the saddest day of the Jewish year, Tisha B'av, the ninth day of the Jewish month of Av. Tisha B'av commemorates the destruction of Jerusalem, first in the year 583 B.C.E. by the Assyrians and second by the Romans in the year 70 C.E. Since weddings should be one of our most joyous days, it would not be fitting to hold one on a sad day on the Jewish calendar.

FACT

There is a difference between Jews of Sephardic background and those of Ashkenazi decent with regard to holding a wedding during these three sad weeks. Ashkenazi Jews do not hold weddings at all during the three weeks. Sephardic Jews can get married until the last nine days, which fall from the first day of the month of Av until the ninth of Av.

The Omer

The Omer or Sefirat HaOmer (literally, the Counting of the Omer) is the name for the fifty days that are counted between the second day of the holiday of Passover and the beginning of the holiday of Shavuot. This counting commemorates the travel of the Jewish people from Egypt to Mount Sinai to receive the Torah. Though in theory this should be a happy time, about 2,000 years ago, all the 24,000 students of the famous Rabbi Akivah died during this period. Today it is a time of mourning and thus not a time permitted for weddings.

Though the general period of the Omer is a sad one, there are two days during this period, aside from Lag Ba'Omer, that are so overwhelmingly joyous that many rabbis will allow a wedding on them. Both dates commemorate recent events in Jewish history. The first is Yom Yirushalayim, Jerusalem Day, which falls on the twenty-eighth day of the Hebrew month of Iyar and commorates the unification of Jerusalem during the Six Day War of 1967. It was on that day that the Jewish people were allowed to return to the place of the holy Wailing Wall and Temple Mount in Jerusalem after 2,000 years. The second is Yom Ha'atzmaut, Israel Independence Day, which is on the fifth of Iyar and commemorates the day the state of Israel was established in 1948.

There are differing customs regarding which thirty-three days during the fifty-day Omer period are days of mourning. Some limit joy during the first thirty-three days of the count, and others start their mourning practices on the first day of the Hebrew month of Iyar, eight days after Passover, and end three days before Shavuot. The thirty-third day in the Omer count is marked by the lesser known holiday of Lag Ba'Omer, on which weddings are allowed.

Especially Auspicious Days

Some days are considered more auspicious for a wedding celebration than others.

- During the first half of a lunar cycle, the waxing moon
- During the week after the full moon
- During the Hebrew month of Adar
- During the Hebrew month of Elul
- During the Hebrew month of Kislev
- During the Hebrew month of Nisan
- The 15th day of the month of Av
- Tuesdays (on this day of creation, the Bible writes "it was good" twice)

Remember these auspicious days would not necessarily push aside practical considerations—for instance, if a beloved uncle can't make it on a more auspicious day. Getting married is a holy act and a mitzvah, and it should not be pushed off just to have it coincide with an auspicious day.

Other Things to Consider

There are lots of factors to consider when setting a wedding date. From a religious point of view, think not just about appropriate dates but dates that might be more auspicious or fitting for your wedding. Include lots of practical considerations in your planning of a date, such as guests' accessibility and ease of transportation. The weather is also an important factor. Icy roads might make it difficult or even dangerous for guests to travel. Having an outdoor wedding in very hot weather can also be hard on you and your guests. Relatives and friends who may be abroad or unavailable are also important to consider. Realize that most factors will not be in your control, and a bright outlook and trust in the beauty and spirituality of the event will keep you from getting overly anxious.

A *minyan*, a quorum of ten, just like the one that is required for public prayer, must be present for the special seven blessings of *sheva berachot*. In Orthodox or more traditional communities, this quorum would consist of at least ten men over age thirteen. In less traditional circles this quorum could consist of ten men and or women over the age of bar or bat mitzvah, which is twelve years of age for a girl and thirteen years of age for a boy.

Sheva Berachot

Another factor to consider in planning a wedding date is the *sheva berachot* celebrations. Traditionally the week following your wedding, the week of *sheva berachot* is considered a week of continued feasting and celebration with family and friends. Many Jewish weddings are followed not by the bride and groom leaving for a honeymoon admid a joyous jumble of just married placards, tin cans, and rice, but with seven days of nightly parties and sit-down meals at the homes of friends and relatives.

These meals during the first week after your wedding are known as the *sheva berachot* (literally, the seven blessings). They get their name from the series of seven special blessings recited at the end of the meal to honor the bride and groom. They are the same seven blessings of joy that were recited under the chuppah at the wedding ceremony, and so they will evoke some of the magical moments you experienced at your wedding.

Sometimes couples will have two or three of these parties in one city and fly midweek to another city for one or more *sheva berachot* meals. Any large meal held to honor and celebrate with the bride and groom during the seven days following their marriage is considered a *sheva berachot* party.

Many couples will have one party on each day of the week following the wedding. While it is wonderful and a bit exhausting, it is not essential. Many couples will opt for one, two, or three parties during the week with a day of respite in between.

Where you want your *sheva berachot* parties to be may be a factor in where you decide to have your wedding, although it is more likely that you will decide what city to have your wedding in and friends and relatives will plan *sheva berachot* around your schedule, travel ability, and convenience. You will read more about the *sheva berachot* themselves in Chapter 19.

There is a requirement that there be at least one "new face" at each *sheva berachot* party in order to be able to recite the *sheva berachot*, the seven blessings at the end of the grace after meals. This new person should be someone who has not been at any of the previous *sheva berachot* parties since the wedding.

Honeymoons and Wedding Planning

Your honeymoon plans may factor into your decision for a wedding location and date. If your dream is to visit India together or cruise the Caribbean, you might want to choose a winter, fall, or spring wedding. If Alaska is your thing, a summer wedding would obviously be a better choice.

Many couples prefer a short engagement period so they can start their life together sooner, but a longer one will often make preparations a little less harried. Some couples who choose simpler weddings will opt for a shorter engagement because less time is required to plan the wedding and the dangers of becoming engulfed in myriad details is less formidable.

Space for Pre-Ceremony Traditions

As always, location is an important consideration in planning your wedding. You will need three or more spaces at your wedding. Many traditional Jewish weddings begin with a *chatan's tish*, the groom's table, in one room and a bride's *kabalat panim*, or reception, in another. If the bride and groom are seeing each other prior to the ceremony, these could be in the same room, but if they are spending the day or week before the wedding apart, they will need two rooms.

The Groom's Tish Room

The word *tish* literally means table in Yiddish, which was the language the Jewish people spoke in Eastern Europe for about 1,000 years. However, the *tish* refers to the gathering, not usually to an actual table. Friends, family, and guests gather at the groom's *tish* before the ceremony to toast the groom, though he usually does not drink because he must be of sound mind and body for the ceremony. Any state or religious documents are often signed at the *tish*.

The room for the groom's *tish* must be able to accommodate a long table and chairs for people to eat and drink a bit. Usually there are bottles of liquor, soft drinks, and cake or hors d'oeuvres. If the wedding is large, there should be ample room for people to stand around the table and watch the proceedings, even if there might not be enough room for everyone to sit at the table.

Be sure to talk to your rabbi and discuss with each other about whether you are planning to see each other the day of the wedding before the ceremony. This will help you decide what kind of wedding space to secure and how many rooms you will need.

The actual table should have seats for guests, a seat for the groom in the middle, and seats for the father of the bride and the father of the groom flanking the groom's chair. Usually there is a chair for the rabbi next to them or opposite them, and sometimes there are chairs for the witnesses who will sign the various documents.

The Bride's Reception Room

At the same time as the groom's *tish*, the *kabalat panim*, the bride's reception, is usually in an adjacent room or in a main reception area. The bride is usually in a special chair since she is considered to be a like a queen for the day. Though this is not always the case, the bride is often on a dais and people come up to see her one at a time or in small groups to wish her well and say mazel tov. Sometimes she is surrounded on both sides—on one side by her mother and on the other by the groom's mother, though they would be seated in regular chairs in contrast to the bride's throne. There are often hors d'oeuvres or some food for guests.

FACT

The word *kabalat panim* literally means the "receiving of faces" or people. It can sometimes refer to the bride's reception, though often it refers to the whole pre-ceremony celebration, on both the bride and groom's sides.

The best set-up for the *kabalat panim* and *tish* would be to have the bride's reception room and the groom's table room near each other so guests can move between them. This is especially relevant if both male and female guests are welcome in both rooms. Following the *tish* and the *kabalat panim*, the groom is usually led to the bride by friends and relatives. A hallway between the two rooms would be ideal, but any space will do.

Ceremony Space

In Judaism, holy space is not required for a wedding, and a wedding can be had almost anywhere—a backyard, a hotel, a garden, a home, or a museum. Any place you love and want to remember or is just convenient and in the right price range can work.

Synagogues Versus Nontraditional Spaces

In Judaism, unlike many other religions, there is no reason to have your wedding in a prayer space. Even though the wedding ceremony is certainly a religious ritual, a synagogue is by no means required. Some people specifically choose not to have their wedding in a synagogue so that it does not seem reminiscent of a non-Jewish "church wedding."

Though it need not be held in a synagogue, it is important to remember that it is a sacred ceremony. In fact, the very word for wedding in Hebrew is *kiddushin*, or sanctity. Thus, the space should be tasteful and not in any way ostentatious or vulgar. If it is a large wedding, there should be a raised platform so all the guests can see the bride and groom.

Under the Stars

There is an ancient tradition of having the ceremony outside, though this is by no means mandatory. In a Jewish wedding, the chuppah is actually the bride and groom's home for the moments of the ceremony, as they enter "under one roof" together. Having it outside makes the chuppah truly a home and a necessary roof. In addition, since the outside is under the stars, we are reminded that in the Bible God promised Abraham that "your children will be like the stars of the sky," and in this way we recognize that every bride and groom are a link in a long line of the Jewish people. Second marriages are often held indoors since they are seen as a bit more of a private affair.

FACT

Though many Ashkenazi Jews (whose ancestors come from Eastern Europe) have the custom of holding the ceremony outside, many Sephardic Jews (whose ancestors hail from Spain, North Africa, and other eastern lands) have the custom of holding the ceremony inside.

Some Jewish wedding halls are actually constructed so that although the wedding ceremony is held indoors, the chuppah at the front of the room stands under an open skylight, thus merging the best of both worlds. Your guests can sit in comfort and your chuppah can stand under the stars.

If the venue does not have a kosher caterer and you plan to stick to Jewish dietary laws, don't forget to ask whether the reception space will let you bring in your own caterer. Verify that there are kitchens for warming up food or cooking the meal.

Another option is to have the ceremony in one place and the reception in another. This is a bit more complicated with *yichud*, which should be done immediately following the wedding ceremony itself. But if your dream has always been to be married on the beach with no room for a reception, it's certainly doable to have your reception somewhere else.

Yichud *Spaces*

Following a Jewish wedding ceremony, the bride and groom retreat to a private room to share their first few minutes of marriage together. This aloneness is called *yichud*, and the room is called the *yichud* room. The guests should be far from the *yichud* room so that the bride and groom can have some quality alone time before greeting the crowd as husband and wife.

Some Jews of Sephardic descent do not have the practice of *yichud* at the wedding. For them, the chuppah, a *talit* spread over them, or the bride and groom's actual home serve this purpose. If you or your fiancé is Sephardic you may consider not having the *yichud* ceremony.

The Yichud *Room*

This room should be away from the crowd and have a lock on the door. There should be a place outside the room for two witnesses to stand or sit; this is actually an official part of the Jewish wedding ceremony, and therefore it requires witnesses. It should be completely private with no uncovered windows. There should be a table in the room and space for the bride and groom to eat their first meal as a married couple together and break their fast if they are observing the customary pre-ceremony wedding day fast.

It is a good idea to have the rabbi or one of your helpers check the *yichud* room to be sure it locks and is fully private on the day of your wedding. In ancient Jewish tradition, this was a time to consummate the marriage. Make sure the room is unlocked and open so you can go right in after the ceremony. Have the witnesses check to be sure no one is in the room and that there is food for you.

For couples observing the Jewish laws of family purity, if the bride has not been to the *mikvah* before the wedding, the couple would not have *yichud* in a completely closed room; instead, they would keep the door slightly ajar. It is wise to schedule one's wedding so that the bride can go to the *mikvah* a few days before the event.

For the Guests

There should be a reception room out of earshot of the *yichud* room for guests to gather while they wait for the bride and groom to reappear and make their grand entrance. Usually guests are served hors d'oeuvres and drinks and can schmooze with each other and wish mazel tov to parents and relatives in another room. This reception room should be large enough for guests to gather, though not necessarily to sit. You may want to have some tables set up for older relatives.

Another option is not to have a side reception room and instead to have the guests go into the main reception space to eat their salad and have drinks while they wait for the bride and groom to finish *yichud*. If you are not seeing each other before the ceremony and have not taken family pictures, you will do that after the *yichud*. Alert the venue of your need for a picture space for you to use after *yichud*. Most couples go back to the ceremony space for posed family pictures under their chuppah. Just be sure the management of your hall or synagogue knows not to take down the chuppah.

CHAPTER 6

Assembling Your Team

Luckily, you are not in this alone; many people will be involved in your wedding preparations, ceremony, and reception. In theory, according to Jewish law, all that is required for a wedding are a bride, a groom, and two witnesses. In practice, though, there are many roles to be filled in a Jewish wedding. Relatives, friends, and your religious leader all play important parts. Your wedding team will help you make your experience less stressful, more meaningful, and very memorable.

Choosing Your Rabbi

You might have a rabbi that you know well, that you have grown up with or studied from as an adult, or you might not have a strong connection to any rabbi. In either case you will need a rabbi, a *misader kiddushin* (literally, one who puts the wedding ceremony in order), to perform your wedding. In addition to actually facilitating your wedding ceremony, the rabbi you choose should be available as a resource for you in the planning process. Your rabbi can be a valuable counselor to help you and your fiancé with matters of disagreement and difficulty and will also help you make the ceremony meaningful and personal.

Where to Find a Rabbi

It is best to look for a rabbi to whom you relate well and one with whom you can have an ongoing connection even after your wedding. If your family belongs to a congregation and you have grown up with the rabbi or know the rabbi and feel comfortable with him, you could consider using him for your wedding. Since most rabbis will want to meet with you and your fiancé several times, you may want to weigh using your family's rabbi with your accessibility to him. Many rabbis will meet with a couple as little as two or three times, but some may want as many as ten or more meetings.

My friend says she can become a certified wedding officiate for a day and perform our ceremony. Should we say yes?
Though there are states in which one can become certified for a day to do a wedding, you would miss out on all the Jewish traditions a rabbi can guide you through and the professional help she can offer with any issues of conflict.

Your rabbi should be more than just someone to perform the ceremony. The rabbi should be someone you feel comfortable with as a person, a guide, and a teacher. This is important since usually rabbis will want to discuss fairly personal things with you and your future spouse prior to the wedding. The premarital meetings most rabbis have with couples should cover at least three major topics: the couple's relationship, the couple's Jewish life and the Jewish home they will build together, and the structure of the wedding itself.

If you don't have a rabbi with whom you have established a relationship, look around for one whose personality and style of doing things appeals to you. It is good to have the rabbi for your wedding be someone you can call even after your wedding with questions about the Jewish home and family. If the rabbi is someone who lives near you, so much the better.

In most states any recognized clergy person can perform a wedding that the state will recognize. Some states require the clergy member to register in advance with the state or city. You should check into this well before the wedding and alert the rabbi of the municipality's requirements.

Obviously, you can look for a rabbi at a local congregation, but different congregations may have different policies about whether their rabbis can perform a wedding for people who are not members of the congregation. Sometimes the rabbi's fee may be higher for a nonmember since the cost of marriage fees may be included in a synagogue's membership dues.

If you recently graduated from college and have a relationship with a rabbi from your college campus Hillel, Chabad, or other Jewish campus organization, this may be a good place to look for a rabbi to perform your wedding. Of course, if you are getting married in your hometown and you have a relationship with the rabbi of your parents' congregation, this could be an obvious choice.

Questions for the Rabbi, Questions for You

If you do not have an obvious choice of rabbi and you are "shopping" for one, you should feel free to call rabbis, tell them you are looking for someone to facilitate your wedding, and arrange a meeting. Meeting with a rabbi to get a sense of his personality, whether you click with him, and to find out about his wedding style does not obligate you to use him as your *misader kiddushin*.

After you have verified that the rabbi will be available on your planned wedding date, find out if the rabbi's denomination and requirements fit you and see if you like her personality and style. If you are planning a nontraditional wedding, ask her what her Jewish wedding requirements are. If you want a more traditional Jewish wedding, see if she has the background and training to facilitate your vision. Discuss with your fiancé whether you would both be comfortable asking this rabbi for advice or assistance in case of bumps in your relationship.

Questions to ask a potential rabbi include:

- When are you available to perform our wedding?
- What is your fee?
- What are your pre-wedding and wedding ceremony religious requirements?
- How many pre-wedding meetings would you have with us?
- What would the meetings consist of?
- What are your limits or requirements for involving friends and relatives in the ceremony?
- Would you be available and willing to meet with our families and answer their questions?

The Bible commands that if a woman's husband dies childless and the husband has a brother, the brother, though usually forbidden to her, must either offer to marry her in levirate marriage to keep the deceased brother's name alive, or perform a fairly simple ceremony called *chalitza*. Today only *chalitza* is done. Some rabbis will want to know that this ceremony was performed before agreeing to perform a second marriage to a new spouse.

Most rabbis will also ask you several questions at your initial meeting. If the rabbi is Orthodox, Traditional, or Conservative, one of the first questions they will want to know is whether either of you, your parents, or even your grandparents were ever divorced. If you were previously married to a Jewish person and subsequently divorced, he will want to be sure you obtained a religious divorce (a *get*). In many cases, remarrying without a Jewish divorce would be tantamount to adultery, since you would still be technically married to your previous spouse.

If the rabbi performing your wedding does not perform interfaith marriages she will also ask if you are both Jewish. If you are, she will want to know if either of you or your parents or grandparents has converted to Judaism. If the answer is yes the rabbi will probably want to know who was in charge of the conversion and how it was accomplished.

Do You Need a Cantor?

Several parts of the wedding ceremony are traditionally sung. You do not necessarily need a cantor to sing these. Your rabbi or a relative who knows how to read Hebrew could sing them. But hiring a cantor can be a good idea if you have a cantor that you are close with or you want a cantor to represent either your family's synagogue or your spouse's synagogue. The rabbi and cantor can both stand under the chuppah and facilitate the ceremony together, the rabbi making some of the blessings and explaining the parts of the ceremony and the cantor singing the sections that are usually sung.

If you do elect to have a cantor, be sure to find out what his fee is beforehand and be sure the rabbi and cantor are in touch to arrange the flow of the wedding ceremony. They must also predetermine which parts of the wedding ceremony each will chant and facilitate.

Cantors will usually sing several specific parts of the ceremony. As bride and groom walk under the chuppah, the cantor will usually sing the *boruch haba*, several phrases of welcome in Hebrew that are sung to the bride and groom as they enter. A cantor will also usually sing the *sheva berachot*, the seven blessings, or at least the last of the *sheva berachot*. The last of the seven blessings is longer than the previous six and contains several lines that are usually sung. In addition, just before the breaking of the glass you can opt to have the cantor sing the traditional song remembering Jerusalem, "*Im Eshkachech Yirushalayim*" ("If I Forget Thee, O Jerusalem").

Working with a Wedding Planner

Not all couples hire a wedding planner (also called a wedding consultant), but having one can save you time, money, and perhaps some sanity. Planning a wedding can easily become a full-time job. According to *Bride Magazine*, more than 50 percent of couples chose to hire a wedding planner. A planner does not take over the wedding planning entirely. She helps you with many of the logistics, no matter how small, and will give advice tailored to your particular budget.

When you interview a wedding planner, find out how many weddings he has planned and ask him for references. You should feel free to call people he has planned weddings for and vendors he has worked with. Interview several planners until you find one you click with and establish a price in writing in advance. Since you will be having a Jewish wedding, be sure your planner is familiar with Jewish weddings or has planned one before.

Different wedding planners are paid in different ways. Some offer free services and are paid by the vendors they hire for you. The disadvantage to this method is that your planner is not really working for you but for vendors who are providing services to you. The only interest the planner has in you in such a situation is the power you will have to recommend them to others after the wedding is over. A second way that wedding planners are paid is by contracting with you to pay them a percentage of the total cost of the event, typically 15 to 20 percent of the entire cost of the affair. The third way is with a flat hourly rate for services rendered. Be sure in this case to specify with the planner the amount of hours she will spend on each aspect of the wedding. Crunch the numbers; depending on the size and cost of your wedding you should be able to determine which fee structure is your best bet.

In any case, a good wedding planner should help you stay within your budget, not stress it. A good wedding planner should also help you stay on a timeline for the planning process and help you negotiate with vendors that he is familiar with, possibly saving you some money. He should be able to advise you when payments are due to your vendors, choose the items you want on the menu, and arrange details such as linens and flowers. In the end, a good wedding planner should be worth the price in the time and frustration he can save you.

The Wedding Party

There is no Jewish law that prescribes the size, composition, or processional arrangement of your wedding party, except that the bride should walk down to the chuppah sometime after the groom. Wedding parties usually consist of a best man and a maid of honor, siblings, family, and sometimes friends. The Midrash describes that when Adam and Eve were married in the Garden of Eden by God (the first rabbi!), the angels Michael and Gabriel accompanied this first bride and groom to the chuppah. Today, the groom is usually accompanied by his parents and the bride by hers.

FACT

The Talmud speaks of both fathers walking the groom to the chuppah and both mothers walking the bride. The Zohar, Judaism's most basic work of mysticism, prefers the parents of each to walk them down to their chuppah.

Shushvinin

After God made Eve, He "brought her to Adam." The Midrash interprets this as a sign that God acted as the "best man" and "maid of honor" at the first wedding. In the book of Aruvin, the Talmud concludes that no one should feel it is below her dignity to spend the day as a bride or groom's right hand person. These helpers at a Jewish wedding are referred to as *shushvinin*.

There is an ancient custom for every groom and bride to have one or two *shushvinin* who are their close friends, each to act as their helpers throughout the day. These helpers can be relatives or friends. On this day the bride and groom are seen as a king and queen and should be treated as such with attendants and people to walk or dance before them and behind them.

The *shushvinin* may have many jobs. She may help the bride with things the day of the wedding, hold her *ketubah* after she is presented with it, or act as a go-between if she needs to get a message to the groom or a relative. For the groom, the *shushvinin* might hold the ring he will give his wife or help to fetch things he needs earlier in the day.

Maid/Matron of Honor and Best Man

In the American tradition the maid of honor has several roles, including helping the bride shop for her veil, assisting with invitations and a shower, lending a hand as the bride dresses and has her makeup and hair done, and holding her flowers. The duties of the best man sometimes include assisting the groom with his clothes, making a toast, and returning the groom's tuxedo if he has rented one.

FACT

The day God was reveled to the Jewish people at Mount Sinai and they received the Torah, which is described in the Bible in the twentieth chapter of Exodus, was considered by the rabbis as a type of wedding between God and the Jewish People. Moses and his brother Aaron were said to be the two *shushvinin* for the people of Israel on that day.

Bridesmaids might walk in the processional, help to mingle at the wedding, and perhaps attend the shower. Groomsmen might help with the seating and ushering of the guests, walking in the processional, and mingling with the guests to be sure everyone has what they need. Sometimes small children in the wedding party will toss flower petals before the processional or hold the ring on a pillow before it is given.

The following is a list of blessings, honors, and witnessing opportunities for you to give out to friends and relatives. Some of these can be combined:

- ✓ Two witnesses for the *tanaim*
- ✓ Two witnesses for the *ketubah*
- ✓ Two witnesses for the giving of the ring
- ✓ Two witnesses to stand outside the *yichud* room

- ✓ Six or seven honorees to each chant one of the seven blessings
- ✓ Six or seven honorees to each translate one of the seven blessings
- ✓ One honoree to make the *hamotzie* blessing
- ✓ One honoree to lead the grace after meals
- ✓ Six or seven honorees to each chant one of the seven blessings following the grace after meals

Wedding Party Attire

The notion of the bride being specially adorned goes far back in Judaism. The Midrash says that God adorned Eve with twenty-four adornments for her wedding to Adam in the Garden of Eden. White is a symbol of purity and forgiveness, and since the wedding day is a small Yom Kippur, or day of atonement, for the bride and groom, it is fitting that they both wear white. At many Jewish weddings, the groom wears a white robe over his suit or tuxedo while he is under the chuppah. This robe is called a *kittel.* There are no requirements in Jewish tradition that dictate the color of the clothing of the rest of the bridal party.

Modesty in Appearance and Expenditure

In Judaism, modesty in dress is very important. In Jewish thought God is seen as omnipresent; we are always standing before the Divine, and our dress should befit such an audience. The wedding ceremony is a holy one. Therefore, even if it is not held in the synagogue, our dress should befit such a ceremony. Some rabbis will require that the bride's dress and the dresses of the bridesmaids modestly cover their legs and upper body.

In some cities, finding dresses that will conform to traditional Jewish expectations of modesty, or *tzniut*, may be a challenging task. Start searching early and seek out bridal salons that can help you find a gown that can be altered. Bridesmaids' dresses will be an even bigger challenge because manufacturers may not alter the design. You can design jackets, and many brides purchase fabric for their attendants, who pay to have custom dresses made in accordance with standards of modesty.

If you are being married by a rabbi who requires that your shoulders be covered under the chuppah but you are not planning to have a dress that will conform to this, you might want to consider discussing with the rabbi whether a shawl that matches your dress could be worn during the ceremony. Discuss with your rabbi his requirements for head coverings for men and women.

If you don't plan to keep your wedding dress or the bridesmaids' dresses, you might want to consider donating them to a wedding dress bank for people who cannot afford a new dress for their own wedding. Many Jewish communities and synagogues have these, and charitable organizations in many cities provide formal dresses free of charge.

Before ordering dresses for your wedding party, call a meeting of your bridesmaids and have a discussion about what style and color will work with the overall plan and what they like. Some brides choose a color and some overall criteria, and each bridesmaid is responsible for procuring her own dress. This way, money and effort is not wasted on a dress that will only be worn once. Indeed, wasting time and money is forbidden in Judaism as part of the Bible's commandment against wanton waste and destruction, *baal tashchit.*

Rabbi and Witnesses

As a performer of myriad weddings, the rabbi is usually given much leeway in dress. Some rabbis will have a tuxedo for black tie weddings, but even if the wedding is a very formal one, the rabbi will often wear his own dark suit. If you want the rabbi to wear a tuxedo, it is appropriate to offer to rent it for him.

Several parts of a Jewish wedding ceremony may require witnesses. The witnesses do not need to be an official part of your wedding party. If they are not a member of the wedding party they do not need to walk down the aisle or have the same clothing as the rest of the wedding party. They can simply be called up at the proper times to do their duty and honor.

Involving Parents

The parents of the bride and groom are perhaps the most important part of the wedding party other than the bride and groom themselves. They will usually walk the bride and groom down the aisle, be there for them in support, and play many roles throughout the ceremony and reception.

If the parents of the bride and/or the groom are divorced, deceased, or remarried, the configuration of the wedding party and the processional can become a bit complex. If parents are divorced and it would be awkward for them to accompany the bride or groom, one option is to revert to the older Jewish custom of having the two fathers accompany the groom and the two mothers accompany the bride. Alternatively, several couples might walk in front of the bride or groom and then the bride or groom themselves might be accompanied by only one parent with or without a close friend or sibling. It is important to remember that whom and how many people walk down with the bride or groom is not nearly as important as avoiding hurt feelings and rejection.

7

CHAPTER 7

Ritual Objects

The Hebrew word for wedding is *kiddushin*, which means "holiness." Judaism teaches not the rejection of the physical but the sanctification of it to a higher level. Your Jewish wedding, too, is not just a symbol but a holy ritual that makes a profound difference in the spiritual and, consequently, the physical world. The spiritual tools you will use are thousands of years old and can help not only to solemnize your commitment to each other but also to sanctify it.

Choosing the Rings

The ring that a man gives a woman under the chuppah is considered in Jewish tradition to be the thing that makes the marriage official. It is given in the presence of witnesses because it is not just a symbol of love but an act that plays a legal and ritual role. With its giving the groom says a phrase that begins, "*harey at mikudeshet li*" ("you are sanctified unto me").

Jewish law writes that the ring that is used to effect *kiddushin* should belong to the groom before he gives it to the bride. It should be plain, but its value should be apparent. The ring usually would not contain unique artwork or stones whose value is in the eye of the assessor. It is most commonly a plain gold, silver, or platinum band whose value is assessed based on its weight. Some feel a ring is used because it represents the perfect circle that bride and groom will form together.

FACT

In the time of the Talmud, a marriage could be effected in one of three ways—by giving something of value, by writing a document declaring the marriage, or, though deemed inappropriate for use as a wedding ceremony in the Talmud, through having sexual intercourse. None of these though would count as an official wedding if they were not done with the specific intent on the part of groom and bride to become married through the act.

In Judaism, a marriage is a concrete change of status. Before it you were accessible to all, and now you are committed and permitted only to your spouse. The famous Talmudic commentary of Rash"i, in tractate Kiddushin, makes clear that this is not, heaven forefend, a purchase of a spouse. For this reason, in traditional Jewish law, one would not use the American custom of exchanging rings because that was often used for purchases. Rather, the ring given represents the legal consideration to effect a *kinyan*, a legal pact binding two people exclusively to each other.

Technically, a ring is not necessary and any object of value will do. In fact, according to the Talmud, if the husband was a good dancer, he could dance before the bride, thus effecting the *kiddushin* with the value of the dance if she were to accept it.

There is evidence that the custom of using a ring for a marriage may go back even to the biblical period. It has been suggested that the giving of a ring from husband to wife is symbolic of the bride and groom's desire to be equal partners, similar to when Pharaoh transferred his ring to Joseph when he wished to give Joseph authority over the kingdom of Egypt.

The Talit: Prayer Shawl

It is a longtime custom for the family of the bride or the bride herself to buy the groom a *talit*, a prayer shawl. The *talit* is actually just a four-cornered shawl; since it is four-cornered, the Bible requires fringes on each corner called *tzitzit*. Though it is one of the commandments for which we do not know the reason, it is a mitzvah, and so such a shawl has been worn to honor prayer services for millennia. Sometimes the bride and groom will use this *talit* with each of the corners tied to a wooden pole for a chuppah, the wedding canopy they are married under, and have friends hold up the poles.

In the Book of Numbers, the Bible describes the *tzitzit*, the fringes that are tied to the corners of the *talit*, and then states, "And you shall see them (the *tzitzit*) and remember all of God's commandments and perform them, and not go after your heart and your eyes after which you lust." Thus the *talit* is seen as a spiritual guidepost for being faithful both to God and to one's spouse.

While all married Orthodox and Conservative men wear a *talit* for morning prayers, many Conservative and some Reform and Orthodox women also wear a *talit* for prayers. If this is so for you, you may both want to give each other a *talit* for your wedding and use both *talitot* (the plural of *talit*) for the chuppah. Another option is to use one *talit* for a chuppah and the other to wrap yourselves in for the *sheva berachot*, following a sometimes utilized Sephardic custom.

Talitot come in many different sizes and colors. The *talit* should be large enough to cover the whole upper body, but the color of a *talit* cloth does not make a difference in Jewish law. Many are white with black or blue stripes, but others are rainbow, multicolored, or tie-dyed. The only requirement is that it be woven, preferably of natural material, usually wool.

You have two choices when it comes to the type of *tzitzit*, fringes, that are on the corner of your *talit*. The Bible commands that among each corner's fringes should be one blue thread. For the past 1,900 years, until very recently, all the *talit* fringes were white because the source of the biblical blue dye for this thread was lost. In the past several years a snail has been found in Israel that is thought to be the original species from which the biblical blue dye (*ekchelet*) for this blue thread of the *tzitzit* is derived.

Many Judaica stores today carry *talitot* with one blue string among the white strings on each corner, the way the *talit* would have looked in biblical times. Though it is significantly more expensive for this type of *talit*, it is thought by some to be much closer to the authentic biblical form of the *tzitzit*, and you and your fiancé may want to consider this type.

Since the wearing of a *talit* is a mitzvah, a blessing is recited prior to its donning. The blessing is, "*Boruch atah Adoni Elohaynu melech haolam asher kidishanu b'mitzvotav v'tzivanu l'hitatef ba'tzitzit.*" ("Blessed are You God, Sovereign of the Universe who has sanctified us with Your commandments and commanded us to wrap ourselves in the *tzitzit*.")

Subsequent to one's wedding the *talit* is worn at all daily, Sabbath, and holiday morning prayer services and on Yom Kippur eve at the Kol Nidrey service. The large *talit* prayer shawl which is worn when praying is mirrored by a smaller *talit* that many people wear under their clothing in order to fulfill this biblical commandment all day long.

Chuppah: Wedding Canopy

The chuppah that you will be married under is a canopy which represents the home that you and your beloved will build together. Part of a Jewish wedding ceremony is accomplished by literally entering under one roof together. This roof is the chuppah. Though it represents the home that you will build together, it does not have any walls. The chuppah is a mirror of the original Jewish home, the tent of the first Jewish couple, Abraham and Sara. The Torah tells us that their tent was open on the sides in order to welcome guests in. Abraham and Sara would go out of their way to welcome people into their home, even strangers and desert travelers they did not know.

Inside this first Jewish home, the Midrash tells us, several miraculous things happened in the merit of our foremother Sara. One of these was a divine light, a godly aura that was constantly present. It is the hope of the Jewish people that couples aim to build the type of home Abraham and Sara built, one that is open to others, thus fulfilling the mitzvah of *hachnasat orchim*, of welcoming guests. Such a home is considered one that also is a dwelling place for the divine presence through its holy atmosphere.

Your chuppah canopy can be made out of any material. Some couples choose to use a *talit* held up by four friends or relatives or tied onto four poles that are supported by people. If you are using your *talit* as a chuppah, use care when tying the *tzitzit* on each corner onto the poles. If the *tzitzit* tear off, it is no longer considered a kosher and fitting *talit*.

Some Judaica stores and artists sell more elaborate chuppahs designed by hand and made of cloth that has been handwoven or painted. If you do not want to use a *talit* or buy a chuppah, you can ask the rabbi who is performing your wedding if his synagogue has a chuppah. A caterer or florist that does many Jewish weddings will sometimes have a chuppah on hand.

Wine and Wine Cups

You will need two wine cups and a bottle of wine for the wedding ceremony under the chuppah. Most brides prefer to use white wine just in case it spills. White wine on a white dress is not nearly as great a dilemma as red, and most rabbis will recommend white wine for this reason.

The two wine cups will be used for the two sets of blessings recited under the chuppah. The first set is said at the beginning of the wedding ceremony, and it consists of two blessings. The first blessing is the *hagafen*, the blessing over the wine itself. The second blessing sanctifies the wedding and acknowledges that becoming married is a mitzvah.

We make a blessing over wine as part of the wedding ceremony because the wedding is considered especially holy. Not only is a wedding a mitzvah, but the Hebrew word for a wedding ceremony is *kiddushin*, sanctity. Just as the *kiddush* is said over wine on Friday night to sanctify the Sabbath, so, too, the holiness of a wedding ceremony demands sanctification over a cup of wine.

FACT

The Talmud writes that significant Jewish ceremonies and blessings are to be recited over wine because it is the drink that not only was considered regal but brought joy because of its alcoholic content. Joy is considered an essential part of any blessing or Jewish act.

The second cup of wine is filled during the later part of the ceremony and is the cup over which the *sheva berachot* are recited. Though technically the cup that is used for the first two blessings could be rinsed and reused for the *sheva berachot*, the universal custom is to prepare a second wine cup for the seven blessings. This is especially appropriate since the second half of the wedding ceremony, the *nisuin*, during which the *sheva berachot* are recited, was originally a completely separate ceremony held at a later time after the *erusin*, at which the ring is given and the first two blessings are said over the first cup of wine.

These cups can be traditional silver *kiddush* cups from family or friends or they can be two glasses from your own home or from the wedding hall. Though many brides and grooms prefer to treasure these as keepsakes, if you just want to use two glasses from the caterer or hall that is fine.

A Glass to Break

If you have ever been to a Jewish wedding, the sound of a glass breaking and shouts of mazel tov will resonate in your memory. At the very end of a Jewish wedding ceremony, a glass is smashed with the foot, usually by the groom, to symbolize that even at our times of greatest joy we acknowledge that the world is not whole. Even though our people have our land back, in the holy land of Israel things are not at peace.

For millennia the Jewish people have prayed for a time of peace and wholeness, a messianic era that would usher in a more perfect world. For a people that has been through so much over its history—times of great joy and success and times of terrible destruction—our moments of greatest joy are not ones of complete abandon. Even at that moment under the chuppah there is the realization that life is real, that our history is part of us, and there is a tinge of sadness. Conversely, for such a complex people as the Jews, the rabbis teach that even at times of great sorrow there is also some joy mixed in.

Some couples ask their rabbi to say a few words before the breaking of the glass, not only about remembering the destruction of Jerusalem and our people's history but also about personal losses for the bride or the groom, such as loved ones who are no longer here. Sharing these memories of loved ones is appropriate just before the breaking of the glass.

You can choose any type of glass to break under the chuppah, even one of the glasses that was used for the blessings. In contrast to the breaking of the plate by the mothers of the bride and groom earlier in the ceremony, glass is used, not earthenware. In his book *Made in Heaven*, Rabbi Aryeh Kaplan suggests this is because earthenware cannot be melted down and reformed but glass can. This demonstrates that even a broken world or mortal life is always redeemable. In *The Jewish Way in Love and Marriage*, Rabbi Maurice Lamm writes that the breaking of the glass represents the bride and groom breaking with their own pasts to start a new life together as a truly new being.

Some couples care little about the glass's sentimental value and use a burned-out lightbulb wrapped in a cloth napkin; other couples opt for a glass that will have sentimental value. Many Jewish bookstores sell handcrafted colored glasses that are used for this breaking and then send the pieces back to the artist to be fashioned into a work of art for the couple's home.

Kittel: *Groom's Traditional White Robe*

At many traditional Jewish weddings, the bride is not the only one in white; the groom also dons a paler shade. Though the groom usually wears a tuxedo or suit, he often wears a traditional *kittel* over his clothes for the wedding ceremony. The *kittel* is usually a special white robe made of linen or cotton with no pockets and a belt that ties in the front.

FACT

In contrast to most men's clothing, the *kittel* usually buttons right over left. The reason for this is found in Kabbalah, Jewish mysticism. God is seen as having many characteristics that are sometimes laid out on a kind of map. The right side is called *chesed*, kindness, and the left is *gevurah*, strength. When wearing the *kittel* we hope mercy and kindness will outweigh judgment and strength.

The *kittel* is worn by men for the first time at their wedding and subsequently each year at the Passover Seder and on Yom Kippur. The *kittel* is a symbol of purity due to its white color. In addition, its similarity to the simple white clothing that Jewish people are buried in helps us realize that life is limited and precious. The *kittel* has no pockets to remind us that we cannot take anything with us when we leave this world, and what we do while we are here matters most. At this most joyous and auspicious moment under the chuppah, the *kittel* helps us focus our thoughts on the proper intentions and goals for life and what is truly meaningful.

Benchers: *Booklets for Grace after Meals*

At the end of the reception, as after every meal, the grace after meals is recited to thank God for the food. The Bible expresses this commandment in a verse in the eighth chapter of Deuteronomy: "And you shall eat and be satisfied and bless God for the good land which God has given you." The notion of giving thanks is deeply embedded within Jewish law and custom. Jews say many blessings to give thanks, whether to a person who has given us something or to God to Whom we are constantly grateful.

The grace after meals, or in Hebrew the *birkat hamazon*, is the only blessing whose recitation is clearly commanded in the Bible. It is interesting that the blessing for thanking God is not said when we are hungry but after we have eaten and are full. It is at that time that perhaps humans are most vulnerable to not giving thanks, to feeling we have everything we need. Especially at a wedding meal when we are extra thankful, taking a few minutes for the tradition of *birkat hamazon* is appropriate. Most Orthodox and Conservative prayer books will have the entire traditional grace after meals, which can cover several pages with some additions for a wedding meal; some reform prayer books may contain a shorter version.

The grace after meals booklets include the name of God in Hebrew and so should be treated with respect and not disposed of after the wedding meal. If you have many of the booklets left over you can keep them or give them to a synagogue to be buried, which is how Jewish holy books are usually disposed of.

It has become a widespread custom to have these grace after meals booklets specially printed and monogrammed with the date of the wedding and the names of the bride and groom on the cover. These are usually left on each table with one by each place setting and taken home by guests as a keepsake by which to remember the bride and groom and their special day each time the booklet is used at home. These *birkat hamazon* booklets are sometimes called *benchers* after the Yiddish word which means "to bless."

A Plate to Break

In addition to breaking a glass under the chuppah, the mother of the bride and the mother of the groom usually break a plate following the signing and reading of the *tanaim* at the *tish*. There are no Jewish legal requirements for the look or materials of this plate. One thing to be careful of is that the breaking, which is often done by hand over the back of a chair, can be difficult. You do not want anyone to get hurt by pieces of the broken plate, so be sure the plate is thin and well wrapped. It is best to use ceramic or china and not glass since glass can create sharper pieces.

Many couples opt to have their mothers use a hammer to break the plate, especially if it is thick. Though it is less dramatic and a bit less traditional than smashing it over the back of a chair, it is much safer. Rabbis who have witnessed an embarrassed mother of the bride or groom take several tries to break the plate often recommend using a hammer. Sometimes the hammer is decorated with paint or ribbon. This makes an especially attractive and safe alternative and a nice memento that can be saved for the weddings of the couple's children or for other siblings or relatives.

Kippot: *Head Coverings*

In addition to personalized booklets for the grace after meals, many Jewish weddings provide personalized *kippot*, or head coverings. From the time of the Talmud more than 2,000 years ago, some Jewish men and women developed the custom of covering their head at prayer times—some wear one all the time—as a sign of remembering that they are covered from above by the Divine. This covering creates a sense of humility and recognition that we are not alone but that God watches over us.

How do I keep this kippah on my head while dancing?
Most people who wear a *kippah* use bobby pins or plain metal hair clips to hold it on. There are also some Velcro options that can be purchased at Jewish bookstores for those with short hair. Works better than staples!

There is no definition within Jewish law or custom for what a head covering must consist of. In some Jewish communities hats are often worn, and in other communities a smaller *kippah*, sometimes called a *yarmulke*, is worn. These small head coverings, or *kippot*, come in all colors and a variety of materials. You can order them from any number of Jewish bookstores or Judaica suppliers in person or over the Internet. You can also buy *kippot* that match the colors of your wedding and usually are personalized with the name of the bride and groom and the date and place of the wedding celebration for people to take home.

Kippot come in many different colors and materials. You can order *kippot* made of satin, which are usually less expensive, or ones made from velvet or suede. You can even order multicolored *kippot* that are crocheted, usually by machine to make them affordable. All *kippot* are available personalized and in bulk. The number of *kippot* you decide to order will depend on how many people you think will choose to wear one and how many of your guests will bring one of their own.

CHAPTER 8

The *Ketubah*: Covenant Between Groom and Bride

8

The *ketubah*, which literally means "that which is written," was created and enacted during the period of the Mishna and Talmud, approximately 2,000 years ago. Though written with Hebrew letters, the original ketubah was written in the Aramaic language, the language used by Jewish people during the Babylonian exile. The rabbis of the Talmud decreed that all Jewish marriages be accompanied by the writing and signing of a *ketubah*.

Why Is It Necessary?

The main part of the *ketubah* outlines the duties that the husband has to the wife during their marriage and the amount of monetary compensation that he will give her in case of divorce. The basic form of the *ketubah* we have now dates from the Talmudic or latter Gaonic period after the exile of the Jews from the Land of Israel in the year 70 C.E.

The Talmud writes that in ancient days men would marry women and if they wanted to divorce them they would do this with no monetary obligations to their wives. The Talmud felt that this gave men the power to marry a woman and too easily divorce her, moving on to another wife. The rabbis felt that to be sure the groom was sincere in his desire to marry, to be sure he would think twice about the gravity of marriage, and to be sure the wife who might not have a livelihood was provided for, a *ketubah* contract should always be written.

You will keep your *ketubah* for a long time. If it is a decorated ketubah, it will probably hang on the wall of your home. Be sure to bring a pen or felt tip marker that will not fade for the witnesses to use to sign the *ketubah*. If you prefer, select a pen whose ink will match the text's color.

The *ketubah* also ensured that the obligations men had to provide for their wives, to respect them and satisfy them, were clearly delineated and obligated of them in written legal form. The *ketubah* for its day was a wondrous and innovative protection device for wives who may not have had much power in relationships.

Obligations

The *ketubah* contains provisions for the wife in case of divorce, but it also outlines a husband's obligations to his wife during the marriage. Though wives also have obligations to their husbands, it seems the rabbis felt it was the man whose obligations needed to be clearly spelled out and made legally binding, perhaps because women had less power.

The traditional *ketubah* that is agreed upon by the groom at the *tish* just before the wedding and signed by witnesses states that the husband must provide his bride with food, clothing, and shelter, and that he will meet her sexual needs. He is also implicitly agreeing to do work around the house as is customary in their locale for husbands to do. Indeed, the Torah itself not only obligates a man to honor his wife and provide for her but also to engage in sexual intimacy with her if she so desires at regular intervals during the time of month in which it is permitted.

Alimony

The *ketubah* states that in case of divorce or the death of the husband, the husband agrees to pay his wife 200 zuz, an ancient measure of silver, if it is the bride's first marriage, and any additional extra funds that he obligates himself to. If it is the bride's second marriage the amounts are lessened. This money can be exacted, as it is written in the *ketubah*, even "from the shirt that is on his back."

Since the *ketubah* is a legal and binding document, it also contains the date on which it is signed and the signatures of two witnesses who are present at the time the husband agrees to the terms of the *ketubah*. Because the rabbis required the *ketubah* for the wife's protection, they enacted a Jewish law that without a written and signed *ketubah* the husband was forbidden to live with his wife, thus ensuring that she would have her *ketubah* and the monetary protection it afforded her as long as they lived together.

Traditional and Nontraditional Texts

Though the traditional *ketubah* text is a fairly businesslike document written in ancient Aramaic and mostly describes the husband's obligations to his wife, having one is a Jewish law and tradition many thousands of years old. Besides the traditional text many alternative *ketubah* texts are also available. Most nontraditional *ketubah* texts come in Hebrew, English, or both and can be purchased from any number of online *ketubah* retailers. Some alternative *ketubah* texts are egalitarian and outline both the bride and the groom's obligations to each other during the marriage and in case of divorce. Others do not dictate the obligations of bride and groom in case of

עוד ישמע בערי יהודה ובחוצות ירושלים

ב_______בשבת_______________לחדש_________שנת חמשת אלפים ושבע
מאות____________למנין שאנו מנין כאן ______________________________
איך החתן______________למשפחת______________אמר להדא ____________
_____________________למשפחת________________הוי לי לאנתו כדת משה
וישראל ואנא אפלח ואוקיר ואיזון ואפרנס יתיכי ליכי כהלכות גוברין יהודאין דפלחין
ומקרין וזנין ומפרנסין לנשיהון בקושטא ויהיבנא ליכי מהר _________ כסף זוזי
_____ דחזי ליכי __________ ומזוניכי וכסותיכי וסיפוקיכי ומיעל לותיכי כאורח כל
ארעא וצביאת מרת _________________________ דא והות ליה לאנתו ודן נדוניא
דהנעלת ליה מבי____________ בין בכסף בין בדהב בין בתכשיטין במאני דלבושא
בשימושי דירה ובשימושא דערסא הכל קבל עליו___________________ חתן דנן
______ זקוקין כסף צרוף וצבי________________ חתן דנן והוסיף לה מן דיליה
עוד _____ זקוקין כסף צרוף אחרים כנגדן סך הכל מאתים זקוקים כסף צרוף וכך אמר
____________ חתן דנן אחריות שטר כתובתא דא נדוניא דן ותוספתא דא
קבלות עלי ועל ירתי בתראי להתפרע מכל שפר ארג נכסין וקנינין דאית לי תחות כל
שמיא דקנאי ודעתיד אנא למקנא נכסין דאית להון אחריות ודלית להון אחריות כלהון
יהון אחראין וערבאין לפרוע מנהון שטר כתובתא דא נדוניא דן ותוספתא דא מנאי
ואפילו מן גלימא דעל כתפי בחיי ובתר חיי מן יומא דנן ולעלם ואחריות שטר כתובתא
דא נדוניא דן ותוספתא דא קבל עליו________________חתן דנן כחומר כל שטרי
כתובות ותוספתות דנהגין בבנת ישראל העשויין כתקון חכמינו זכרונם לברכה דלא
כאסמכתא ודלא כטופסי דשטרי___________ מן _________________ למשפחת
______________חתן דנן למרת_______________ למשפחת________________
_______ דא על כל מה דכתוב ומפורש לעיל במנא דכשר למקניא ביה

הכל שריר וקים

נאום ____ עד
נאום ____ עד

קול ששון וקול שמחה קול חתן וקול כלה

עוד ישמע בערי יהודה ובחוצות ירושלים

ON THE ______ DAY OF THE WEEK, THE ______ DAY OF THE MONTH OF ______ IN THE YEAR 57____, CORRESPONDING TO THE ______ DAY OF _________ 20___

THE HOLY COVENANT OF MARRIAGE WAS ENTERED INTO AT ______________________

____

BETWEEN THE BRIDEGROOM

____

AND THE BRIDE

____

THE BRIDEGROOM MADE THE FOLLOWING DECLARATION TO HIS BRIDE: "BE MY WIFE ACCORDING TO THE LAW OF MOSES AND ISRAEL. I FAITHFULLY PROMISE THAT I WILL BE A TRUE HUSBAND UNTO YOU; I WILL HONOR AND CHERISH YOU; I WILL PROTECT AND SUPPORT YOU, AND WILL PROVIDE ALL THAT IS NECESSARY FOR YOUR SUSTENANCE IN ACCORDANCE WITH THE USUAL CUSTOM OF JEWISH HUSBANDS. I ALSO TAKE UPON MYSELF ALL SUCH FURTHER OBLIGATIONS FOR YOUR MAINTENANCE AS ARE PRESCRIBED BY OUR RELIGIOUS STATUTES."

AND THE BRIDE HAS ENTERED INTO THIS HOLY COVENANT WITH AFFECTION AND SINCERITY, AND HAS THUS TAKEN UPON HERSELF THE FULFILLMENT OF ALL THE DUTIES INCUMBENT UPON A JEWISH WIFE.

THIS COVENANT OF MARRIAGE WAS DULY EXECUTED AND WITNESSED THIS DAY ACCORDING TO THE USAGE OF ISRAEL.

BRIDEGROOM______________________________________

BRIDE ____

OFFICIATING RABBI ______________________________

קול ששון וקול שמחה קול חתן וקול כלה

divorce and describe only their sentiments of emotional and interpersonal support to each other.

Whichever *ketubah* text and translation you plan to use, be sure to consult with your rabbi or wedding officiant first. Depending on their Jewish affiliation they may require a certain kind of *ketubah* text and may or may not have a preference or requirement with regard to translations.

Traditional Kitubot

Orthodox and Traditional *kitubot* always include the Aramaic text, though there is some slight variation in textual style, phrasing, and content even among these traditional Aramaic *kitubot*. Often a couple using this type of *ketubah* will choose to include an English translation of the Aramaic text in a separate paragraph. This translation can be literal, though often it is more poetic.

Though artistically fashioned decorative *kitubot* have become very popular among all Jews today, a traditional Aramaic *ketubah* can be obtained for only a few dollars, often copied by machine since there is no reason that the *ketubah* be handwritten or decorated if you do not plan to hang it on your wall.

The English translation can be purchased as part of the *ketubah*, or you can choose to write one yourself and give it to the *ketubah* artist or company to print or write in calligraphy. Though a traditional Aramaic *ketubah* text has only space for the two witnesses to sign, often the English translation will include a space for bride and groom and sometimes the rabbi to sign.

Many *kitubot* today are highly decorated. Though in many religions religious texts were often elaborately illuminated in order to communicate their lessons and stories to those who were illiterate, Jewish religious texts such as prayer books and bibles were rarely illuminated with drawings. This was probably due to the Jewish opposition to rendering images, especially of God. The two exceptions to this, beginning in the Middle Ages, were the Passover Haggadah, the book used for the Passover Seder, and the *ketubah*.

Nontraditional Kitubot

There is a wide array of nontraditional *ketubah* alternatives. Almost all of these *kitubot* are available in Hebrew, English, or in both languages side by side. Some couples, especially from Conservative or Orthodox families, choose to use a traditional Aramaic Hebrew text along with an alternative English translation. Other Conservative and some Reform Jews opt for a traditional-style *ketubah* in Aramaic Hebrew written with egalitarian language. These egalitarian *kitubot* outline both the bride and groom's equal obligations to each other but utilize the traditional Aramaic phrases adapted from the traditional *ketubah* text to do so. Egalitarian *kitubot* of this type can come in Aramaic or more Modern Hebrew language.

Reform *kitubot* can be purchased in Hebrew, English, or both languages and do not usually refer to provisions in case of divorce or separation. If your Reform *ketubah* is to have a Hebrew language section it will most likely be in Modern Hebrew, not Aramaic. Reform *ketubah* texts are always egalitarian.

Some conservative, reform, or Reconstructionist couples have chosen to use a document called a *brit ahuvim*, or a lovers' covenant. This document was written by Rachel Adler in her 1998 book *Engendering Judaism*. It is not a *ketubah* but rather a Jewish legal document that creates a legal partnership. It is written in Hebrew with an English translation. Some liberal couples find it appealing because it is an egalitarian text and binds the couple to a legal partnership, but it does not fit the *halachic*, the traditional Jewish legal parameters of a *ketubah* for *kiddushin*, the classic Jewish marriage ceremony.

Humanistic Jewish *kitubot* are written in any language and sometimes translated into Hebrew. They focus exclusively on the bride and groom's aspirations to build a harmonious family together. Nontraditional *kitubot* usually provide space for the bride and groom to sign but will sometimes provide spaces for the signature of witnesses and the rabbi to sign, while some do not require any signatures at all.

Agunah *Provisions*

The word *agunah* in Hebrew means "one who is chained," specifically one who is chained in a marriage and is unable to receive a *get*, a Jewish divorce, thus rendering them incapable of moving on to another relationship and marriage. According to Jewish law, a Jewish religious marriage must be dissolved by a Jewish divorce. Remarrying without an official Jewish divorce can render the second marriage an adulterous one in the eyes of Jewish law since the party is still technically married to the previous spouse. In this case, if a spouse is unable to attain a Jewish divorce they would remain "chained" to their first marriage and unable to remarry.

Sometimes in cases of difficult divorce, one party will refuse to give or receive a *get*, a Jewish divorce, holding their spouse up for custody wishes or monetary gain. Using one's agreement to give a *get* as extortion is obviously considered a terrible crime in Judaism, but today's Jewish courts have little power to punish the offender or force them to agree to a *get*.

FACT

The benefit of the Lieberman clause was that in theory the couple agrees in writing to pursue a religious divorce in addition to a civil one. The dilemma is that since it is contained within a religious document it is not usually admissible in a secular court and is therefore difficult to enforce.

Legal Clauses

This potential for abuse has been addressed by different Jewish groups in different ways. The Conservative movement requires a clause in the Aramaic text of the *ketubah* that states that the husband and wife will agree to appear before a *Bait Din*, a Jewish court, for a Jewish divorce in the event that the couple is civilly divorced but not religiously divorced. This clause is commonly referred to as the Lieberman Clause after its author, Rabbi Saul Lieberman, who was at one time the head of the Conservative rabbinical school, the Jewish Theological Seminary in New York City.

Reform *kitubot* do not usually contain any language of agreement to a Jewish divorce since the ceremony of Jewish divorce is not a part of Reform Judaism today.

Religiously Required Prenuptial Agreements

Orthodox *kitubot* do not contain such a clause in the ketubah since there is a desire in more traditional communities not to change the text of such an ancient document. The problem of *agunah* is a powerful one in the Orthodox community; in response, many Orthodox rabbis have begun requiring couples to sign a legal prenuptial agreement that is admissible in a secular court. It states that if the couple ever becomes divorced civilly or the couple is separated and the wife has asked for a religious divorce, the husband must continue to support his wife as is his *halachic*, Jewish legal obligation, until such time as he gives her a religious divorce. The results of such a prenuptial agreement have proven to be quite positive and some rabbinical organizations will not allow a wedding to be performed without one. See Appendix D for additional resources.

In the Bible and in traditional Judaism according to the Talmud, when a divorce is executed it must be written carefully by a trained scribe and given volitionally by the man to the woman. This process is based on the biblical verse in Deuteronomy 24:1: ". . . and he shall write for her a document of separation and place it into her hands. . . ." Originally, this verse also gave the husband the power to divorce his wife without her consent.

The rabbis of the Talmud, in an attempt to grant wives power, enacted a set sum of money that the husband was obligated to give the wife with her divorce, thus giving her at least some monetary power, though the husband could still divorce her against her will if he was willing to pay the amount. In the eleventh century, Rabbanu Gershom, the leader of Ashkenazik European Jewry, made a rabbinical decree that no man could divorce his wife without her consent and that no man would any longer be allowed to have more than one wife, even though it was biblically permitted. Since wives now had to agree to any divorce, they gained a great deal of bargaining power over the financial terms of the divorce. Husband and wife needed to come to an agreement together as to the terms of their divorce before they would both agree to it.

Today several problems have emerged with this arrangement. Sometimes Jewish men, knowing that they are biblically permitted to have more than one wife, will leave a marriage with only a civil divorce. Though the wife may want the husband to agree to her monetary terms of the divorce, he may simply find another wife. This violates the rabbinic decree and leaves his first wife essentially an *agunah*, a chained woman, using this power to force his own divorce terms. In addition, if a wife demands a divorce and the husband refuses, though she can obtain a civil divorce in a civil court, for a Jewish divorce to be biblically and rabbinically valid it must be given by the husband to the wife.

To address these problems, in the Orthodox community some groups of rabbis have instituted the binding secular prenuptial agreement which is admissible in a secular court. Though the document can not compel the husband by physical or corporal force to give a *get*, since technically a *get* given under coercion can be declared invalid, the husband is obligated while he is religiously married to his wife to support her fully. In Israel today husbands are sometimes jailed for refusing to give their wives a religious divorce.

This prenuptial agreement works because it obligates the husband to support his wife with a good living wage all the time they are separated or civilly divorced until such time as he gives her a religious divorce, which is truly his obligation.

He supports her with a good, though not outlandish, living wage, currently valued at $150 per day and attached to the cost of living and inflationary indices in order to obviate devaluation over time. Thus, if inflation goes up, the amount he must pay her increases. In the years since this prenuptial agreement has been instituted there have not been any cases of husbands withholding a *get* as extortion in order to obtain additional money or custody consideration beyond what they were legally granted. For a link to this prenuptial agreement on the internet, see Appendix D.

English Translations

Traditionally, *kitubot* were written in Aramaic, which utilizes Hebrew letters but is a language composed of Hebrew and Babylonian words. Although prayer was always said in Hebrew, the Jewish people in the period of the Talmud spoke the Aramaic language. The Talmud requires a *ketubah*, so having one is a rabbinic mitzvah, or religious commandment. However, the actual document itself is not essentially a religious one. It is simply a contract between husband and wife outlining his obligations to her, so an added translation is entirely appropriate.

Today many *kitubot* come with a translation into English. Since it should be seen as a legal document, the Hebrew and English texts should be separate on the page and each should be printed in a defined shape so that the texts themselves cannot be manipulated at a later time without becoming apparent.

Whichever *ketubah* you choose, you can decide if you will have a direct translation, a more poetic translation, or merely a section of the *ketubah* that is not in Hebrew or Aramaic but in your spoken language. You can put anything you like in this section. If you are not using a translation or loose translation of the *ketubah*, you can use a favorite poem or write your own vows to each other.

Finding a Ketubah

There is a large variety of *kitubot* the market today. Some are made specifically for a couple by hand by a particular artist and thus will be quite expensive. Other beautiful decorative *kitubot* are created by artists through computer graphics; since they are not one-of-a-kind, they are less expensive. Of these *kitubot* some will be of a numbered limited series and others will not. These types of *kitubot* usually have the bride and groom's names and the place and date of the wedding set in seamlessly as part of the text so they do not look written in.

A couple who just wants the text of a *ketubah* or wants an inexpensive decorative *ketubah* can opt for a preprinted decorated *ketubah*. The rabbi will write in their names and the place and date of the wedding in Hebrew and English by hand. Couples who do not want a decorated *ketubah* at all and just require the text can copy one by machine that contains blanks for their names and the location and date of the wedding. The rabbi can fill it out for them to keep and treasure just for its meaning and the covenant between them that it represents.

Your *ketubah* supplier should provide you with a form to fill out the names of the bride and groom, their parents' names, and the date and place of the wedding. Be sure to run it by your rabbi to confirm the Hebrew spellings if required, as there can be more than one way to spell these in Hebrew.

If you are purchasing a *ketubah* that will be preprinted with your specific information or one that is being handwritten and decorated by a scribe or artist, you will need to give the artist, scribe, online purveyor, or Jewish bookstore through which you are buying the *ketubah* your information to put in the document. If your *ketubah* is to be in Hebrew and English you will need to supply your names, your parents' names, and the place and date of the wedding in both languages.

Different rabbis may want to use different kinds of information in the *ketubah*. Usually a *ketubah* contains the names of the bride and groom, their fathers' names, and often their mothers' names also. If your *ketubah* is only in English you may be able to supply all the information yourself, but if the *ketubah* is to be in Hebrew also you should check with your rabbi to be sure your wedding location, your names, and the date of the wedding are spelled correctly in Hebrew.

Adding Your Own Vows

You have many options if you want the English component of your *ketubah* to be something more personal than a translation of the Hebrew. Often the

English "translation" is not a translation at all. Instead, it is a summary of the more poetic parts of the *ketubah* that pertain to your obligations to each other. This may be a good opportunity to record your own vows to each other for posterity.

You might want to use the theme of the *ketubah*, that of your commitments to each other and the obligations of support that are an essential part of any marriage. The process of writing this English "translation" can be a very meaningful one for you both. You will take time out during this hectic period of wedding planning to focus or refocus on your relationship, what you give to each other, how you are different, and how you are alike.

Try asking each other a question such as, "What do you love about me?" or "What is unique about this relationship for you?" Write down some words that come to mind and use this list to begin writing about what you mean to each other. Work the words into sentences that reflect how you feel about each other and your hopes for your future together.

This will not only produce a personal unique "translation" for your *ketubah* but the process alone will be an indispensable exercise in appreciating each other, your relationship, and the journey that you are embarking on together. As your wedding date gets closer and the planning process gets more hectic, the time you take to reflect together will remind you of what it is all truly about.

CHAPTER 9

Wedding Tools

No doubt, when you close your eyes and picture your wedding day you see perfection—a seamless, meaningful, and tender celebration. In contrast, the reality of a wedding, with its myriad details, plans, and personalities, can be a hectic whirlwind that may be anything but smooth. Though the details of wedding planning often seem to go on and on and become removed from the romantic scene in your mind, sufficient preplanning with the proper tools can help you create the space and circumstances to facilitate the wedding you have anticipated.

Choosing an Invitation Style

Early on in the planning process, you and your fiancé will need to think about how you wish to invite the guests you want to celebrate your wedding with you. Though invitations are often chosen based exclusively on their visual and design appeal, keep in mind that the formation of your particular and unique wedding style, feeling, and ambiance begins at the first glimpse your guests will have of your wedding—your invitation.

Jewish Aspects of Your Invitation

Since the invitation is the beginning of your Jewish wedding, you may want to consider the Jewish aspects of your invitation style and attempt to reflect the style of your particular Jewish wedding in the invitation. Your invitation can also, of course, reflect other more typical themes that will play a role in your wedding, such as wedding colors or symbols that are sentimental to you and your fiancé.

Many times the invitation to a Jewish wedding contains some Hebrew language and an English translation. When a guest sees such an invitation, he immediately knows that this is going to be a uniquely Jewish wedding. In contrast, if your wedding invitation were to be only in English with none of the traditional phrases that are used in Jewish wedding invitations, the only clue a guest might have to the Jewish tradition might be your name, or the name of the institution, synagogue, or temple if the celebration is to be held at a Jewish venue.

There is a series of traditional Jewish phrases, words, and layouts that are often utilized for Jewish wedding invitations. Some of the Jewish wedding invitation styles contain Hebrew writing on one side of the invitation and English on the other. The English is not necessarily a direct translation of the Hebrew but contains many of the elements that are found in it. You can choose some of the traditional Hebrew phrases and language with your invitation designer to include in the Hebrew and English sections, or just on the Hebrew side. If your wedding invitation will be only in English, you can still choose a Jewish phrase or two to write in translation over the top of the text as a heading.

The following is a list of some of the Hebrew phrases that are commonly utilized in Jewish wedding invitations in translation with their sources:

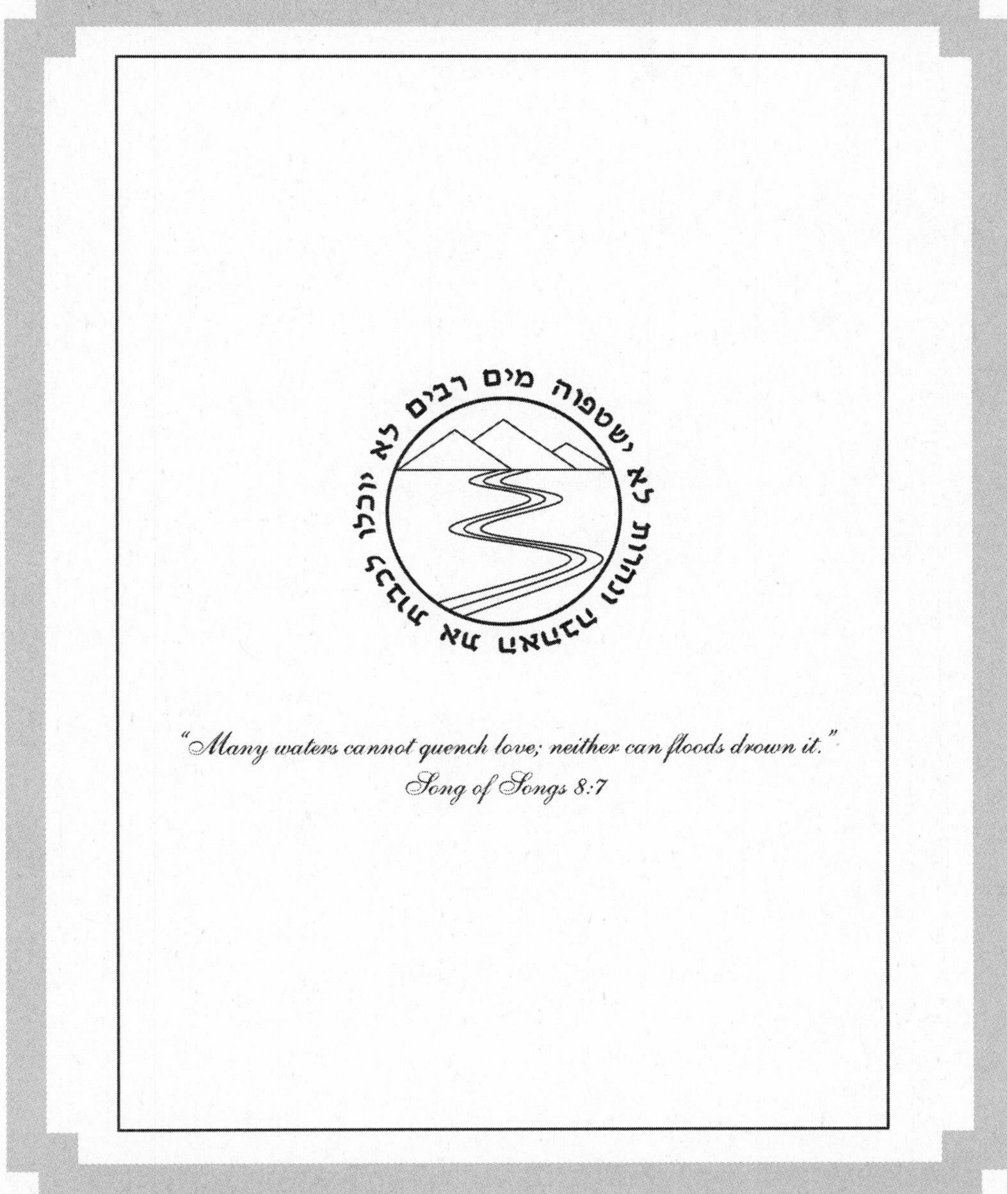

Invitation design by Jeff Glowgower

Suzanne Ruth Pritzker

and

Andrew Dudley Love

together with our parents

invite you to rejoice with us at our wedding

Sunday, the fourteenth of October

Two thousand and seven

Eleven o'clock in the morning

Chuppah at noon

Bais Abraham Congregation

6910 Delmar Blvd

University City, Missouri

Reception to follow

נעלה את ירושלים על ראש שמחתנו
עוד ישמע בערי יהודה ובחוצות ירושלים

קול ששון וקול שמחה
קול חתן וקול כלה

בשבח והודיה לבורא עולם

החתן המופלג — **הכלה המהוללה**

יונתן נחשון — עם בחירת לבו / עם בחיר לבה — **שושנה רבקה**

מתכבדים להזמינכם להשתתף בשמחת כלולותיהם
שתתקיים אי"ה
ביום ראשון פרשת לך לך, ב' חשון תשס"ח

קבלת פנים בשעה אחת עשרה
חופה בשעה שתים עשרה

בבית אברהם קאנגרעגיישאן
סנט לואיס, מיזורי

הורי החתן
אליסון לוב
גורג לוב

הורי הכלה
דוד וזלאטה פרצקר

- I am my beloved's and my beloved is mine. (Song of Songs 6:3)
- This is my beloved, this is my friend. (Song of Songs 5:16)
- Come into my garden, my sister, my bride. (Song of Songs 5:1)
- The mountains and the hills shall burst into song before you, and all the trees of the fields shall clap their hands. (Isaiah 55:12)
- You created joy and gladness, bridegroom and bride, mirth and exultation, pleasure and delight. (Sheva Berachot 7)
- May it be heard once again in the cities of Judah and in Jerusalem, the voice of joy and gladness, the sound of rejoicing with the bride and the groom. (Sheva Berachot 7)
- With the assistance of God, may God's Name be blessed. (Liturgy)
- With great praise and thanks to God. (Liturgy)
- We place Jerusalem at the head of our joy. (Psalms 137:6)
- Give peace, goodness, and blessing. (Amidah Prayer)

If you are uncomfortable with having a Hebrew side to the invitation or feel that it will seem too foreign to some of your guests, you might choose to have an English wedding invitation with no Hebrew letters or traditional phrases but with some indication that this is going to be a Jewish-style wedding. In addition to or instead of using the above phrases, you can write not only the regular Gregorian date on the invitation but also include the Hebrew date in English letters. For instance, you might write the following for the date: "Tuesday, November 20, 2007, corresponding to Tenth Day of the Hebrew Month of Kislev, 5768," or "Tuesday, November 20, 2007/10 Kislev 5768."

General Aspects of Your Wedding Invitation

Just as the Jewish aspects of your invitation will introduce the fact that your wedding will be a Jewish one, the general aspects of your invitation can be a first glimpse into the type of wedding you will have and into your personal style. Some invitations are more traditional and some are more creative. For instance, today many invitations incorporate three-dimensional elements such as ribbon or textures and symbols that reflect your personal image. Some couples opt for invitations that will also use elements and colors that will be encompassed within their thank you cards and place cards. Rubber stamps, monograms, colors, and textures can all become thematic aspects.

Some couples who are having a smaller wedding will have handmade invitations custom made for them. This is a bit more expensive, but if your wedding is not too large it may be affordable and offer you flexibility. In addition, the postal service now offers personalized photo stamps. These are valid postage stamps that you can order online from a number of retailers. Though they are more expensive than stamps from the post office, these photo stamps can be personalized to fit you. For instance, you could use your engagement picture as the actual postage stamp. Reflecting the themes of the *sheva berachot*, you could use a picture of the Wailing Wall in Jerusalem, a Garden of Eden, or of the chuppah. Since Jewish weddings are religious ceremonies, some couples also include a request for guests to dress modestly in their wedding invitations.

Organizational Tools

Staying organized, especially if you are planning your wedding without the assistance of a professional planner, is indispensable for retaining sanity and calm. Several simple, commonsense tools can be helpful if you are not the type of person that is well organized by nature.

Budget Worksheets

As everyone knows, weddings can be quite costly, and it is far too easy to go beyond your preconceived budget. Utilizing a budget worksheet can be a helpful way to let you know how much you can spend on the various parts of your ceremony. This tool may help you sidestep some arguments and conflict between you and your fiancé, family, or vendors, since cost limitations will be in a clear, indisputable format. Several types of wedding budget worksheets and planners are available.

Checklists

If you are doing much of the wedding planning yourself, you will find many helpful organizational tools in libraries and bookstores. Some of these are the many checklists you will want to generate yourself or purchase for ideas and reminders.

Other important checklists are the registry checklist, which is a list of the many kinds of kitchen houseware you may want to register for, a flowers checklist, describing what kinds of flowers you might need and when, and a catering checklist, listing things to think about when arranging he food.

An important checklist specifically for a Jewish wedding is a list of all the rituals and stages of the wedding, such as the *tish*, ceremony, reception, and *yichud*, and which of your guests you will ask to act as witnesses or sign the *tanaim*.

One of the most basic of these checklists is a wedding planning timeline. This is a timeline that goes according to the months and weeks leading up to your wedding and gives you a general sense of what must be done by any number weeks or months before the wedding.

Optional Economic and Religious Prenuptial Agreements

A few years ago, the phrase prenuptial agreement might have brought to mind the very rich or famous nitpicking over which partner in case of certain divorce gets the vacation castle in the south of France and which gets the Aston Martin. Today, however, prenuptial agreements are quite common, and they often address religious and cultural situations as well as financial arrangements. Some couples have several prenuptial agreements and some have one document that weaves together agreed-upon financial considerations as well as cultural or religious values and methods of living together.

Financial Prenuptials

Some couples have a lot of anxiety and doubts about the notion of signing a financial prenuptial agreement. They feel that nothing would quash their romantic wedding feelings like signing a prenuptial agreement that essentially delineates the couple's financial plan in case of divorce and, to a lesser extent, within the marriage.

If a couple does not trust each other and requires a prenuptial agreement for this underlying reason, the prenuptial might be a good idea, but perhaps the couple should consider seeing a counselor to address the mistrust between them and the ways in which those feelings might affect their relationship as a whole. On the other hand, if the couple does essentially trust each other but for tangential reasons thinks it wise to have a prenuptial agreement, there is much to be said for this.

A couple might opt for a financial prenuptial agreement if the couple is marrying when they are older and already have older children, especially if their respective children desire to retain their own parent's inheritance. Another reason might be to protect one spouse if the other is truly not financially responsible or is an addicted gambler or shopper. A prenuptial agreement can also serve to put the financial aspect of your marriage out in the open, and this exercise in honesty and vulnerability can often be good for a couple, especially if one spouse feels less financially equipped, educated, or empowered than the other.

If you desire a prenuptial agreement, be sure to inform your potential spouse of this as early as you can. Be honest about why you want one. Though this may be a difficult conversation, there is no reason to avoid it if you have a trusting, open, and communicative relationship.

When it is time to actually draft the prenuptial agreement, you will each need lawyers to represent you individually. This is wise because each lawyer's job is to represent one of the parties so that no ethical conflicts emerge.

When you write a prenuptial agreement, it is important to be open and honest about your assets. It is also important to express your love and commitment even within the terms of the agreement, to see the prenuptial agreement as a way of providing for each other in case of the other's death or in case of divorce. Express that you hope all goes well but that no one can tell the future and so the prenuptial agreement is there to help protect both of you and your families. View the prenuptial agreement not as an expression of mistrust but more as an insurance policy. Judaism itself believes that if a marriage is based upon not only love but on a clear sense of the couple's obligations and requirements to each other, this will produce a sound foundation upon which to build a long-lasting marriage.

Religious Prenuptials

Some couples also use a prenuptial contract as a way of delineating the practice and provisions of their religious life together. This is especially true if the bride and groom come from very different religious backgrounds and their practices are different or if they have children of their own at the time of their marriage to each other.

For instance, if two people are marrying and they each have children from previous marriages, they may want to come to some basic agreements and ground rules for how to educate and raise their children religiously together.

FACT

Even if it is a first marriage for both parties but their religious practices differ, they may want to outline some basics for how religion will function in their home. This is one way to guarantee that each is able to practice without causing conflict.

One example is the situation of Jonathan and Leah. Their wedding was to be a second marriage for both of them and they each had one child that they were bringing into the marriage. Leah grew up as an Orthodox Jewish person and was observant of the Sabbath and kosher laws; Jonathan did not but was interested in attempting to learn more about this but was unsure how much he would be comfortable committing to. Since they were already a mature couple, they understood that along with the romance of a marriage come many practical curves that must be navigated carefully to live a harmonious life together in which each partner feels that their needs are being met.

In addition to a structured religious prenuptial agreement that addressed the provisions of their commitment to a religious divorce if they were to become divorced, Jonathan and Leah wrote a prenuptial agreement that outlined the aspects of their commitments to religious life as they formed a new family. Through this agreement, they made room for Leah to have a kosher home and for her child to have a religious education. Jonathan, as someone who was newer to Jewish religious life, was able to clearly say how much he was willing to be expected to do religiously. In the prenuptial agreement, Jonathan agreed that both their children would be given a similar religious education and that Jonathan would attend services at times with Leah at her Orthodox synagogue. Leah agreed that it would be acceptable if Jonathan occasionally chose not to attend Saturday services and played golf instead.

For Leah and Jonathan, the delineation of some of their religious commitments in a written agreement allowed each to clarify and voice their expectations, needs, and potential areas of compromise. Leah agreed not to pressure Jonathan religiously as long as his actions did not affect the basic Jewish functioning of their home together and its religious spirit. In this way, Leah was assured that it would be enough of a religious Jewish environment for her and her child to feel comfortable, and Jonathan was assured of the freedom he needed and was able to outline what would and would not be expected of him. This kind of clear delineation often gives both parties security in their own personal lives. This freedom removes a potential source of religious struggle and can make room for both to actually grow closer together in their love and in their religious lives.

An Explanatory Wedding Booklet

Preparing an explanatory wedding booklet or program so that your guests know exactly what is happening at your Jewish wedding is of paramount importance, especially if not everyone attending your celebration will be Jewish or familiar with the Jewish aspects and rituals of the wedding. Such a booklet is also a convenient place to thank family and friends and to outline exactly what will be happening and when. You will find two sample wedding booklets in Appendix C.

A wedding booklet usually contains explanations about all of the steps and rituals in a Jewish wedding. It also lets your guests get to know your wedding party. A booklet will usually say who is walking down the aisle, the name of the rabbi, and contain any thank-yous or memorials that the bride and groom wish to make.

As you write your wedding booklet, keep in mind those people that may have never attended a Jewish wedding before or know little about the rituals involved. You can include reasons for each part of the wedding ceremony and some of its history as well as the significance of the practices generally and for you and your fiancé in particular.

Some couples begin the book with a page they wrote together, a welcome letter to their guests expressing their delight in having them at the celebration and mentioning some of the special aspects of the wedding or the meaning of having a Jewish wedding.

The cover of the wedding booklet usually contains the name of the bride and groom and the date and location of the wedding celebration. Some couples devise a monogram for their wedding and place this on the front of their booklet as well as on their *bencher*, their grace after meals booklet. This logo is often designed by a friend or relative and regularly uses the first letters of the couple's Hebrew or English names as well as a meaningful symbol that resonates with them. Some examples are trees, the branches of which are formed by the first letters the couple's names, or a house, the walls and roof of which are formed by their monogram.

The following is a list of headings usually found in a typical Jewish wedding booklet:

- A Welcome Letter
- The Wedding Day as a Personal Reflective "Yom Kippur"
- The Groom's *Tish*
- The Bride's *Kabalat Panim*
- The *Bedekin*

- The Procession
- The Circles of Wholeness
- The Ring
- The *Sheva Berachot*, Seven Blessings
- The Breaking of the Glass and People to Remember
- *Yichud*

The sections of a wedding booklet are placed at the discretion of the couple, but they usually reflect the stages of the ceremony. In addition to writing about each ritual itself, you can also write a sentence or two about its significance for you and your fiancé and any ways you are tweaking the ceremony to fit your style and your path of Jewish observance.

Choosing a Photographer and Videographer

Years after your wedding, you will treasure the wonderful experience of looking at your photos and your video and showing them to your children. This can bring back so many memories for you both, and the experience can give your children a glimpse into who you were before they were born and the romance and holiness of the Jewish wedding that brought you together. Hiring the right photographer and videographer now and being savvy about how you hire and instruct them will help to ensure that your wedding memories are accessible in years to come.

Questions to Ask

Photographers and videographers are an expensive but important part of your wedding. When you interview potential photographers and videographers, you will want to find out if they are familiar with Jewish weddings that are similar to yours or are willing to learn. Many of the powerful moments at a Jewish wedding that you will want captured do not exist in non-Jewish wedding ceremonies. You should ask to look at some of their past work; if you know people who have used them, find out if they were satisfied with the result. Try to get a clear sense of what will be included in the package and what will not. Ask if there are any additional charges for nighttime versus daytime weddings, for retouching photos, for negatives, for a disk so that you can make reproductions at will, or extra fees for assistants or overtime charges.

The photographer will probably show you examples of previous wedding photographs and videos she has taken. Be sure to realize that these are set up well, that the locations, clothing, and makeup are probably done by professionals, and that the bride and groom may be models. Don't be taken by only the romance you see in the photos. Ask your potential photographer and videographer the right questions so that you may go into the deal with your eyes open and without breaking your bank account.

Some couples attempt to save money by asking a friend or relative to be their photographer, but be wary of this option. Ask yourself the following questions: If you are not happy with the results, what toll will it take on your relationship with the photographer? If the designated photographer is sick or has an emergency on the day of your wedding, is there a backup? Will your friend be able to take the type of photos you desire without feeling they missed the wedding themselves?

Photography at Jewish Weddings

There are several types of photos, both formal and informal, that you may want to have in order to remember your wedding day. Some photographers are very adept at studio-type formal photos that you will probably take before the *tish* and after the *yichud* but are less comfortable with informal shots. A Jewish wedding often has some raucous dancing and celebrating at the beginning of the reception, and the photographer and videographer might need to jockey for position among hundreds of guests dancing in a big circle, some of them perhaps juggling fire or skipping rope. Will he be able to handle this? Has he ever photographed a wedding like yours or one that had similar challenges?

Some rabbis do not like to have flash photography or an intrusive videographer at the wedding ceremony, and other rabbis do not mind at all. It can be helpful if the rabbi speaks to the photographer before the ceremony to point out where the members of the wedding party will stand and explain the procedures of the ceremony. Be sure to discuss this with your rabbi or wedding officiate well before the wedding and tell the photographer and videographer of your officiant's requirements. Sometimes even a rabbi who prefers no intrusive photography will be fine if there is no flash or if the photographer is a bit farther away using a zoom lens.

If the photographer has not worked at many Jewish weddings before, be sure to give her a sense of the different parts of the wedding, such as the pre-wedding ceremonies like the *tish*, the *kabalat panim*, and the *bedekin*. Give her an outline of exactly what will be happening at each stage of the wedding and what parts you want photographed. In addition, if there are any members of your family or friends that you want to make sure are included, give the photographer a list of these individuals beforehand.

If you are not seeing each other on your wedding day until the ceremony, be sure to alert the photographer and videographer of this. They will need to schedule themselves accordingly to take photos of both your families with you before the *tish* and then of the two of you together and with your families after the *yichud*, when you are able to see each other again.

Traditional Versus Modern Music

When you choose the type of music you will have at your wedding and the band you will hire, it is important to consider that the main mitzvah of a Jewish wedding is to give the bride and groom great joy, and for your guests and the atmosphere of your wedding to make the happy couple laugh and celebrate. One of the most essential ways in which this happens is through the music at your wedding reception.

Although at most American weddings the music is used as accompaniment to the meal or for couples' dancing, the hallmark of a Jewish wedding is the upbeat Jewish music that accompanies the *simcha* dancing. The Hebrew word *simcha* means joy. This type of dancing is usually done in big circles, and sometimes circles within circles, with the bride and groom always in the middle, up on chairs, or being taken by the hand and danced in the buoyant crowd.

Some Jewish weddings include only Jewish *simcha* music and its lively circle dancing, while other Jewish weddings may have a combination of *simcha* music, slower American music for dancing in couples, and more upbeat American dancing music for dancing in a big group. Still other Jewish weddings may have only some slow instrumental Jewish music at the processional and wedding ceremony, and the music and dancing at the reception may be secular music.

The *simcha* dancing at a Jewish wedding is often one of the most engaging parts for the guests since they help make it happen and it requires much movement and big smiles. Many couples find that years later, after the type of food is long forgotten, the *lebedic* (Yiddish for "joyous") dancing is remembered. Choosing *simcha* music and the traditional dancing that accompanies it is one good way to guarantee joyous wedding memories for you and for your guests for many years to come.

After deciding together what types of music you plan to have at your wedding celebration, be sure that you ask the bands you interview about their specific experiences with Jewish weddings. Ask to see a video of a wedding that was similar to the one you plan to have. Ask for a list of songs that the band is familiar with. If you will have both Jewish *simcha* music and secular music, be sure they are adept at both and can switch easily from one type to another.

Many Jewish wedding bands do a wide variety of different types of Jewish weddings and can easily handle not only Jewish music (which may be their main talent) but also lots of typical non-Jewish wedding music. As you meet with a potential band, try to paint a picture of the wedding you are planning and the ambiance you want. If it is to be *lebidic*, let them know. If it is to be a combination of fast and slow music, klezmir or sefardic, describe that for them too.

If you have your heart set on a band that plays only Jewish or only secular music, consider using them and augmenting their selection with music from an iPod or CD player. Check with the band beforehand to see if they will let you connect it to their sound system while they are on a break. A deejay who is accustomed to Jewish weddings should be able to provide a wide array of choices, but these deejays may be more difficult to find.

CHAPTER 10

Couples from Different Backgrounds

If you and your fiancé come from different types of Jewish backgrounds, whether in terms of your observance, culture, or familial customs, it will take some negotiation, compromise, and honest conversation to be sure both of your needs are met and your comfort levels addressed. This goes not only for your wedding but also for your life together afterward. As you build a home you will often need to compromise, and in some instances you may have to create new ways of doing things so both of you can feel comfortable. Remember that in today's varied world you are not the only couple to face this challenge.

Denominational Differences

Since a Jewish wedding is very much a Jewish ritual with many Jewish legal aspects and traditions, if you and your fiancé come from different Jewish denominations or levels of observance, you and your families may come into conflict over certain aspects of the wedding.

Sources of Conflict

In addition to conflict with your fiancé about religious matters, you may find that your views differ from those of your own family. Even though you grew up with them, you may have grown or changed religiously and in many other ways since you were a child. Sometimes this can create conflict between the bride or groom and their own families. At times like this, it is important to realize that your parents probably want the best for you and for you to make your own path, but on some level they may feel rejected.

Many parents whose children are unlike them religiously wonder why their way was not "good enough" for you, their son or daughter. They often fear that since you are different you may reject them and become distant. Since weddings are such sensitive, public moments, people tend to be very opinionated when it comes to their planning and execution, and this can lead to conflict.

It is important to have open and honest conversations with your parents or future in-laws about how much you value your relationship with them. This way, when you do differ in your opinions, you can assure them that you are not arguing out of disrespect but out of your own convictions.

For many couples, their wedding brings to light their religious differences with each other for the first time. Making matters more complicated, a wedding is a big party in which you will both inevitably feel quite invested; at the same time, its very public nature leaves both of you—along with your personal practices, style, and Jewish path—quite exposed to all of your friends, relatives, and family members. For couples, though individuals rarely fit neatly into one Jewish classification, a little education and discussion about each other's denominations can help to make your wedding a time of showing off your life together instead of being in conflict about it.

Judaism today has several different groups that are often referred to as denominations. Some of the major Jewish denominations are Orthodox, Reform, Conservative, Reconstructionist, and Humanist. In addition to these some would also include Jewish Renewal as a denomination.

Orthodox Judaism

Using the word Orthodox as a label for a type of Judaism is new. The use of the label Orthodox began in the eighteenth century as a response to the first modern denominational break-off in Judaism, that of Reform. Some would argue that Orthodoxy is not a denomination because it never broke off from the mainstream and it lacks one central organizational body. Whatever you like to call it, Orthodoxy is the oldest form of Judaism.

For several thousand years, from the time of the destruction of the Jerusalem Temple in 70 C.E. until the late eighteenth century, there was some uniformity among the way individual Jewish communities saw their relationship to the rest of the Jewish people and to the commandments of the Torah. Though different Jewish communities had different customs, they saw the Torah and its laws as the word of God.

Though personal levels of Jewish observance might not have always been uniform, most Jewish communities and the people within them subscribed to the written Torah and the Talmud, Judaism's oral tradition. Orthodox Jews believe this tradition should remain constant and that the Judaism they practice is indeed this same Judaism that has been practiced over the past few millennia.

Orthodox Jews are observant of Jewish law as it is codified in the *Shulchan Aruch*, the pivotal sixteenth-century code of Jewish law written by Rabbi Yosef Cairo, and other less central codes of Jewish law. They often turn to these books for direction. The source for these codified Jewish laws is the Talmud, which is often studied by Orthodox Jews in the Jewish schools they attend from elementary school through college and daily on their own even after they are no longer in school.

Most fully observant Orthodox Jews pray three times a day, are observant of the Sabbath in a very traditional way, and will not eat foods that are not kosher or are made in kitchens that are not kosher. In addition to these basic laws, Orthodox Jews subscribe to many Jewish laws and guidelines that govern life and their spiritual path. The name for the system of Jewish law that Jews subscribe to is *halacha*, which literally means "the way."

FACT

Though all Orthodox Jews subscribe to *halacha* and from the outside their practice may look the same, there are some differences within Orthodox that pertain to Jewish weddings. For instance, some Orthodox Jews will insist that all the blessings and prayers at the wedding be recited by men, whereas other Orthodox Jews will allow women to recite the English translations of the blessings and some of the blessings and prayers in Hebrew.

If one or both members of the couple are Orthodox Jews they will probably want a very traditional wedding ceremony. This would include most of the blessings being said by males and several of the witnesses to be male also. They will probably want the blessings to be said in Hebrew, with or without translation into English, and for the dancing at the wedding to be Jewish and to be primarily separated by gender.

Conservative Judaism

Conservative Judaism began in the late nineteenth century in Germany and grew on American shores during the first half of the twentieth century. It was originally formulated to "conserve" Judaism, first against the tide of change within Reform Judaism and later for an American population that was quickly assimilating into secular American culture. The Conservative movement believes that the Jewish people are bound by *halacha* but that the law can be consciously changed through a voting process by the Conservative movement's Committee on Law and Standards to fit the society in which it is practiced. Though a law might be set down in the Talmud, it can be changed to fit modern mores.

If you or your fiancé is conservative, you will probably require a fairly traditional Jewish wedding performed by a rabbi with or without a cantor. You will probably desire a mix of men and women to recite the blessings and prayers and to act as witnesses. You might not need all of the music to be Jewish and will probably be comfortable with mixed-gender dancing.

In practice, however, as with most groups there is much diversity of observance among Conservative Jews. The bride and groom should discuss in depth what they will require and be comfortable with before the planning starts.

Reform Judaism

Historically, the first denominational break from traditional Judaism in the modern period was Reform Judaism, which had its beginnings in late-eighteenth-century Germany during the European enlightenment. The early Reformers were learned Jews who changed their beliefs about the Bible's origin through their study of biblical criticism. They also felt that Jewish people needed to be less insular and more like the surrounding German culture both in their personal religious lives and in their synagogues. In an attempt to make Judaism in the early 1800s more attractive and accessible to Jewish people, the early Reform movement made such changes as the use of organs in the synagogue, replacing the Hebrew language of prayer with German, and declaring their country of Germany the new Zion in place of Jewish hopes for restoration to the Land of Israel.

Though Reform Judaism today has become increasingly more traditional, it is very much a liberal movement in which there is a great deal of leeway with regard to weddings. Though Reform and Reconstructionist weddings often use the outline of a traditional Jewish wedding, there are few Jewish legal requirements, and the bride and groom can usually adjust these rituals to fit their particular spiritual sensibilities.

Reconstructionism and Humanism

Reconstructionism and Humanism are the most recent Jewish denominations. Both had their start in the United States in the twentieth century. Reconstructionism is based on the ideas of Mordechai Kaplan and established its rabbinical school in the late 1960s. Reconstructionist Jews see

Judaism as a culture and a civilization and are usually quite liberal with regard to Jewish beliefs. At the same time, they tend to incorporate many traditional Jewish practices and *mitzvoth*. While Reconstructionist Jews would probably utilize various Jewish wedding traditions, if a ketubah is used it would be a creative one of the couple's own choosing.

Humanistic Judaism

Humanistic Jews see Jewish practices and traditions as the accumulated cultural ways of the Jewish people. Judaism is human-centered, and God is not seen as playing an active role. While humanistic Jews might utilize certain Jewish practices in a wedding such as a Hebrew blessing and a chuppah, the form, structure, and content of the wedding would be entirely up to the feelings and desires of the couple.

Ashkenazi and Sephardic Differences

In the early Middle Ages when the Jewish people left Babylonia and spread out across the globe, some went to Eastern Europe, mostly Germany, and some to Spain and North Africa. The Jewish communities that were in Eastern Europe for about 1,000 years are referred to as Ashkenazi Jews (literally, "German Jews"), and the Jewish communities of Spain, North Africa, and the Middle East are known as Sephardic Jews (literally, "Spanish Jews").

Since these major Jewish communities were separated by many miles for a millennium with little easy communication, they developed differing customs with regard to many aspects of Jewish life. They were vastly different in the languages they spoke and the dress they wore, as well as in some Jewish legal decisions and the form of the customs they observed.

If one partner in a couple comes from a family of Ashkenazi descent and one from a Sephardic family, you will find that some of the customs your families expect at a wedding are slightly different.

Some Sephardic Jews, depending on their particular land of origin, have a henna ceremony for the bride and her female friends and relatives the night before the wedding. Henna is a temporary plant-based dye used in some countries to create complex patterns on the skin. In Sephardic countries such as India and Kurdistan, the bride's hands and feet are intricately colored with the henna dye the night before the wedding as part of a great pre-wedding celebration. This custom does not exist among Ashkenazi Jews.

Some Sephardic Jews also have a custom of wrapping the bride and groom in a *talit* under the chuppah, which many Ashkenazi Jews do not. Some Sephardic Jews do not use the *yichud* room at all for the bride and groom to retreat into after the ceremony, though almost all traditional Ashkenazi weddings would require this. Some Sephardic weddings include customs such as the eating of sugar under the chuppah or the offering of gifts of clothing. In addition, though many traditional Ashkenazi Jews fast on the day of their wedding and almost all have a *bedekin*, not all Sephardic Jews do.

Interfaith Marriages

While virtually no Orthodox or Conservative rabbis will perform an interfaith wedding between a Jewish person and a person of another religion, some Reform rabbis and many Reconstructionist and Humanist rabbis will perform an interfaith wedding between a Jewish person and non-Jewish person. Marrying when you are both from different religions is no easy task. Knowing in advance what some of these differences are and identifying probable areas of tension between you and your fiancé and between your two families can help you minimize some of the potential conflict.

Religious Differences

There are vast differences between, for instance, Judaism and Christianity in general and in the ways in which both religions view and celebrate weddings. In both Judaism and Christianity, weddings are considered a holy event, and some priests, ministers, and rabbis will have similar requirements for the modesty of the bride's and bridesmaids' clothing. However, almost all of the traditions, except for the use of a ring, are entirely dissimilar. In Judaism weddings are both a religious and a contractual ceremony while in most other religions (with the possible exception of Islam) weddings are a religious ritual.

Christian weddings are very different from Jewish weddings in many religious and cultural ways. At a Jewish wedding, the groom walks down the aisle and the bride walks down last; at a Christian wedding the groom waits at the front with the clergy for the bride, who is "given away" by her family. At Christian weddings, vows are recited by both the bride and groom; at a Jewish wedding, the details of the couples' commitments are outlined in the *ketubah*. Many Christian weddings are held in churches, and Jewish weddings today are more and more often held in hotels and reception halls, though synagogues are also used for wedding ceremonies to some degree.

In Catholicism the wedding is a sacrament, meaning it is performed in the context of a mass. Depending on the depth of your families' Jewish background, this ceremony, as it includes the imbibing of the body and blood of Jesus, may be jarring to them. Some priests may perform intermarriages without sacrament.

Jewish Views of Intermarriage

The reason Judaism is and has been historically so opposed to interfaith marriages is not out of prejudice. Indeed, Judaism does not believe that non-Jewish people should become Jewish. The Talmud itself states that righteous non-Jewish people have a share in the world to come. Rather, the opposition comes from the fact that it is very difficult to have an encompassing and fulfilling religious life that you cannot fully share with your spouse. Thus, not only is the wedding itself often difficult to negotiate, but certainly the raising of children and the observance of your religion in depth can be quite a challenge also.

It is advisable to take the planning of an interfaith wedding slowly so that you can make time to discuss it as a couple. Go over your differences in custom, culture, and point of view. Well before your engagement, you might engage a rabbi and a priest or minister that you both trust to have a frank conversation about the potential challenges of an interfaith wedding and marriage. Ask the rabbi to paint a picture for you from his experiences. What are the points of difficulty you may encounter? Many couples wish to become more involved after their children are born. Will being of different faiths make this process more difficult? This can help to facilitate later conversation between you and your fiancé as you begin to envision your marriage together.

Economic Differences

The economics of who pays for what and how lavish a wedding to have can be very tricky to negotiate. So many factors come into play. In different parts of the country and in different Jewish communities, the expectations for the expense of your wedding are very different. In the past, the bride's family paid for most of the wedding, but today much has changed and it is quite acceptable for the bride and groom and their families to split the cost of the wedding two or three ways.

FACT

Bride and groom must serve as the go-between among their families. Though it can be intimidating, it will often be up to the couple themselves to create some openness and understanding about who can pay for what and what each party's financial expectations are. It falls to the couple to make decisions about what they can give up in order to make their wedding more doable for everyone.

Financial Pressures

What happens if one family is much more economically secure than the other? What happens when the groom's family expects the bride's family to pay for the wedding but they cannot afford it? What about when the bride and groom come from very different economic backgrounds and families and everyone in the wedding party has vastly diverse economic expectations for the wedding?

If one of the members of the couple comes from a family of great means and the other comes from a family of lesser means, and both families are going to split the cost of the celebration, the bride and groom must tactfully approach the family of means and explain the situation. The family of means must be willing to pay more than the other family without embarrassing them or the couple must find a way to plan a less expensive wedding that is just as tasteful and holy.

What's Really Important?

Though there can be much pressure in the Jewish community to have a wedding that is as expensive as the Schwartz's next door, remember, too, that Judaism values the meaning and spirituality of the wedding much more than the amount of money that is spent on it. Sometimes spending large amounts of money on a wedding can detract from its ability to be deeper and more meaningfully Jewish.

Make some decisions with your fiancé about what is truly important to you both. Use your wedding as an educational opportunity to make a statement that bucks the trend and focuses less on the things that cost lots of dollars and more on that which takes personal engagement and giving.

One couple opted for a backyard wedding and used the money they would have spent on a hall and large scale caterer on the music instead. They loved a certain Jewish singer and guitarist and felt this would add heart and soul to their wedding. Though the wedding did not have as much in the way of flowers or food, it more than succeeded in inspiration and joy.

For instance, you might decide to forgo the expensive wedding cake and opt for ice cream instead. You might nix arranging flowers on every table and instead put your energy into writing a beautifully worded introduction to your wedding booklet or a wedding covenant.

Geographic Diversity

Weddings and wedding expectations are different in different places. Though the ceremonies and rituals may be essentially the same, a Jewish wedding in Israel is vastly different in look, culture, size, and formality than the average Jewish wedding in America. In Israel the groom will rarely wear a tuxedo, the invitation might not come with a reply card, and just because you did not RSVP does not mean you won't go to the wedding. Such is not the case in many other countries, where weddings are more formal.

In New York, it may be hard to find a Jewish wedding without a smorgasbord, but in the Midwest there may be only passed hors d'oeuvres at the *tish*. If one member of the couple is from New York or Chicago and the other from a smaller town in the South or Midwest, the bride and groom and their respective families may have very different expectations of some of the wedding details. Don't let such issues and expectations derail you. Use it as an opportunity for communication and for appreciating how different you are and the beauty in diversity.

Premarital Counseling and Guidance

Inevitably, when a couple comes together to marry they realize that as similar as they thought they were, they are in fact very different. They were brought up differently, in different families, with different genes, and no matter how similar they are, they have had very different experiences. This, too, is the beauty of getting married. You are so different and yet you trust each other, get along well, and learn from each other. To marry someone just like yourself would be more comfortable but a lot less challenging. It would be much calmer, but less growth would result.

The other side of this beauty, of course, is that inevitably there will be conflict and frustration. One of the keys to navigating the natural tension of becoming one is practicing your communication skills. Sometimes we have issues to discuss, but resist out of fear. It is essential that the rabbi marrying you also spends a bit of time counseling both of you together. The rabbi can help you reflect on your relationship, what you love about each other, and the difficulties you have encountered. The rabbi or another counselor can also help to create a safe space in which both the bride and groom feel heard and feel safe to express themselves and the issues they are having to each other.

Sometimes couples are tempted to talk to the rabbi separately, each person complaining about their fiancé or asking for help understanding him. In truth, your counseling session should include you and your fiancé talking face to face with each other. Use this neutral space to hear your future spouse talk directly to you about the things that bother him, about the things that make him uncomfortable in the relationship, and also about what he loves about you.

CHAPTER 11

Nontraditional Weddings and Diverse Families

Though a lot of wedding advice is geared toward first-time brides and grooms, more and more couples come from or are entering into multifaceted families. When planning a wedding, thinking about the complexities of your particular family will help you avoid unneeded conflict and alienation. Take a few moments to put yourself in the shoes of those who will be most affected by your wedding. Understanding how they might feel will help you make sure everyone feels comfortable, joyous, and inspired by your wedding celebration.

Second Marriages

Approximately 35 percent of couples who marry today will divorce, and 75 percent of those who experience a divorce will marry again. In the present day, second marriages are quite common. Second weddings differ from first weddings in feel, in meaning, and in the couple's expectations for the wedding ceremony and experience.

The Uniqueness of Second Weddings

Though many couples who are marrying a second time prefer to have a formal wedding, it is often expected that second weddings will be smaller, less formal, and more creative. The rules of etiquette do not have as tight a hold on second weddings as they used to. Some brides wear white dresses, and some second weddings have as full a wedding party as a first wedding.

Since friends and families don't expect second weddings to be as elaborate as first weddings, make your second wedding your dream wedding. If you held your first wedding at a traditional location because of expectations, this is your chance to get married on a mountain top or the seashore.

Though first marriages in Judaism are traditionally followed by seven days of feasting and special recitation of the *sheva berachot*, if this is a second marriage for both partners it is followed by only one day of *sheva berachot*. This is not to say that it is less joyous, rather less communal and more personal.

It is quite common for brides and grooms to pay for a second wedding themselves and to ask guests not to bring gifts. This is especially true if the bride and groom already have the things they need for a home. If, of course, all of your silverware is monogrammed with the initials of your previous spouse, or if you and your new partner are moving into a larger house, you may need to think about restocking. A wedding registry can help you accomplish this.

Financial prenuptial agreements are more common in second marriages than first marriages. This is so because the bride and groom often bring more assets into the marriage and may have children from a previous marriage. Couples that are marrying for the second time can be more set in their way of life and may need to outline certain ground rules, methods of living, and religious observances with each other to be clear on what they need and expect.

Second Marriages after Divorce

If your first marriage ended in divorce, set aside some time to let yourself think before you enter into a second marriage. Honestly evaluate why your first marriage failed and think of how to avoid something similar this second time around.

Usually a bad marriage is not one person's "fault." The responsibility belongs to both partners. Before marrying again, ask yourself what you would do differently this time if things were not going well. You might think about turning to counseling with a new spouse earlier, changing your attitude, or laying certain expectations on the table from the beginning. In Judaism, the goal of remarrying is not just to start again but to learn from past challenges and to personally grow from them.

When one partner has been married before and the other has not, the second-timer may want a smaller wedding. He may feel he has already had a big wedding and does not want to repeat the experience, or he may have feelings of hesitation or raw feelings of failure from his previous marriage.

In contrast, the partner who has never been married may desire an all-out shindig and may have lots of exciting wedding energy. Each party has different expectations and hopes for their mutual wedding celebration. Realizing this can help each partner remember that their fiancé may not be experiencing the wedding preparations in exactly the same way. A conversation about the way in which this experience is different for you both can help make your wedding suit you both.

Second Marriages after the Death of a Spouse

Surviving spouses sometimes experience a sense of guilt at the prospect of remarrying. In truth, marrying a second time demonstrates that the first marriage was a good one since you desire to be married once again.

Of course, your former spouse is always there in spirit and it can be comforting to think he would have approved of your new prospect.

Judaism teaches that after a sufficient mourning period, usually one year, life should go on. Holding onto valued memories as you embark a new road is difficult, but it can be seen as a tribute to your spouse and everything she taught you about relationships and the world. If she loved you, she would probably want you to live in joy and not to be alone. It is also important to remember that Judaism counts marriage, whether a first marriage or a subsequent one, as a mitzvah. Thus, remarrying is not forsaking your former spouse but a divinely ordained obligation.

FACT

Tension can arise if one partner's former spouse passed away and the other partner divorced. The divorced partner can feel that the end to her previous marriage was not as dignified as her fiancé's. Couples must bring any such underlying feelings out into the open so that these issues cannot undermine the second marriage.

Your departed spouse was dear to you and so his memory must be honored, but at the same time the person you are about to marry is worthy of your full love and attention. This may be hard for both partners, but—especially if there are children involved—it is vital that this balance of memory and moving on coexist.

Including Children and Other Family Members in Second Marriages

As you prepare for a second marriage, it is imperative to pay special attention to the children and other family members whose daily lives will change as a result of the new union. Take great care not to make children choose sides between a new spouse and their other biological parent. Children have many fears when parents remarry. They may be afraid that a new stepparent will take away their biological parent's attention or that the new stepparent will not love them or like them enough. Sometimes children with such feelings may try to undermine their parent's budding second marriage. To address your child or children's apprehension, engage them in conversations about your relationship with their prospective stepparent. Child and family counseling can also be helpful. Tell your children what a holy thing and a mitzvah it is in Judaism to marry again, thus shifting the focus from their immediate concern to the much bigger picture.

Getting Off to a Good Start

Just as it is important for children to form a positive relationship with their parent's new spouse, it is also crucial that parents realize children have an obligation to honor both their biological parents and their stepparents. For the sake of their children, divorced parents should do their best to have a civil relationship with each other, and any new spouse must realize this. The alternative is to place one's children in the terrible situation of choosing between their biological parent and their new stepparent.

Second weddings can present complex situations with regard to the inclusion of family members, especially children, in the ceremony, the reception, and the planning process. It is important to include children—particularly younger ones—in the wedding process. If you share custody of your children with your former spouse, let him know that you plan to include your children in your wedding. Handling the matter openly can prevent children from becoming caught in the middle.

Involving Everyone

Your wedding is a kind of cover page to your marriage. Take advantage of the opportunity to include children who will be part of the blended family you are about to form. Be sure to treat your children and your future spouse's children equally and give them roles in the wedding that befit their ages and personalities so that their first experience as a new family will be a positive one.

Try involving younger children in concrete and easy parts of the planning process. Let them help make place cards or mail invitations, or give them a small appropriate role in the wedding itself. Talk them through the upcoming ceremony and reflect on its meaning and holiness. This focus on the bigger picture can help with their personal transition. Your wedding will be a time of upheaval for them, but you can help them see the holiness and the greater significance in it. This can help alleviate some of their anxiety.

Jewish Considerations in Second Weddings

If one or both spouses were divorced, be sure that there is a proper religious divorce, a *get*. In Jewish law and tradition, remarrying without a religious divorce from a previous marriage is tantamount to adultery and can affect the status of children born into the subsequent marriage and whom they may marry. In addition, if your wife-to-be's first husband passed away and there were no children from that marriage, consult with your rabbi about the Jewish biblical process of *chalitza*. In Jewish law, *chalitza* serves to sever the automatic marriage-like relationship the Bible creates between the wife of the deceased and the deceased husband's brother. For more information regarding rabbinical organizations that can help you to obtain a *get*, see Appendix D.

The Bible and Jewish law forbid remarrying a former spouse after they marry someone else. Some people reason that divorcing, marrying, and then remarrying one's spouse could be used as a way of violating the sacred monogamy of one's marriage.

There are several differences in the wedding planning process and in the traditional Jewish wedding ceremony when people are marrying for the second time. The *ketubah* is a bit differently worded and there does not have to be a *yichud* room or *bedekin* ceremony. For a second wedding *sheva berachot* are recited only on the day of the wedding itself, though the couple should celebrate three days of joy and feasting.

Older Couples

When couples marry at an older age, whether it is a first marriage or a second one, they may be presented with a unique set of challenges. Many people erroneously believe that couples who are marrying latter in life will have more conflicts with each other regarding monetary issues, values for living, and social predilection. The opposite is actually true.

Special Considerations

Older couples may face more potential hurdles, but older couples are often more mature and more open about what they feel, think, and need in a relationship. The ability to lay an issue out on the table and discuss how you see potential areas of conflict can nip potentially explosive conflicts in the bud.

If you are marrying at an older age it may be important to consider purchasing long-term care insurance for both of you to help guarantee that neither of you will be a burden upon the other. In fact, it can be less expensive to purchase long-term care insurance as a couple than as separate individuals.

How to spend shared assets and deciding who will inherit what if one partner has children and one does not can be sources of great tension among older couples. Additionally, if one partner is older and one is younger, children may worry about the older spouse becoming a burden finically or physically on the younger one. If this is a concern, children and parents should evaluate the available options for long-term care together.

Great love can bloom for couples in their seventies, eighties, and nineties, but sometimes children are not sure what to make of it. Some children are thrilled that their parent has found a mate, but others are not sure how to view the love and sexual desire of their parent at a significantly older age. It is important for children of older couples to realize that just because people are older does not necessarily mean there is less need and desire for intimacy and companionship.

Intimacy and Older Couples

Older couples sometimes have a better intimate life than younger couples. They may be more knowledgeable about what works and what doesn't work sexually and emotionally for themselves and for a partner. They may be wiser and more emotionally mature than younger couples. Older partners are often better at being able to view sex as the product of an intimate emotional life with each other, not just as a source of their own pleasure. In addition, older couples may finally have the time for each other that they did not have when they were younger. No matter the age, a couple must not be embarrassed to talk to each other about their intimate life, which is an important part of a healthy marriage.

FACT

Sara and Abraham, the first Jewish couple, had a child when they were both well into their golden years. Though their situation was the result of a divine miracle, the notion of older people being loving and close and having sex is not shunned in Judaism. It is considered a mitzvah as for any other couple.

Older couples must consciously realize that as we age our bodies change, not just physically, but emotionally and sexually, too. Older partners, unless they are in good physical shape, may not be as spry or as flexible. The male's penis may not get as erect and the female's vagina may not be as lubricated. As a result, it may take longer for partners to become aroused. This can sometimes have the benefit of equalizing male and female times for arousal.

Divorced Parents

If the parents of the bride or groom are divorced, complex issues can arise in the wedding planning process. It is equally important to involve both parents and avoid any undue tension. If divorced parents are on good terms with each other and with the child who is getting married, they will both be involved in the proceedings and will be seated with their own families. If they are not on speaking terms the situation will be more difficult.

Wedding Planning

If you are getting married and your divorced parents are not on good terms with each other but both are in close contact with you, take care to avoid potential conflict. Sit down with each of your parents and let them know how important your wedding is to you, what a great and holy moment it is in Jewish life, and how you want to be sure your whole family is there with you. You might ask your parents' close friends to sit near them to help minimize any conflict. They can be a buffer and a source of calm and support for your parents. Before the wedding, you might also want to brief each of your parents about what an important role they play in the wedding. Give them a sense of the specific tasks and responsibilities they will have as special honored parents.

Think about how to seat your parents. Seating your mother and father equally near you and your fiancé but not close to each other is often a good approach. Talk honestly to your mother and father about their own feelings and let them know that both of them are being invited and that it is important to you to have them there. Express how important it is to you that the wedding be joyous and civil.

The phrasing of engagement and wedding announcements may be affected by the status of the relationship between divorced parents. If the parents are affable, the engagement announcement may come from both; if not, it can come from the bride's mother and list the bride as her father's child on the second line of the announcement. The bride and groom themselves may also announce the marriage.

Wedding Logistics

With regard to the processional, if the relationship between the divorced parents of the bride or groom is amicable and they each have a relationship with their child, it would be ideal to have both parents walk their child to the chuppah together. If the parents are not on speaking terms with each other, this may be a difficult situation to resolve. Stepping back and letting the two of them decide who goes to the wedding or who walks down the aisle and when can work if you have a relationship with both parents.

Assuring parents that they do not need to sit near each other or interact can help settle their minds. If your parents are close with their rabbis, you might want to ask their advice. If the rabbi has a good relationship with your parent and commands their respect, he may be able to influence a difficult parent.

If you want both of your parents to be at your wedding and they do not want to be in the same room together, stay calm and reassure each parent that you want them there for you and your fiancé. If you think it will be helpful, you can also mention that being in the wedding will help them stay close to you and your spouse. It will strengthen your relationship with them and ensure that they have an ongoing relationship with any children you have now or will have in the future.

Judiasm demands that you honor each of your parents, and you must not compromise on that. Open, honest communication is essential to finding a resolution that satisfies everyone. Gently remind feuding parents that it means a great deal to you that both of them be involved in your wedding.

If you are looking to both of your divorced parents to help you pay for the wedding, get a clear sense of how much they are willing to contribute toward the celebration and consider doing the planning yourself. This way, you can avoid having them both involved or overlapping in the planning process.

Deceased Parents

If the bride or groom has lost a parent, the wedding planning process and the ceremony itself can be emotionally painful. It is important for you to anticipate the bittersweet moments, but your support group can include your fiancé, close friends and family, and your rabbi.

Remembering and Honoring

In the wedding announcement, the deceased parent's name can be listed, followed by the words "of blessed memory" or the equivalent in Hebrew, *zichrono l'vracha* or *zichronah l'vracha* for a departed female. In Judaism, though it is traditional for parents to walk the bride and groom to their chuppah, there is no rule that it cannot be someone else. In the past, this was not uncommon, especially with those who survived the Holocaust and had no relatives. Friends who walk the bride or groom to the chuppah are much honored in Judaism. In Hebrew they are called *shushvinin*, and in Yidish they are given the special title of *unterfirers*, escorts.

FACT

Every Jewish wedding ceremony ends with the breaking of a glass to remember and mourn the destruction of Jerusalem. If you have a parent whom you would like to remember at the ceremony, invoke their name, memory, and blessing just before the breaking of the glass. You can also mention them in your wedding booklet.

Recent Deaths

It can be difficult to decide whether to go ahead with a wedding if a parent passes away just before the wedding. In Jewish law, it is acceptable to go ahead with the wedding if it cannot be postponed without losing all of the food, money, and preparations. Otherwise, the wedding should be postponed until mourning is completed. If the death occured just after the wedding day, the bride and groom complete their seven days of feasting before beginning the observance of *shiva*, the traditional seven days of mourning.

Same Gender Couples

Though there is no precedent in the Bible or Talmud for same gender weddings, in recent years Reform and Reconstructionist rabbis and more recently Conservative rabbis have begun performing unions for homosexual couples. Since there is no historical model for same gender marriages in Judaism and it exists only in liberal Jewish denominations, there is much ceremonial experimentation and leeway in the way in which same gender weddings are conducted.

Same Gender Couples in the Orthodox Community

Since in Jewish law *kiddushin* is seen as a ceremony that applies only to a couple made up of a woman and a man, there are virtually no same gender marriages performed in the Orthodox community. *Halacha*, Jewish law based on the Bible and Tamlud, forbids sexual activity between men and—on a rabbinic level—between women. Gay Orthodox couples do exist, but they are typically less public about their relationships and almost no ceremonies have been held since same gender relationships are seen as a violation of Jewish law. Being gay and Orthodox is a great challenge to individuals who feel at times that they must choose between ever loving another person deeply and their religious love of and dedication to Jewish tradition and law.

Same Gender Couples in Liberal Denominations

For Jews who desire to stay closer to tradition but are having a same sex union, the question of how similar their ceremony should be to a traditional wedding can be difficult to navigate. Often, same gender weddings reflect traditional ceremonies with the use of Hebrew and familiar wedding tunes, but the content and structure of the ceremony is altered to fit better with the meaning of the ceremony for the particular couple. Some couples have utilized the structure of the *sheva berachot* by rewriting the seven blessings from scratch to reflect the nontraditional makeup of the wedding and the couple.

Some same gender couples choose to have a commitment ceremony since same sex marriages are not recognized in many states. Other couples wish to have something more akin to a wedding ceremony since they recognize it as a higher level of commitment. Some liberal rabbis use a recently developed ceremony called a *brit ahuvim*, a lover's covenant. The *brit ahuvim* that is used is an agreement between the couple to be committed to each other as partners.

The *brit ahuvim* utilizes some traditional Jewish language and methodology derived not from Jewish marriage law but from the world of business partnerships. The *brit ahuvim* document itself is often at the center of the ceremony, but other aspects of traditional Jewish weddings are added to it, such as the breaking of a glass, the use of witnesses, the inclusion of traditional tunes, and the blessings bestowed upon the couple by parents and friends. Couples will often add their own vows, tunes, and poetry to the ceremony to express their love to each other.

CHAPTER 12

Harmonizing Religious and Cultural Differences

If you and your fiancé are from differing religious backgrounds or have strong cultural differences as a result of where and how you were raised, it can be difficult to harmonize your expectations and desires within one cogent wedding ceremony and celebration. In addition, your religious life may be different than that of your parents. You may have become less or more religiously observant than your family of origin, or perhaps you have just come to see Jewish weddings differently than they expect.

What to Serve

What food to serve can be a source of contention if you or your fiancé are of different religions or if you are both Jewish but observe the laws of kosher differently. If one partner's family is more observant than the other's, the more observant family will probably expect kosher or more strictly kosher food to be served. This would include not mixing meat and dairy or even serving them both together at the reception, as well as being sure the food itself is produced in a kosher kitchen. Preparing meat—and most other foods—requires supervision to be sure it is produced in accordance with kosher standards and laws. The less observant family might not require kosher food, sometimes even feeling that the quality or creativity of the food may suffer if the dining options are limited to kosher caterers.

Making a Decision

One way to deal with some of these tensions is to invite both families to a tasting that the caterer, or several caterers vying for your business, will have for you to taste different dishes. You can choose for yourself what to serve at your wedding, and both families can feel empowered to make an educated decision about the food.

Some older Jewish people who remember the era in America when little quality kosher food and wine was available may be under the impression that all kosher food is nineteenth-century Eastern European food. This is no longer true, and lots of great kosher international food and wonderful French and Israeli wines are now de rigueur in most large cities.

It may be necessary to compromise if all the parties involved cannot come to an easy decision. If one family or person keeps strict kosher, they will not be able to eat meals cooked by a non-kosher caterer. If one family prefers kosher food but does not require it and the other family does not want to use a kosher caterer, you may want to ask the non-kosher caterer to serve only dairy or fish and not meat. This may work for people who do not fully keep kosher, and it will allow you to preserve the peace between your families.

When negotiating the question of kosher food, the manner in which you present the question is vital. No one wants to feel as if they are less Jewish because they are not committed to eating kosher food. One suggestion is to broach the question with lots of "I" statements. Something like the following may be helpful: "Mom and Dad, thank you so much for all of your help in planning and paying for my wedding. Given my current spiritual commitments I would feel uncomfortable having non-kosher food served at my wedding." If both the bride and groom are involved in wedding planning, it may be important for them to speak in advance, decide together what they want, and present their wishes in a unified way.

Individual Kosher Meals

If you and your fiancé and your families do not require kosher food but a small number of relatives or friends do keep kosher, the option exists to order them a special meal from a kosher caterer. This is especially true if the rabbi is the only person requiring a kosher meal and will be eating with you. It is important to note that not all Rabbis will officiate at weddings where non-kosher food is served.

Why does the oven affect the kosher status of food?
Kosher food can become un-kosher if it is cooked or heated in a non-kosher pot or oven since the walls of the vessel or oven are porous and absorb some of the taste of the non-kosher food that was cooked in it previously.

If you order special meals from a kosher caterer, be sure the kitchen at your event knows how the meals should be heated and served. The meals should not be heated uncovered in a non-kosher oven; usually the kosher caterer can arrange to have the meals wrapped and sealed so they can be heated in a non-kosher oven and still retain their kosher status. The kosher guests themselves may want to oversee the opening of the package before it is served to them. Your wedding helpers or the wait staff will need to be sure to provide the guests with plastic plates and silverware or new plates and silver so that it meets kosher standards. Be sure to let your guests know what the arrangements will be.

Dancing Differences

One of the strongest ways in which religious and cultural differences can surface is through the question of what kind of dancing to have at your wedding. Since weddings are seen in Judaism as a holy act and a kind of prayer service, most observant Jewish weddings, due to the considerations of modesty that guide traditional Jewish social interaction, have separate circles of dance for men and women. Such dancing is usually to Jewish music in big communal circles.

If you and your fiancé are facing conflicts in your own relationship over religious or cultural differences, you may want to think about how these differences will play out after your wedding in your marriage itself and especially when raising children. Talk it over now and come up with some general guidelines and productive ways of communicating about the issues in the future.

Mechitza and Other Options

Within Orthodoxy, there are some differences in the way that people separate the genders for dancing. Some will put a *mechitza*, a divider, between the circles of men and the circles of women. Others will have a table or plants in between to create a kind of separation. Still others erect no physical separation at all and simply designate one side of the dance floor for men and the other for women.

If you and your fiancé or your families come from different Jewish backgrounds, denominations, or levels of observance, the question of how to structure the dancing at your wedding can be an especially sticky subject. If one partner's family is Orthodox and the other's is not, it is not uncommon for the Orthodox family to expect that there be only separate dancing and for the non-Orthodox family to assume that there will be only mixed dancing for couples and perhaps for any group dancing.

This kind of dilemma can pit one family against another and can be a source of tension between the couple as they express their desires for their own wedding and advocate for their families' needs. What are you to do when both families want opposite things at the wedding and are each motivated by deeply held beliefs, traditions, and desires?

Negotiation and Compromise

These situations, especially if both families are involved in planning and paying for the wedding, will require careful discussion and compromise. First, each side should be given the space to respectfully explain why they feel the way they do and why it is important to them. Families may talk to each other or the couple can act as a go-between.

In most situations, some kind of compromise will need to be reached. For instance, if one family wants a *mechitza* for dancing and the other is opposed to having one, you might suggest having separate dancing and using different sides of the dance floor for men and women's dancing or separating the two sides of the dance floor with small plants, a dessert table, or both. Another possible compromise might be to have some separate dancing at the wedding and some mixed. A third way might be to let each family have influence over different parts of the wedding. One family could have their way for the parameters of the ceremony and the other for the reception. Remember that although your wedding is an important day and statement, it is not the end all and be all of how you will live your life as a couple.

Musical Differences

The music that each family or partner listens to and feels is appropriate at a Jewish wedding may differ also. If one family or partner is more traditionally Jewish, they may want more traditional Jewish music and dancing. A less traditional family or one that is not Jewish may be unfamiliar with Jewish wedding music or dancing and may not want any, feeling that it might make them, their relatives, or their guests feel uncomfortable or less included.

It is very important to remember that a wedding is essentially a time for each family to show themselves and their values to everyone they know. Religious and cultural convictions are powerful. Less religious families worry that their friends and guests will be put off or think them extreme, and religious families worry that they will be seen as too lenient or compromising. Within Judaism, if one family subscribes to Jewish law, *halacha*, and the other does not, it is difficult for one committed to religious law to be asked to compromise, though they should be encouraged to speak with a rabbi for guidance. The couple should try to seek out a rabbi who can understand both sides and cultures and can take into account the religious and cultural sensitivities of each family.

Work toward a compromise that encompasses a combination of types of music and dancing. Perhaps you could structure the reception to feature Jewish dancing at the beginning of the reception and mixed couples dancing during courses, following the grace after meals, or during the afternoon prayer service for those who observe the traditional thrice-daily prayer service.

When to Take Pictures

When and how to take pictures is sometimes a thorny issue for couples and parents, depending on their religious traditions. If you follow Jewish traidition, the bride and groom will not see each other for as long as seven days before the wedding. This is tradition, not Jewish law. Though in Judaism longheld traditions sometimes gain the standing and importance of law, many Jewish legal authorities allow the couple to see each other prior to the wedding.

If the bride and groom are not seeing each other on the day of the wedding before the ceremony, on the morning of the wedding the bride and groom will usually take pictures with their individual families. Group portraits with both families are taken after the chuppah and *yichud*. During this time, the guests usually have cocktails and hors d'oeurves before the actual reception.

The dilemma for some brides and grooms is that taking pictures after the ceremony prevents them from being with their guests during that time. In addition, some brides may worry that their makeup may not be as fresh, especially if the ceremony has been a moving one. Other considerations such as time of day may also come into play. If you want pictures outdoors but yours is a late afternoon wedding, the sun may be setting by the time the ceremony and *yichud* are over and it is time for pictures.

You might consider taking as many separate pictures as you can before the wedding and leave the photographer a list of what posed pictures you want taken while you are in *yichud*. The photographer can take as many photos as possible without you while you are in *yichud*. After you and your fiancé re-enter, he can take pictures with you for fifteen minutes or so. This means you still have some less formal time with your guests at the cocktail hour. You can also talk to your photographer about minimizing the number of posed photos and strategizing for more candid shots, using more than one photographer's assistant if need be.

The Importance of Explanations

If your fiancée or her family is not from a Jewish background or from as Jewishly knowledgeable a background as you or your family, one of the most important things you can do is provide explanations. Consider borrowing a Jewish wedding video that will be similar to your own wedding to show them. Open up for discussion which parts of the wedding were unfamiliar or may make them uncomfortable. If some of your guests have never attended a Jewish wedding before or have not attended a traditional one, do not assume they will know anything about the steps involved in the ceremony and reception or about the traditions and their meanings.

Write a detailed booklet of explanations, but also talk with your rabbi about what parts of the ceremony you would like to make sure are carefully explained. Give the rabbi a good sense of who will be at your wedding and how diverse the crowd will be in their knowledge and background of Jewish practice. Ask the rabbi if he has done Jewish weddings at which many in the audience were not familiar with Jewish practices. Get a sense of how comfortable the rabbi will be explaining all the steps and traditions and their meaning as the ceremony progresses. Your wedding will not only be a meaningful moment for you but an educational and enlightening experience for your family members and guests.

In some ways, planning a big public party for all your friends is a good first thing to do as a couple since it will bring out many issues between you. Though a wedding seems like a very hard event around which to find common ground, peace, and compromise, this skill will be important all through your marriage and especially when raising children.

Take time with your fiancée and her family to read about and discuss the different Jewish traditions involved in a wedding ceremony. If members of the family are worried that your wedding is going to be too Jewish, foreign, and confusing, use explanations as a way to include everyone.

Another way to deal with religious or cultural differences in a Jewish wedding is to read parts of the wedding ceremony in English rather than or in addition to the original Hebrew. If your *ketubah* has both a Hebrew or Aramaic and English section, you could opt to read only the English section or vows written by you and your fiancé entirely in place of the Hebrew reading.

Working With Your Rabbi

If you and your fiancé are from different Jewish backgrounds or your families are of different levels of Jewish identity or observance, be sure to inform your rabbi of this. Your rabbi can do a great deal to smooth over differences and make everyone comfortable. Your rabbi should be able to understand where each of you or each of your families is coming from religiously or culturally and should help each family be heard and feel that their concerns matter.

If you have decided on a very traditional Jewish weding but one family is less observant or knowledgeable, have your rabbi make a special effort to call or meet with the family, hear their concerns, and give them some explanations and teaching. Sometimes less observant or knowledgeable parents feel they do not know what their role should be and the more knowledgeable parents can unintentionally end up playing a more central role in the wedding simply because of their knowledge of the ceremony and its blessings, language, and traditions.

Despite prior lack of knowledge regarding the ceremony and its blessings, language, and traditions, both sets of parents can play a central role in the wedding. Ask your rabbi to meet with the less knowledgeable family and help them carve out a part of the ceremony that will be theirs. For instance, a blessing that the rabbi could put on tape for your parents to memorize and recite under the chuppah will help them feel a part of your ceremony.

No matter what kind of Jewish wedding you are having, if you know that many of your guests will be unfamiliar with your Jewish wedding ceremony, discuss with your rabbi or wedding officiate the importance of explaining the key parts of the ceremony as you do each one. This will help your guests appreciate your particular wedding and gain a deeper understanding of Jewish weddings.

CHAPTER 13

The Wedding Weekend and Sabbath

13

The week prior to your wedding is a time of building anticipation and inner preparation for the transformative moment of unification with the person you love. The most exceptional day during this wedding week is the Shabbat, the Jewish Sabbath, which extends from Friday night until Saturday night. Jewish tradition teaches that every Shabbat is not just a day of rest but such a time of intimacy between the human and the divine that in Kabbalah, Jewish mysticism, Shabbat is compared to an actual wedding each week.

To See or Not to See, That Is the Question

There is a Jewish tradition for the bride and groom not to see each other for a period of time before the wedding. Even if you do not consider yourself very religious or strongly observant, you may find great meaning in this custom. Of course, not seeing each other just before your wedding can be stressful also, since you are on the verge of committing your lives to each other and are so much in love. Perhaps, though, that is precisely the time to let your heart grow fonder, to reflect on your loved one and what it is like to be without him.

In addition, the period just before the wedding is very stressful. Some brides and grooms find that although they love each other, the pre-wedding stress of last minute plans can actually take a toll on their relationship. Some brides and grooms become stressed and edgy and just need to focus on the last details of the wedding. It is perhaps one of the least romantic times to be together.

The custom of bride and groom not seeing each other before the wedding is actually a relatively recent one, and there are several customs that have emerged regarding how long this separation should last. The most common custom is not to see each other for the week before the wedding, but some couples do not see each other for several days before the wedding. Many couples do not see each other before the ceremony on the day of the wedding. Customs in Judaism are very important, but the couple must weigh the spiritual power of being apart with the difficult logistical problems it can sometimes create. Today many couples who do observe this tradition of separation talk on the phone and communicate through e-mail and text messages.

What Is an Ufruf?

Due to its special nature, the Shabbat preceding your wedding is associated with many unique and ancient Jewish customs. The most well-known Jewish custom on the Sabbath before a wedding, at least among Ashkenazi Jews, is the *ufruf*. *Ufruf* is a Yiddish word that means "the calling up," since traditionally it was the day that the groom was given a special *aliyah*, a special calling up to the Torah in the synagogue.

The bride and groom are considered to be a king and queen. The Torah commands that a Jewish king must always carry a Torah with him in order to remember that it is not his honor but the honor of the Torah, of God, and of the people that he represents. So, too, a groom just before his wedding is like a king, and he must see the Torah as central to what he is about to do in the world. Accordingly, he is given a special *aliyah* on the Shabbat just prior to the wedding day. Some people even walk the groom or bride to the synagogue on this Shabbat in recognition of their royal status.

The Kabbalah teaches that the intimacy between the divine and our world is so intense on Shabbat that we reflect this in our own actions. This is one of the reasons that on Shabbat sexual activity between husband and wife is a special mitzvah, in that it mirrors the divine unity of the Sabbath day itself.

This day of the *ufruf* is a special one in the synagogue. The service might center around the groom and bride and their family and friends, perhaps with them leading the service and receiving *aliot*, which means they are called to the Torah to kiss it, make a blessing on it, and stand up on the *bimah*, the stage at the front of the synagogue, as it is read.

When the groom—in liberal Jewish denominations, usually the groom and the bride—are called to Torah, they are called up with a special tune, as if announcing the approach of royalty. Following the *aliyah* in most congregations people yell mazel tov and also sing "*Simon Tov U'Mazel Tov*," a joyous Hebrew song. Some even have the custom of singing other special wedding songs or poems in honor of the bride and groom on this day.

One of the most memorable moments of most *ufrufs* is the throwing of candy or other sweets. In many synagogues, after the Torah portion is read and the last blessing is made, the congregation throws bags of candy at the honored couple. In the past candy, nuts, or raisins were thrown but today in most synagogues only candy is thrown. One reason given for the historical throwing of nuts, despite the slight risk of injury, is that in Hebrew each letter of the alphabet is associated with a number and the Hebrew word for nut, *egoz*, adds up to the number seventeen, which is also the numerical equivalent of the Hebrew word *tov*, which means "good." In any event, avoid using rock candy or half-pound bars of chocolate as these can bruise the groom or bride before their big day.

Though it is a sign of hope for a sweet life, being pelted with candy or nuts can hurt. If you are the one who is being honored remember to duck when the shower of candy starts. If you are wearing a *talit*, a prayer shawl, try spreading it over your head for some added protection.

The throwing of candy at an *ufruf* symbolizes our hope that the couple will have an overflowingly sweet life together. Some also say that it is a reference to the verse in the biblical love poem *Shir Hashirim*, the Song of Songs, in which one lover in the poem sees his lover's beauty as he walks into the garden: "I went down into the garden of nuts to see the fruits of the valley, and to see if the vine had blossomed, to see if the pomegranates were in bloom." Jewish tradition teaches that this book of love poetry is not only a literal depiction of the passion and beauty of human lovers but an expression of the love and intimacy that can be cultivated between humans and the divine.

In the first Temple in Jerusalem built by King Solomon, there were two gates—one for mourners and one for people about to be married. This ensured that each would be greeted appropriately. To those about to marry, the people would say, "May the one Whose presence dwells in this house rejoice you with sons and daughters."

In some synagogues, the singing of the traditional song "*Siman Tov U'Mazel Tov*" is followed by spontaneous dancing with the groom or with the bride and groom if they are both in the synagogue for the *ufruf*. Dancing and singing with them for a few minutes on the Sabbath is an expression of love and joy, and it prepares them for the joy of their imminent wedding. If you want the congregation to dance with you at your *ufruf* and are not sure if this is always done in your synagogue, talk to the rabbi beforehand. Some more formal synagogues do not follow the custom of dancing.

Throughout much of Jewish history, the Shabbat before the wedding—or for some Sephardic Jews, the Shabbat following the wedding—has been a special day for groom and bride. Many liturgical poems were sung for them, and during different eras in Jewish history special Torah portions were even read in their honor.

Groom's Torah Honors and Bride's Torah Honors

The public synagogue honors that those who are about to marry will receive depends very much on what type and denomination of synagogue they attend. In all Orthodox and most Conservative synagogues there are seven *aliyot*, seven people called to the *bima*, the raised platform on which the Torah is read, to make a blessing on the Torah. One additional person is called up at the end to read from the *haftorah*, a section from one of the books of the prophets. In addition, there is the honor of lifting the Torah up at the end of its reading and showing it to the congregation, which is called *hagbah*, and a second person who is honored with tying the Torah up after it is lifted, called *gililah*. These honors are often divided among the families of the wedding party along with any others who need to be honored in the synagogue that Shabbat.

In most Orthodox synagogues, if the groom is at the synagogue for the *ufruf* he will receive an *aliyah*, meaning he will be called to the Torah to make a blessing on it. In Reform synagogues and in most Conservative synagogues, both bride and groom are in the synagogue for the *ufruf* and will probably both receive an *aliyah*, perhaps the same one together or two separate ones.

In some synagogues if you are knowledgeable enough to recite the longer blessing on the *haftorah* and read the *haftorah*, you may receive the last *aliyah*, the *maftir aliyah*. Following it, you will make the blessing on the *haftorah* and read it. The *haftorah* is an additional reading to the Torah portion. Each Sabbath in most synagogues, in addition to the weekly Torah portion, a portion of one of the books of the prophets is read. The reading from the prophets usually corresponds in some thematic way to that particular week's Torah portion. If you plan to get the *maftir aliyah* and read the *haftorah* you will want to study the reading of it beforehand since it is in Hebrew and is read with a special tune and musical notes.

If you are given the honor of *hagbah*, of lifting up the Torah at the end of its reading, be careful when you lift it because dropping a Torah is considered a grave thing and people usually fast for several days if this happens. Make sure to use the leverage of its table to help lift. If you have any back trouble you might want to pass on this honor.

In some synagogues the *haftorah* is read from a scroll of the prophets just like the Torah scroll. Such a scroll will not contain any vowels with the Hebrew letters or any *trop* notes, the musical notes used to chant the Torah or *haftorah*. Thus, in these synagogues, unless you are quite familiar with *haftorah* reading, you will need to memorize the *haftorah* section before you are called up.

Can I have an aliyah to the Torah even if I do not know Hebrew?
Yes. Next to the Torah, most synagogues have a printed page of the Torah blessings not only in Hebrew but transliterated into English letters also.

In many synagogues today, though the Torah itself is read from a scroll without notes or vowels, the *haftorah* is read from a book that does contain both vowels and the *trop*. If you are in a synagogue that uses a book for the *haftorah*, you might be able to read it without much preparation if your Hebrew is good and you are familiar with the musical notations for the *haftorah*.

Since it is within a week of the wedding, if the bride and groom are not seeing each other, the bride will not be at the synagogue with the groom.

On this Shabbat after the *aliyah*, a special *mi shebarach* is made by the rabbi or another appointed synagogue official. *Mi shebarach* literally means "the one who blesses," and it is a short prayer asking God to bless the bride and groom in preparation for their wedding. Charity is usually pledged to the synagogue by the parents of the bride and groom as part of this *mi shebarahch* blessing. In many synagogues, the Hebrew names of the groom and bride are mentioned as part of the blessing and the cantor or the rabbi may need this information. If the bride or groom do not have Hebrew names, an English name can usually be substituted, or a Hebrew name can be taken.

The Kiddush

In most synagogues, a *kiddush* usually follows. The *kiddush* is a light but festive meal, sponsored by the parents of the groom and sometimes by the parents of the bride or both families together. The *kiddush* can be a good way to celebrate with and include members of the host congregation that the bride or groom's family may have connections with but are unable to invite to the ceremony and reception. The joy of this communal celebration is a good prologue to the wedding itself.

The *kiddush* can be cake and drinks or it can be an entire meal, depending on when the wedding is, the custom of the congregation, and how many out-of-town guests you have to feed. It is good to make a *l'chaim* at the *kiddush* toasting the bride and groom and offering them *berachot*, blessings, for a joyous wedding and a fulfilling life together. A *l'chaim* is the Jewish word for a toast over an alcoholic beverage, and it literally means "to life." After offering words of blessing to the bride and groom one says "*l'chaim*" loudly and drinks.

The *kiddush* gets its name from the Hebrew word for sanctity and refers to the blessing made on a cup of wine prior to the Sabbath meal. Interestingly, wedding ceremonies are also called *kiddushin*, from the same Hebrew root word, and begin with a blessing on a cup of wine. In some synagogues, this blessing over the wine to sanctify the Shabbat is made by the rabbi or cantor, but if this is not necessarily the practice, the bride or groom's family may be allowed to choose who will make the *kiddush* blessing and the *hamotzie* at this meal. The *hamotzie* is the blessing over bread that begins each

Sabbath meal. If they allow you to do so, you can use the opportunity to give this honor to someone in the synagogue that you or your family is close to but will not be able to honor at the wedding itself. In addition, there is usually a *bentching*, a grace after meals blessing, and said after the *kiddush* and after every meal, and this can additionally be led by someone you would like to honor who is familiar with the blessing.

FACT

The *kiddush* blessing that is made over a cup of wine before the Shabbat meal is one of the ways in which Sabbath meals are made special and by which we fulfill the biblical commandment in Exodus to "Remember the Shabbat day and make it holy," which is the fourth of the ten commandments.

If the congregation at which the *ufruf* is to be held is not your regular congregation or your parents' congregation, be sure to arrange the *ufruf* and *kiddush* far in advance. In some larger synagogues there can be many celebrations, such as weddings or bar mitzvahs, and your *kiddush* date could already be booked by another family far in advance.

It is acceptable to have more than one *ufruf*. If the groom lives in one city and the bride in another and both families would like to participate, consider having an *ufruf* two weeks before the wedding in the groom's home town and one the weekend before the wedding in the bride's home synagogue or wherever you will both be for the wedding weekend. If the one partner is being called to the Torah in a synagogue that her fiancé does not feel comfortable having a Torah honor in, she could suggest coming up to the *bimah* together for a blessing of good wishes from the rabbi.

Shabbat Kallah: *The Bride's Sabbath*

There is a long-standing custom for the friends of the groom and his family members and the friends of the bride and her family to spend time with the bride and groom separately on this Shabbat, bringing them support and joy. This is especially true if the bride and groom are not seeing each other during this Shabbat before the wedding. Today, if the bride will not be at the ufruf, this Shabbat with the bride has come to be known as the *Shabbat Kallah*, the bride's Sabbath. The same Shabbat spent with the groom is known in many circles as a *Shabbat Chatan*, the groom's Sabbath.

In traditional Ashkenazi Jewish circles where the bride and groom do not usually see each other, the *Shabbat Kallah* has taken on much importance as a celebration focused on the bride to complement the *ufruf*.

Usually a *Shabbat Kallah* is marked by a gathering at the home of the bride or one of her close relatives or friends. Sometimes the invitation is an open one for anyone in her community who is close with her. Everyone gathers around the bride to give support and love. This time just before the wedding can be fraught with anxiety, but Shabbat should be a time of rest and joy. Stories about the bride are told, food and drinks are consumed, and words of Torah pertaining to wedding joy are usually shared.

If the *kallah* and *chatan*, the bride and groom, are not seeing each other for the week or Shabbat before the wedding but the bride wants to be available to go to the *ufruf*, you could consider holding an *ufruf* in the synagogue two weeks before the wedding and a *Shabbat Kallah* the week before.

Sephardic Pre-Wedding Customs

There are many kinds of Sephardic Jews, and their wedding and pre-wedding customs will vary depending on what community and locale they are from. Sephardic Jews come from Spain, Asia, the Middle East, or North Africa.

The Sephardic Henna Ceremony

Several days before a Sephardic wedding, the bride and her family and friends—and sometimes the groom and his family also—gather for the henna ceremony, usually at the bride's home. There is music and dancing and very colorful clothing and jewelry for the bride. The highlight of the henna ceremony is the painting of the bride's hands with henna dye. Henna dye is temporary and is made with powder from the leaves of a henna plant, a small desert tree. This powder is mixed with rose water, forming a vivid orange-colored paint. The dye is used to make elaborate decorations and patterns on the hands and sometimes feet.

After the bride's hands are painted with henna dye, other women may have their hands painted also. The henna is painted into various designs and symbols, some of which are meant to ward off any evil eyes. Special sweets are consumed and sometimes incense candles are lit. The henna ceremony is especially popular among North African, Indian, and other Sephardic Jews but less so among Syrian Sephardic communities.

Some say the word henna is related to the Hebrew word *chen*, which means grace or charm; others say its three Hebrew letters—*chet, nun,* and *hey*—are a reference to the three home-based *mitzvoth*, commandments that were always unique to the woman of the house. These are challah, the baking of bread for the Sabbath; *nida*, the observance of the laws of family purity; and *hadlakat nerot*, the kindling of the Shabbat candles each Friday evening before sundown.

Other Sephardic Pre-Wedding Customs

Since the *ufruf* and *Shabbat Kallah* are Ashkenazi customs, most Sephardic Jews do not celebrate them in the same way. Instead, a special Shabbat before or after the wedding, depending on custom, is celebrated for the groom, often together with the bride. On this Shabbat, in addition to the regular portion, the portion of the Torah that describes Abraham sending his servant Eliezer to find a wife for his son Isaac is read in honor of the couple and a *kiddush* is provided. Among Syrian Jews, this is done at the Shabbat prior to the wedding and it is usually not attended by the bride herself. Among other communities it is celebrated with bride and groom together on the first Shabbat after they are married.

An additional Sephardic pre-wedding celebration that does not exist among Ashkenazi Jews is a special *mikvah* party for the bride. A few days before the wedding, the bride has a party with her female friends and relatives at the *mikvah*. The bride will go to the *mikvah* in preparation for her wedding day and subsequently after every menstrual cycle. This first trip to the *mikvah* is accompanied by sweets, special gifts, and much singing, dancing, and joy. If you are not Sefardic but like the idea of the festive *mikvah* party, consider starting the custom yourself since it is the celebration of a momentous and holy act.

CHAPTER 14

The *Mikvah*: Natural Waters of Renewal

In Judaism there are notions of *taharah* (purity) and *tumah* (an absence of *taharah*). They have nothing to do with good and bad but rather with different states of being, and they are most often related to life and death and to holy spaces and times. Jewish concepts and guidelines of purity and impurity come from the Bible and from Judaism's oral tradition as recorded in the Mishna and Talmud, Judaism's central books of law and tradition.

Rebirth and Renewal

The Bible tells us that contact with a dead body renders one *tameh*, impure. In English, the word "impure" has negative connotations, but in Hebrew it merely connotes a certain state of being. The result of being impure in Judaism is for the most part associated with practices in and guidelines surrounding the ancient Temple in Jerusalem and its precursor the Mishkan, the tabernacle that traveled with the Jewish people in the desert during their biblically recorded journey from Egypt to Israel.

Jewish Philosophy

Being human is a strange thing. Humans are endowed with higher knowledge, the ability to be self-reflective and knowledgeable, a sense of a larger divine harmony, and a unique ability to love. Yet we die after a short and fragile life, seemingly no different from any animal. This conflict between life and death is the source of perhaps the greatest human anxiety and existential conflict.

FACT

The mitzvah of burying the dead is so important that if a corpse has no one to burry it, even a *Kohen Gadol*, the High Priest in the Temple in Jerusalem, was commanded to do such a burial even though he was usually never allowed to become *tameh* by being in the same room or coming in contact with a dead human body.

Though the Bible does not give reasons for the laws and spiritual concepts of purity and impurity, many commentators point to the fact that all sources of impurity in Judaism are connected with death in some way. There is nothing embarrassing or bad about death in Judaism; in fact, the physical body is seen as a holy temple that holds the soul.

In the story of Adam and Eve, the Bible relates that the human body is made from dirt and then the soul, an actual part of God, is put inside us to animate us. The soul, Judaism believes, is in many ways our true self. When the soul departs from the body and returns to its maker the body returns to dust. This body, Judaism tells us, is a holy thing and deserves respect because it houses us and our true self, our divine soul.

Cleansing the Body

It is a great mitzvah, a holy act of kindness, to take care of the body and prepare it for burial. In Judaism, the body is so important and respected that it is ritually washed before it is put in white shrouds and buried with a little bit of dirt from the Land of Israel placed under the deceased's head.

Though burying the dead is such a holy act, whenever one comes in contact with a source of death or something related to it—for instance, if you have gone to war or been to a funeral—you must go through a purification process before retuning fully to regular life, especially before entering the ancient Holy Temple, the source of Judaism's spiritual life.

Female menstruation and male ejaculation are also considered sources of impurity in Judaism, though less so than a dead body. Both menstruation and ejaculation are perhaps sources of impurity because in both instances the possibility of new life, of forming a new child, did not come to fruition. As a result, neither a man who has ejaculated nor a woman who has menstruated could go into the Holy Temple without first immersing in a body of rain water, an ocean, or a spring-fed river. A body of rainwater that is used for this purification process is called a *mikvah*.

Menstruation and Mikvah

According to the biblical book of Leviticus, a woman cannot engage in sexual relations with her husband during or after menstruation until she bathes her entire body in a mikvah. After the mikvah she and her husband are then permitted to engage in sexual relations again. The same cycle occurs each month.

Nida

Today, Jewish women observeing *mikvah* wait seven "white" days after menstruation with no bleeding before going to the *mikvah*. The state of a menstruating woman before going to the *mikvah* is referred to in the Bible as *nida*, the word for "separated" or "apart from" in Hebrew. This status, regardless of how long it has been since she last menstruated, remains until her immersion in a body of *mikvah* water and and starts again with the next cycle of menstruation.

The status of *nida*, though it requires immersion in a *mikvah* before the woman is permitted to engage in sexual activity, is not bad in any way. The process of immersing in a *mikvah* generally is one that just transforms us from one spiritual state to another. Many men go to the *mikvah* every morning and many go every Friday afternoon in preparation for the new spiritual state that will be experienced on the Shabbat.

Times for Mikvah

The *Kohen Gadol* used to immerse in a *mikvah* ten times on Yom Kippur, the holiest day of the year. Though the *Kohen Gadol* was on perhaps the highest spiritual level of all people after exiting from the Holy of Holies in the Temple once a year on Yom Kippur, it was even then that he would immerse in the *mikvah* after changing his clothing and moving to a new spiritual state in a different part of the Temple.

The amount of rainwater a *mikvah* must hold is forty *saah*, an ancient biblical liquid measure. Forty is always the number associated with rebirth in Judaism, such as the forty days of the flood of Noah, which was a rebirth for the world, as well as the forty years in the desert which the Jewish people spent being "born" into a nation.

Mikvah always indicates a changed state. When a person converts to Judaism, one of the greatest changes of spiritual state, the main act of transformation in the process of their conversion is immersion in a *mikvah*. Since the immersion in a *mikvah* requires one to be totally immersed under the water, a place where one cannot survive, their emersion from the waters signifies a new rebirth and a new beginning in life.

Reasons for Mikvah

In *Waters of Eden: The Mystery of the Mikvah*, Rabbi Aryeh Kaplan points out that a *mikvah* represents a womb, the place from which every human is born, a place where one is surrounded by the waters of life. He explains that the *mikvah* also hearkens back to the Garden of Eden, the birthplace of the human race and the place of the first wedding, the marriage of Adam and Eve.

According to the biblical account, the Garden of Eden was a place in which humanity dwelled before the concept of death had come to the world, a time when the divine was more accessible and palpable. After Adam and Eve were expelled from the Garden of Eden, the Midrash says they wanted to find some connection back to their primordial state of spiritual perfection. They could not go back to the garden, but they saw one of the rivers that came from Eden as it flowed past them and realized that immersing themselves in this river could reconnect them, to their past in Eden.

This event, writes Rabbi Kaplan, is part of the mystery of the *mikvah*. That all waters in their natural state are "connected" to the Garden of Eden, our birthplace as humans and a source of rebirth for us as individuals. Since marriage is the movement from one life to a completely new one, it is additionally appropriate to go to the *mikvah* in preparation for this enormous transformation.

Many women who might not be planning to observe the mitzvah of going to the *mikvah* each month do choose to go before their wedding, and some traditional rabbis will require it. In fact, grooms should also go to the *mikvah* in preparation for their wedding because a wedding for the couple is a day of great rebirth and transformation for them both, from being one person to becoming a completely new entity of two people together, a true rebirth.

Your Cycle

It is ideal to plan your wedding so that it will take place more than seven days after the end of the bride's menstrual cycle, enabling her to immerse in the *mikvah* a day or two prior to the wedding day. Every *mikvah* has an attendant through whom an appointment to use the *mikvah* can be made. Women usually immerse in the mikvah during the nighttime after dark.

When calling your local *mikvah* to make an appointment, tell them that you are a bride, what day the wedding will take place, and what night you would like to go to the *mikvah*. Then speak with the *mikvah* attendant on the phone to arrange a time and other details. Find out the cost and when and whom to pay. When scheduling a night for the *mikvah* it is best for it to be as close to the wedding as possible, though within several days is usually fine.

Some brides today, even if they do not plan on using any kind of birth control, will begin, under their doctor's guidance, a schedule of birth control pills in order to regulate their menstrual cycle and have their period finish at least seven days before the wedding so that they can go to the *mikvah* just before the wedding.

Mikvah attendants are usually knowledgeable and used to having brides who know little about *mikvahs* as well as those who might know a lot about the process. Feel free to ask the *mikvah* attendant on the phone any questions and details you may not be familiar with. If you have never seen a *mikvah*, it is a good idea to arrange a tour several weeks before you will actually be going to the *mikvah* to immerse. Becoming familiar with how it looks and what amenities are available there for your preparation and immersion can help to remove much of the anxiety you may naturally have about going to the *mikvah* for the first time. Consider bringing a female friend or relative along for company; this will be fine with the *mikvah* attendant and is encouraged.

Learning about It

Taharat hamishpacha, family purity, is historically one of the foundations of the Jewish family. Observant Jewish husbands and wives do not engage in sexual activity or things that can lead to it from the day of the month that the wife usually begins menstruating and then for seven days following cessation of bleeding, until after immersion in a *mikvah*.

Boundaries

Some couples cannot imagine putting boundaries on their sexual life, essentially amounting to not having sexual intercourse or other sexual activity for two weeks each month. On the other hand, many couples find that this process helps them reach a much deeper level of relationship. For two weeks each month they must interact with each other only through conversation, without being able to fall back on any physical touching.

FACT

During the nine months of pregnancy during which a woman does not menstruate, unless there is other bleeding, she and her husband will be permitted to engage in sexual activity. After the birth of the child a woman is considered a *nida* and not is permitted to her husband sexually for several weeks, after which she goes to the *mikvah* again.

The laws of Jewish family purity are a bit detailed. To keep them, one usually needs to study them, preferably with some guidance. A local Orthodox synagogue, Chabad House, or some Conservative synagogues can usually supply you with an understanding and sensitive teacher.

There are also several good books and websites from which one can learn the basics of these family purity laws and traditions and can find some answers to commonly asked questions that inevitably come up. If you are not familiar with the laws or processes of this tradition, these resources can be a good place to begin. For the names of some books and websites where you can read about and study these laws please see Appendix D.

Many women and men who have not grown up expecting to keep these laws may feel overwhelmed by the notion of separation or of bringing Jewish tradition into their bedroom. However, it is a powerful spiritual statement to see Jewish law and tradition as applying to and sanctifying even one's most intimate life.

If you find it hard to keep these laws or are nervous about trying them out, start by calling a local rabbi or *mikvah* and seeing if you can schedule a visit to the *mikvah* to see it and have someone knowledgeable explain to you the procedure for immersing. Today many *mikvahs* are beautifully constructed with additional whirlpools and salons to make the experience of going to the *mikvah* a true physical pleasure as well as a spiritual one.

If you decide to keep the laws of family purity but do not feel you can commit to keeping them fully, begin just by counting seven clean days after your period each month and going to the *mikvah*. The experience of the *mikvah* is a profound one that you may find purifying and fulfilling. Over time you and your groom can learn more about the laws of family purity and the separation of husband and wife. Learning about a Jewish commandment and tradition such as *mikvah* can help to make it meaningful and organic rather than uncomfortable.

QUESTION?

How long have people been using the mikvah?
Mikvahs go back to the Bible. On the south side of the Temple Mount in Jerusalem and other places in Israel, archeologists have uncovered hundreds of *mikvahs* from approximately 2,000 to 3,000 years ago.

The separation and rapprochement process that brides and grooms go though and that husbands and wives experience each month can be a powerful one for your relationship. You will spend two weeks of each month cultivating your deep and intimate relationship in a nonsexual way. This is followed by a coming back together sexually and can make your sexual relationship truly about coming together as one—physically, emotionally, and spiritually. Perhaps since it is so easy for sex to become about one's own pleasure, Judaism's process of separation and rekindling intimacy can help facilitate a sexuality that is about the other person and becoming one together, rather than the fulfillment of one's own sexual pleasure.

Admittedly, the process of physicial separation and togetherness can be a challenging one. Though the two or three weeks a couple are together after being apart can make their sexual life much more powerful, it can also lead to a heightened pressure to have sex since they have only two or three weeks at a time of being accessible to each other.

Conversely, as life becomes busier and children enter the picture, husbands and wives sometimes find that they have very little time for each other and their relationship, and whatever time is left will be spent in the most heightened and physically intimate way possible. But if for two weeks a month they are not permitted to each other sexually, those few precious minutes of together time will be spent not in immediate sexual activity but in interrelating in other ways. This can lead, some couples find, to a relationship that is more multifaceted than it might have been without the laws of family purity and *mikvah* immersion.

If you are keeping the laws of Jewish family purity, it is important to have a rabbi you are comfortable consulting in case questions come up. Sometimes married women or brides experience some bleeding or spotting during their white days and will need to consult with a rabbi to know if additional days must be counted.

For the *mikvah* process to work it is important for bride and groom, or husband and wife, to talk honestly about their needs and how they are feeling about being separate and together. If you have not kept these laws before or considered it, try some of the *mikvah* process and check in with each other often as to how it is going for each of you. For instance, though fully observant couples do not touch at all while the wife is a *nida*, if you have not considered keeping these laws fully before, trying to do it all right away can lead to keeping none of it and just becoming frustrated.

Experimenting with Regular *Mikvah*

If you are going to try keeping the laws of *nida* and *mikvah* after your wedding night you may want to experiment with this important tradition in stages. For instance, first try not having sexual intercourse from the beginning of menstruation until after *mikvah* immersion. As time goes on, add some additional physical distancing such as not hugging and kissing during those two weeks and instead making specific times to talk about your lives together, dreams for the future, and spiritual life together.

Consider spending some time studying Torah together. This can be a new level of deep intellectual and emotional interaction resulting in a heightened level of respect and appreciation for each other and for Judaism. If this is not a good place to begin, change nothing in your sexual life but schedule a trip to the *mikvah* seven days after the end of your monthly period and grow and experiment with more from there.

Everyone is at a different place when it comes to this mitzvah, which is admittedly easier said than done. Grow into it while you study it and talk about it even before your wedding. In this way it can become an organic part of your life and your relationship, and will not feel like a burden but an adventurous spiritual path.

How and When

Here is a brief outline of the process of counting the days of *nida* and the process of *mikvah* renewal for a bride and subsequently for married women after each menstrual cycle. After a woman has menstruated, she checks with a white cloth, packs of which which can be obtained from the *mikvah* attendant, to be sure there is no more blood. This is colloquially called "checking," and when she finds no blood it is often referred to in English as a "clean check." Obviously, different women have different length menstrual periods, so how long it will take until she has a "clean check" will depend on her cycle. In Jewish law if a married woman has a period that lasts less than five days, she waits five minimum days before counting her "clean" days.

After cessation of menstrual bleeding a woman counts seven "white" days, during which she checks each day to be sure there is no blood and usually wears white undergarments. During this week one should call the *mikvah* to schedule an immersion on the night following the seventh white day. At the end of these seven days she can immerse in the *mikvah*. The night after a wife has gone to the *mikvah*, when husband and wife will be coming together for sexual intimacy after almost two weeks of separation, is considered very special.

Though sexual intimacy between husband and wife is always considered holy in Judaism, sexual activity this night after her visit to the *mikvah* is considered a special mitzvah, a uniquely holy commandment. In addition, each Friday night is also a special mitzvah for wife and husband to engage in sexual intimacy.

FACT

Some say that on Friday nights there are two mitzvoth, commandments, fulfilled though sexual intercourse. The first is the regular mitzvah of sexual intimacy between wife and husband, and the second is the deep pleasure one is supposed to have in honor of the Shabbat itself.

Preparations

Since nothing can come between between us and the waters of the *mikvah*, before immersing in the water of the *mikvah* one bathes in a bathtub for about half an hour, carefully cleaning the hair and combing it of any knots and cutting and cleaning the fingernails until they are free of dirt and polish. If you are having your nails done for the wedding be sure to schedule your manicure and hair appointments for after your visit to the *mikvah*.

On the night of your scheduled visit to the *mikvah*, probably a day or two before your wedding, you will meet the *mikvah* attendant at the *mikvah* building and then you will bathe and clean yourself. If your *mikvah* has a whirlpool you can take advantage of this also. When you are all cleaned and ready let the *mikvah* attendant know, and after you disrobe she will check to be sure there are no stray hairs or dirt that could block the mikvah waters from encompassing you.

You then walk into the *mikvah* waters and the *mikvah* attendant will watch to be sure that when you dunk under the *mikvah* water all of your body and hair go fully under the water. For most women, the most efficient way to immerse the entire body is to bend at the knees with your arms straight out in front.

When immersed in the life-giving waters of the *mikvah*, think about the step you are about to take in your life and the blessings it can bring for holiness, joy, and the new life you may bring into the world in the form of children. Feel the *mikvah* waters as a kind of womb and rebirth into a new state of merging with your future husband to become one new and powerful entity at your wedding.

After emerging from the water and robing you can then change back into your clothing and let the *mikvah* attendant know you are finished. Before leaving she may bless you and wish you mazel tov. Among Sephardic Jews, the *mikvah* attendant will often give the bride a kiss on the cheek and a *beracha*, a blessing, for children and joy.

Sephardic and Ashkenazi Traditions

For most Ashkenazi Jews a bride's first trip to the *mikvah* is a very private and subdued affair. She may be accompanied by her mother and mother-in-law and perhaps a friend who offer support and blessings. Few others will know about her *mikvah* attendance. If she is close with a female rabbi, *rebbitzin*, or teacher, they may accompany her, but her main interaction within the mikvah will be with the female *mikvah* attendant. In general, in this community, personal *mikvah* attendance is rarely spoken about even with one's children.

In contrast, among many Sephardic communities the mood of the bride's first *mikvah* attendance is just the opposite of subdued. In these communities the bride is accompanied to the *mikvah* by her mother, sisters, relatives, and many friends. This first trip to the *mikvah* is a big party at which they eat sweets, open special gifts sent by her groom and friends, and celebrate with singing, dancing, and joy. Some also partake in special sweet almond milk.

Among Sephardic Jews this celebration is called by various names. Spanish Jews refer to this festive *mikvah* party as *Noche de Novia*, literally "the Night of the Sweetheart." Syrian Jews call it the *Swehnie,* a reference in their language to the special fancy trays on which the night's gifts to the bride are placed. Among the gifts presented on the special *Swehnie* tray is an expensive white handbag sent to the bride by the groom containing money to pay for the *mikvah* and party.

During the party the bride is accompanied to the *mikvah* itself by her mother, the groom's mother, and perhaps very close friends. According to Herbert Dobrinsky's detailed book, *Treasury of Sephardic Laws and Customs*, in some Sephardic communities the groom has his own party at which he celebrates with friends and rice is thrown at him as a symbol of future fertility and blessings.

CHAPTER 15

Your Wedding Day

Your wedding day is one of the most special days of your life. You become a new and enhanced person, part of a unique partnership. Give yourself the gift of focus on this day. There will be a lot of expectations put upon you that can serve to remove you from the spiritual, emotional, and inspirational aspects of this day. Jewish traditions and values can help to make this day one that is truly and personally significant to you and your fiancé forever.

A Day of Transformation

In Judaism, your wedding day is considered a day of transformation from being one person to becoming a new entity of two. Jewish tradition teaches that on your wedding day all of your sins are forgiven since you truly become a different person. Who you are now is someone new; the person you were yesterday, with his sins and faults, is gone. Often, because of this spiritual phenomenon, the wedding day is seen as a personal Yom Kippur, a day of atonement.

A Personal Yom Kippur

Though we sometimes see Yom Kippur, the annual Jewish day of atonement, as a sad day, it really is not. Yom Kippur is a solemn day, as, in truth, a wedding day should be, but Yom Kippur, like your wedding day, is also a great joy, offering the chance of making your life more perfect and complete. To become transformed into a new entity with entirely new potential is truly a moment of incredible joy.

It is this side of the wedding day, with its Yom Kippur–like power of transformation and spiritual growth, that colors the day for the bride and groom from the time they wake in the morning until the end of the chuppah. In Judaism, there is a long-standing custom for the bride and groom to fast from dawn on the day of their wedding until the *yichud*, when they break their fast alone together right after the ceremony.

For many of us the idea of fasting is not a pleasant one. A Jewish fast is one that allows no food or water at all, though brushing one's teeth and rinsing is permitted on this fast day since it is not actually Yom Kippur. Fasting, though difficult, serves many productive purposes. When fasting, one realizes how frail human life is. Without food we feel a bit weak and reaffirm our knowledge that life is tenuous and precious. Experiencing our personal frailty and humility is a great way to prepare for making room for another person in our life.

The following is a list of the days in the Jewish calendar on which a bride and groom would not fast even if it is their wedding day:

- Rosh Chodesh, the new moon
- The day following a festival

- Hanukkah
- Purim
- Tu B'Shevat, the new year of the trees
- The fifteenth day of the Hebrew month of Av

Fasting also makes room for thought. You will have extra time because there are no meals to worry about, and fasting is also a good way to become a bit more spiritually aware and open to God and to others. We fast on Yom Kippur, the Jewish day of atonement, because fasting in Judaism is thought to help lead us into the process of *tishuvah*, return.

Fasting on your wedding day is not as important as fasting on Yom Kippur. If it is hard for you to fast or if fasting makes you sick, you do not have to. Nevertheless, even if you are not fasting on your wedding day you should make time for reflection and return. In addition, if you are not fasting on your wedding day, since one of the primary reasons for this fast is to be sure the bride and groom are of sound mind, you should refrain from consuming any alcoholic beverages this day prior to the chuppah ceremony.

FACT

In many Sephardic lands there was no custom for brides and grooms to fast on the day of their wedding. Some rabbis even felt that they should not fast so as to not weaken themselves for the wedding ceremony. Of course, the wedding day still retained proper overtones of *tishuvah*, repentance, renewal, and solemnity.

In Judaism, we don't simply repent for sins we have done; instead, we return. *Tishuvah*, or return, is the process of changing who we are, not to become someone we are not, but to become the person we truly are, the best we can be. Judaism believes we each are endowed with a divine soul and so our essential nature is a good and holy one. At times of transformation and return, we have only to return to our true, holy, and sinless selves and the day of marriage is precisely this.

Deeper Meanings

Yom Kippur might bring back many bad memories of feeling bored, hungry, and lost in a synagogue. This day of your wedding, a personal Yom Kippur, is just the opposite. Unlike Yom Kippur, there is no sitting in a synagogue or temple with lots of people. It is a personal journey that utilizes the very valuable ideas of personal perfection, return, and the shoring up of our relationships with ourselves, others, and God. It can be a most inspiring day of spiritual reflection and growth.

In his book on Jewish weddings, *Made in Heaven*, Rabbi Aryeh Kaplan suggests another reason for fasting on the day of one's wedding. At first in a relationship, we are drawn physically to the other person, but for a good relationship to endure this physical attraction we must have a deeper emotional and spiritual bond. Fasting, separating yourself from your primary source of physical nourishment on the day of your wedding, shows that you and your fiancé are not linked only to the physical but to that which is deeper. This reflects the deeper nature of your relationship.

In addition, this day is akin to the Jewish people standing at Mount Sinai when they became "married" to God. On that day they were on such a high spiritual level that they did not eat and drink. According to the Bible, Moses did not eat or drink for the full forty days during which he ascended the mountain to receive the Torah for the people.

The problem with a wedding day, of course, is that there are often myriad things to get done. Questions about the ceremony, guests that want to wish you mazel tov, hair to be done, makeup to be applied, tuxes to be picked up, and on and on. Everyone and everything demands your attention, so how can you utilize your wedding day as a day of personal return and spiritual transformation?

Making Your Wedding Day Meaningful Through Prayer

Judaism teaches that our spiritual and religious life is supposed to be led in the real world and not just in the synagogue, religious school, or on a mountain top. Rituals and prayers that help to create this focus are programmed into Jewish everyday life. This allows us to do all the mundane things we need to and have our deeper spiritual reflection, too. To facilitate the wedding day's Yom Kippur atmosphere, in addition to actually abstaining from food and drink, time is created for the bride and groom to reflect and recite special prayers.

The *amidah*, which is traditionally recited three times a day, is the most basic Jewish prayer. It is the only prayer actually referred to as "prayer" in the Talmud and is said completely silently and alone, even in a large group. The *amidah* is an intimate experience between you and God, and the only person who should be able to hear your *amidah* is yourself.

The *amidah* opens with praises of God, and then contains a long section in which we humans ask God for the things we need. The prayer closes with words of thanks. Brides and grooms usually insert two special prayers into the *amidah* on this day if they are accustomed to regular Hebrew prayer.

If not everyone knows that you are fasting on your wedding day, tell your maid of honor or best man and ask them to tell people so that you are not offered food or thought strange for not eating. In addition, they should help you find a time and place to be alone for reflection the morning of your big day.

The first special prayer added to the *amidah* on one's wedding day is the *anaynu* prayer. This is a paragraph added on every fast day petitioning God to answer our prayers. This prayer asks God not to see the bad that we have done and to answer our prayers quickly. The *anaynu* prayer also asks God to be present to us and askes God not to "hide Your face from us."

The function of the *anaynu* is to help us feel the closeness of God through our fasting and to ask that God answer our prayers, especially today since we are experiencing discomfort in a spiritual effort. On a wedding day the bride and groom are not only praying for personal *tishuvah* but for years of happiness, joy, and fulfillment together in their marriage. Asking God to grant our wishes in light of our intense fasting efforts is especially appropriate on this day.

The other prayer that is formally added to the *amidah* is the *viduy*, the traditional confessionary prayer. Even if one is not fasting, the *viduy* prayer should still be said and this time taken for reflection and return.

Make sure to pack a *siddur*, a Jewish prayer book for yourself if you will be praying alone the day of your wedding. You can certainly pray from the heart, but having the special penitential prayers printed can help you jumpstart your personal *tishuvah* and prayer.

Tishuvah: *Repentance and Return*

In Judaism, the process of *tishuvah*, of return and repentance that we emphasize on Yom Kippur or on our wedding day, has several steps. The first is to think about what we have not done right and what sinful actions we have taken that we would like to change. The second step is to verbalize how we want to change. In Judaism, this act of confession is not done in front of other people, but it is between ourselves and God.

On Yom Kippur we confess by reciting the *viduy* prayer ten times throughout the day. Some people recite a smaller version of it every day in their prayers. A day of fasting and return such as a wedding day is especially fitting for these confessionary prayers. The third step in *tishuvah*, return, is to ask forgiveness of those we have sinned against, whether ourselves, other people, or God. The fourth step is to truly change—to make an inner decision to act differently in the future and transform into a different person than we were before the process of *tishuvah*.

The *viduy*, the confessionary prayers, can be found in the Yom Kippur prayer book. The prayer usually consists of a list of sins or bad traits that we may have engaged in and that we wish to change and be forgiven for. We express how we are humbled before God and before the things we have done wrong and how much we want to change for the future, and then we recite a list of things we might have done wrong that we wish to change. You can use this list as it is for confession between you and God or you can make your own list or take aspects of both.

Take some time before this prayer to reflect upon your life and what you would like to change as you embark on your new life with your fiancé. Ask God for help in seeing what to change and in helping you see how to shed parts of your old self to uncover more of your divine self. When both bride and groom have engaged in this process independently they will no doubt be ready to enter a relationship of humility and positive growth with each other.

In order for this personal day of atonement to be productive, the bride and groom must set aside time to be spent alone by themselves. You can certainly pray with a community if that is what you usually do, but before or after communal prayer you should find a special place to reflect where no one will bother you. It does not have to be a long time—just long enough to focus on the significance of the day and your personal *tishuvah*, the significance of the life-altering day you are about to embark upon.

Jewish and Not-So-Jewish Wedding Day Customs

There are popular American customs associated with the wedding day and the weekend preceding the wedding. It is important to realize that not every one of these customs, no matter how time-honored, is considered by Judaism to be appropriate for a Jewish wedding, though some might be. A classic bachelor party, rife with debauchery, obviously would not lend itself to the foundation of a Jewish wedding day. At the same time, customs that are not necessarily Jewish—such as gifts given to the wedding party—are commendable. In the best of worlds, a bride and groom will find ways to transform the American customs they like into customs that are productive for their Jewish wedding.

Bachelor Parties

Bachelor parties are not a Jewish tradition, but you can transform yours into a fun, meaningful, and potentially moving tradition of your own. Many grooms feel that the orgiastic bachelor parties of the past are not in keeping with their personal vision of their wedding day. Titillating thoughts of other women as objects have no place within the day they are about to share with their bride.

A groom's wedding day should be his most meaningful day together with his bride, celebrating an equal relationship of honoring each other, not doing things of which he could not comfortably inform her. More and more grooms today are opting for bachelor parties that are very different from the decadence of the past. Some popular ideas are golfing parties, fishing parties, and catered affairs with friends at which toasts are made to the groom. Some grooms even choose to go with their friends to perform community service together, an honorable way to prepare for one's new life as a married man while bonding with buddies.

In some Jewish communities, family and friends make a meal for the bride and groom, together if they are seeing each other the night before the wedding, or separately if they are not seeing each other for several days before the wedding. These meals are a far cry from something that one would be reluctant to share with one's future spouse. Though very celebratory, such a pre-Jewish-wedding meal would celebrate the change and growth the bride and groom are about to undergo at their wedding, not lament it as a lost freedom.

Though Jewish law does not forbid rehearsing the wedding procession, a rehearsal is usually discouraged for Jewish weddings since the moment of the actual ceremony is a religious one and should be unique. But there is nothing wrong with having a meal and calling it a rehearsal dinner.

These meals are sometimes held in the home of the bride or groom or, similar to a rehearsal dinner, at a hotel or restaurant. They are small meals of the bride and groom's family and friends at which toasts and a *l'chaim* are made to them offering encouragement and wishes of mazel tov. Usually a *divar torah*, a word of Torah, or some Jewish spiritual or religious thoughts, are said to the bride or groom. These words are important since they serve to sanctify and focus the meal on the bride or groom and on giving them insight into the great step they are about to take. They emphasize how meaningful, important, and holy a day it will be.

Cakes and Other Wedding Day Traditions

There is nothing wrong with a four-tiered wedding cake in Judaism's eyes, especially if this is something you have always dreamed of and is kosher. Yet at the same time, Judaism does discourage wasted opulence or haughty show. If the cost of your cake will be exorbitant and it will be a work of art only to be consumed momentarily, perhaps you should consider a more modest cake by a less well-known cake artist and donate the money you save to a deserving charity. Indeed, in Jewish tradition the act of giving to others in need is considered one of the greatest joys.

The custom of carrying candles down the aisle is found at both Jewish and non-Jewish weddings. At non-Jewish weddings they are usually referred to as unity candles. Those accompanying the bride and groom carry candles and then at the end of the ceremony the couple lights a third unity candle symbolizing the two partners coming together as one. There is a similar Jewish custom in which those accompanying the bride and groom each carry candles, but the couple does not light a unity candle. Often, the candles are braided *havdalah* candles, those used at the end of the Shabbat in the *havdalah* ceremony each week to mark the separation of weekday from Shabbat.

Giving Away the Bride

In many non-Jewish, especially Christian, weddings, the bride is "given away" by her father. This custom dates back to a time when the ownership of a daughter was transferred from father to husband. This is not a Jewish custom. In Judaism, a woman who reaches the age of twelve becomes an adult and is considered independent. She therefore must agree to the marriage on her own. If she does not fully agree to the marriage she is not, in the eyes of Jewish law, married. Though it is fine for the bride to be escorted down the aisle by her father, the marriage ceremony itself takes place solely between the bride and the groom with no one acting as an agent.

Flowers

Flowers seem to be ubiquitous at Jewish and non-Jewish weddings alike. Flowers at weddings go back to the Roman era when different kinds of flowers were seen as representing various virtues such as love and fidelity. Some claim that flowers at a Jewish wedding represent the Garden of Eden and the first wedding of Adam and Eve or the *Midrashic* sources that describe flowers blossoming at Mount Sinai when God gave the Jewish people the Torah and thereby "married" them. Flowers are not considered particularly Jewish or not Jewish; provided exorbitant amounts of money are not frivolously spent paying for them, decorative flowers are certainly in line with the joy and celebration of a Jewish wedding.

Tossing Rice and Other Customs

Rice is usually seen as a particularly non-Jewish wedding day custom. Except for certain Sephardic communities who have a tradition of throwing rice as a symbol of fertility, rice-throwing along with tying cans to the car of the bride and groom, are usually seen as attempts to mimic non-Jewish wedding traditions.

In addition, making efforts to wear something old, new, borrowed, and blue, or placing money in one's shoe are seen as particularly non-Jewish superstitions. Public removal of a garter from the bride is very much a violation of Jewish ideals of modesty and the intimacy reserved solely for the bride and groom.

Practical Wedding Day Preparations

The morning of your wedding, recheck to be sure all the Jewish ritual "tools" you will need have been brought to your wedding space, or that you have sufficiently instructed a helper or wedding planner to be sure everything you will need is present. Appoint someone to be in charge of transporting the big things such as boxes of wedding booklets, *benchers*, *kippot*, and the chuppah. In addition, the following is a checklist of the smaller things, both ritual and practical, for you to have brought to the wedding space:

- ✓ *Ketubah*
- ✓ White wine and two wine cups
- ✓ Wedding license
- ✓ Wedding rings
- ✓ *Kittel*
- ✓ Pen for signing the *ketubah*
- ✓ Plate for the mothers to break and recommended hammer
- ✓ Wrapped glass to break
- ✓ Copy of the blessings and readings people will be saying

Gifts for Members of the Wedding Party

From a Jewish point of view, gifts are not required to be given to attendants and others by the bride and groom since accompanying the bride and goom is considered itself a great honor and mitzvah. At the same time Judaism does require *hakarat hatov*, the recognition of the good that people have done for us.

In American tradition, the bride and groom usually give gifts of thanks to their attendants and to the maid of honor and best man. In addition, the ring bearer, flower girls, and parents are usually recognized and given gifts as well. These gifts are usually things such as jewelry and are often monogrammed. Typically they are bestowed before the wedding at a special dinner.

Giving gifts to the attendants and certainly to one's parents and others who have helped make your special day possible is an appropriate act of thanks and *hakarat hatov*. Some Jewish brides and grooms choose to give something Jewish that people will use often, such as a leatherbound prayer book embossed with the name of the recipient and the date of the wedding.

CHAPTER 16

Pre-Ceremony Traditions

Jewish tradition requires a bride and groom to know each other and to partake in a formal or informal engagement prior to marriage. The Talmud says this is so for practical reasons. To marry without first knowing who one is marrying could lead to not loving one's neighbor—or in this case, one's spouse—as oneself. Marriage cannot be jumped into; it must be preceded by certain preparatory activities. So, too, a wedding itself is preceded by certain moving rituals that serve to deepen one's subsequent wedding ceremony and marriage.

What Is a Tish?

A traditional Jewish wedding begins not with the wedding itself but with a joyous celebration of and preparation for the event. The *tish* and the *kabalat panim*, the reception, serve certain practical purposes, such as a forum for the signing of the *ketubah*, but they also set the tone for the moment of marriage to follow. Through it, the bride and groom and their guests can ease into the wedding ceremony, rather than jumping into the solemnity and power of the chuppah itself.

The word *tish* is a Yiddish word that literally means "table." The tish is also known as the *chatan's tish* or the "groom's table." The *tish* ceremony receives its name from the table at which the groom—at some weddings the groom and bride—are seated. This is the table at which the *ketubah*, the *tanaim*, and any state documents such as the license will be signed.

Though serious documents are signed at the *tish*, its atmosphere is jovial and celebratory. Traditionally, only the *chatan*, the groom, will be seated at the head of the *tish.* If this is the case, the bride will be seated at the head of a different room, sometimes on a dais, at what is often referred to as the *kabalat panim*, the reception. If the bride and groom are seeing each other before the wedding ceremony they may choose to have a bride and groom's *tish* together, or just to call the ceremony a *kabalat panim.*

Sometimes the word *kabalat panim*, reception, or literally, "the receiving of faces," refers only to the bride's reception and the groom's table is called the *tish.* Other times both the bride's reception and the groom's table are referred to as the *kabalat panim.*

Traditionally at a *tish* the refreshments are fairly simple, consisting of cake and liquor, often scotch and vodka for a *l'chaim* to be offered as a blessing to the couple. If the groom and bride are having one *kabalat panim* together, there often will be hors d'oeuvres. If the bride is to be in her own room, the more elaborate victuals will usually be served there and something simpler at the groom's *tish*.

Usually a *tish* begins with singing. Several traditional wedding songs such as "*Od Yishamah*" are usually sung, along with clapping or banging on the table to energize the atmosphere. Then the *tanaim*, the conditions of the wedding—essentially an agreement made by both families to proceed with the wedding—is signed. In generations past, the *tanaim* were signed many months prior to the wedding as a legally binding agreement to go through with the wedding before any money was spent on food and location. Today, though, in most Jewish communities the *tanaim* are signed as a matter of custom. Since there is less reason to legally bind the families before the wedding today, they are usually signed at the *tish* if they are signed at all.

The *tanaim* is an agreement between the two fathers, mothers, or families to go through with the wedding. They are signed only by the two witnesses. The rabbi will usually explain what the *tanaim* is to the fathers, have them agree to the terms of the document, and then ask the witnesses to sign the *tanaim*. After it is signed, a previously appointed honoree reads it in Hebrew. This is followed by the breaking of a plate together by the mothers. With the shattering of the plate, everyone present shouts, "Mazel tov!" It means "good luck" or it should be a "good sign."

The groom and bride should by no means drink alcohol at the *kabalat panim* since it is required that they be of sound mind at the moment of entering into their wedding bonds with each other. This, many suggest, is one of the reasons for the bride and groom's fast on this day.

Making a *l'chaim* is usually a mainstay of the *tish*, and anyone can make a *l'chaim*. Sometimes it is made with just a few people at one end of the *tish*, or sometimes, especially if being made by the rabbi, it is said louder and addressed to the entire room. A small shot glass or the bottom of a soda glass is filled with an alcoholic beverage of choice and the word *l'chaim* is said in a loud voice, after which people take a drink.

A Jewish wedding consists of many religious rituals and traditions. Here is a reference list to help you remember what comes next at each stage of your wedding:

Tish

1. Sign the *tanaim*
2. Read the *tanaim*
3. Break the plate
4. Sign the *ketubah*
5. Optional *l'chaim* and *divar torah*
6. *Bedekin*
7. Parents bless the couple

Ceremony

1. Procession
2. Circles
3. Words of welcome
4. Blessings on the first cup of wine; bride and groom drink
5. Groom presents bride with wedding ring
6. Reading of the *ketubah*
7. Groom hands the *ketubah* to the bride
8. Rabbi may speak
9. *Sheva berachot* over the second cup of wine; bride and groom drink
10. Optional blessing by Rabbi or Kohen
11. Optional ring presented to groom by bride
12. Break the glass
13. *Yichud*

Reception

1. *Hamotzie*
2. Grace after meals
3. *Sheva berachot*

Kabalat Panim: *Greeting the Bride*

If the bride and groom are not seeing each other before the wedding, then during the groom's *tish* the bride will be in her own room welcoming guests. This is called her *kabalat panim*, or welcoming. In traditional circles the bride is seated at the front of the room, on a special "throne." This special chair symbolizes the bride's honored status as a queen on her wedding day.

At many traditional Jewish weddings the mother of the bride is seated to her right and the mother of the groom is seated to the bride's left. The custom of the bride being seated on a "throne" may be a very ancient one. The Talmud in tractates Ediyot and Yivamot speaks of a special bride's chair, and later commentaries identify this as something elaborate.

If you cannot find a special chair for the bride, speak to those in charge of the location about putting a few pillows or a decorative sheet on a chair for the bride. Another alternative is to buy a large wicker chair at a home decorating store. These chairs are inexpensive but usually have a large back and resemble a throne.

The bride's friends and guests file by her, wishing her mazel tov. Usually a band plays in the same room and there is a more elaborate array of foods served than at the groom's *tish*. Today there may be a smorgasbord or hors d'oeuvres at the *kabalat panim*, and though this is primarily for women, men are usually welcome to partake.

If the bride wishes, the *tanaim* may be signed on the bride's side even if the bride and groom are having their *kabalat panims* in separate rooms. Neither the groom nor the bride sign the *tanaim*, rather it is agreed to by representatives of their families, usually a father or mother, and signed by designated witnesses. Thus, the groom is not required at all for this ritual, and signing the *tanaim* on the bride's side might be more convenient for the two mothers who will break a plate after the signing. Though at many weddings the *tanaim* are signed at the groom's *tish*, signing them on the bride's side may help to involve those in the bride's room in a more official capacity.

Licenses and Required State Documents

In addition to the religious documents such as the *ketubah* and *tanaim* that might be signed at the *tish*, most states require that a license or wedding certificate be signed by the rabbi and two witnesses. Of course, there are no Jewish religious requirements of witnesses for the wedding license; they may be any United States citizen over eighteen years of age. After the marriage license is signed by your officiant and the witnesses, it must be mailed back to the proper state office to be officially recorded and recognized.

You will need to apply for your state wedding license in advance of your wedding in most states. If you have been married before, states require proof of the dissolution of your previous marriage. Some states require a blood test. While a state marriage license is of no significance in the eyes of Jewish law, without a marriage license your wedding will not be recognized by your state government, which might be problematic when you try to pay taxes or buy insurance as a couple.

FACT

You and your fiancé will obtain a wedding license and marriage certificate from your state before the wedding. The rabbi and witnesses will sign a marriage certificate to prove that the wedding ceremony was correctly conducted. It is this certificate section of the licensure that is then mailed back to the state's recording office.

Most states charge fees of approximately $50 for marriage licenses, and some have a waiting period of several days. Most states require that both the bride and groom be at least eighteen years of age without written parental consent, and people under certain ages may only be married with the consent of parents and a local judge.

Signing the Ketubah

One of the main proceedings at the *tish* is the signing of the *ketubah*. The traditional ketubah is essentially an agreement between the bride and groom outlining, for the most part, the groom's obligations within the marriage and in case of a divorce. Since the *ketubah* is an agreement between bride and groom, both must agree to the terms. This is especially true for the groom since he is obligating himself to most of the terms within the *ketubah*.

Names and Places

The *ketubah* may be written on plain paper and can be preprinted with all the necessary information, such as the names of the bride and groom, the city in which the wedding is taking place, and the date of the wedding. If the *ketubah* used is one that has blank spaces for the names of the couple and the place and date of the ceremony, these will need to be filled in by the rabbi at this point in the *tish* before the groom accepts the terms of the *ketubah* and the witnesses sign it.

Some cities have various ways in which their names can be spelled in Hebrew. The rabbi should check whether the city has a traditional spelling for its name in a *ketubah*. This information can usually be obtained from a local rabbi who has performed weddings in that city before.

If the *ketubah* is fully preprinted, the names of the parties and the city and date of the ceremony will not need to be filled out at the *tish*, and only the signatures of the witnesses will be required. Sometimes *ketubahs* are left with a word, a letter, or part of a letter missing so that the *ketubah* may be completed just before it is signed. The word usually left incomplete is the word *v'kinyanah*, which translates as "the kinyan" or "the agreement" and appears close to the end of the *ketubah* text. If this is to be filled in by the rabbi at the *tish*, be sure to bring an appropriate pen that has the same color ink as the *ketubah* text itself. If only a letter or part of a letter is to be left out, this is usually the letter *kof* in the word *v'kinyanah*.

The Kinyan

There is a class of acts in Talmudic law called *kinyan*. A *kinyan* is a symbolic way of facilitating a transaction, usually monetary in nature. If one buys a field it is not truly the buyer's until he has performed a symbolic act of acquisition upon it, for instance, built a fence around it or walked its width and breath.

Since the *ketubah* is truly a contract, the methods used to confirm the groom's agreement to undertake what is outlined in the *ketubah* come from the section of Jewish law having to do with business contracts. As such, if the *ketubah* is one that conforms to the traditional Talmudic *ketubah* contract, the bride and groom do not actually sign the *ketubah*. Instead, it is signed by two witnesses who have witnessed the groom formally agreeing with the bride or her agent to undertake the obligations of the *ketubah*.

FACT

In Judaism there is not really a bifurcation between ritual and civil law. They are both commanded in the Torah and are equally important. Nearly a quarter of practical Jewish law is business law, from torts to acquisitions to the details of contract law such as a *ketubah*.

The *kinyan* used here to signify the groom's acceptance of the terms and obligations of the *ketubah* is called a *kinyan chalipin*. Such a *kinyan* is actually an exchange. The bride or her agent, usually the rabbi, takes an object and gives it to the groom. In exchange for the object, known as consideration in common law, the groom assumes his obligation to the terms of the contract before him, in this case the *ketubah*. The *kinyan* object is passed to the groom from the rabbi or the bride, and he lifts up the object, thus "acquiring" it. Usually the *kinyan* object is not kept by the groom but promptly returned. The witnesses who have watched the act of *kinyan* then sign the *ketubah*, signifying their testimony.

The concept of *kinyan* as an exchange is derived from the following verse in the book of Ruth, "This was the ancient practice in Israel . . . to confirm all things, a man would remove his shoe and give it to the other party. This among the Israelites would create a confirmation." Though in biblical times a shoe was used, today we usually use an object such as a handkerchief or a pen.

Variations

A variation of the *kinyan* of the *ketubah* was recently suggested by Rabbi Dov Linzer, head of Chovivey Torah, an Orthodox rabbinical school in New York City, and has been used by some Orthodox couples who wish to be sure the bride, as well as the groom, is fully engaged in each part of the ceremony.

If the bride and groom will not see each other until the *bedekin* and the bride would like to make the *kinyan* over the *ketubah* herself instead of relying upon the rabbi to be her agent, she can give the *kinyan* object to the groom herself under the chuppah, just before or after the start of the wedding ceremony.

Some Sephardic Jews such as those of Syrian ancestry do not make the *kinyan* with the groom at the signing of the *ketubah* but later under the chuppah just before the giving of the ring. In addition, though Ashkenazi Jews all read the *ketubah* under the chuppah, not all Sephardic Jews do this.

The *ketubah* witnesses, of course, need to be present under the chuppah at this time to watch the *kinyan* and promptly sign the *ketubah*. If the bride wishes, the *kinyan* object that she might give to the groom, instead of a handkerchief, pen, or shoe, might be a wedding ring for him to wear ever after or a silver kiddush cup for Sabbath and holiday use.

The Witnesses' Signatures

If your *ketubah* is written in Aramaic with Hebrew letters, the most common practice is for the witnesses to sign the *ketubah* with their Hebrew names followed by the name of their father, mother, or both. The Hebrew word used for son is *ben* meaning, "son of" and for daughter, *bat*, or "daughter of." According to Jewish law, the witnesses on the *ketubah* should be males who are observant of Jewish law. At observant weddings the witnesses usually sign their names, for purposes of *ketubah* signing, using the word *ben* after their name and then writing their father's name. At the end of each of the witnesses' names, if it is not preprinted, the work *ayd*, witness, in Hebrew, should be written.

Conservative, Reform, and Reconstructionist rabbis will allow women as well as men to sign the *ketubah* and will almost always use the witnesses' mothers' names in addition to their fathers' names. In traditional Jewish law, the use of anyone other than an observant Jewish male would pose a problem. What is considered observant for this purpose is the subject of some legal debate, but most traditional opinions would require the witnesses to be at least Sabbath observers. Be sure to consult with your rabbi regarding what kind of witnesses would be appropriate and to inform your rabbi prior to the ceremony who the witnesses will be.

FACT

During most of Jewish history, people did not have last names. They were called by their given name and their parent's name. In Orthodox synagogues, some rituals, such as calling to the Torah, utilize a person's father's name; other rituals, such as blessings for recovery, utilize their mother's name. In non-Orthodox circles, father's and mother's names are usually used together.

According to *halacha*, Jewish law, since the act of witnessing the *ketubah* is no different from being a witness in a court of law, the two witnesses must not be related to each other or to the bride or groom, neither directly nor by marriage. The requirement of not utilizing fewer than two witnesses comes from the verse in Deuteronomy, "By the mouth of two or three witnesses is a thing established." According to Jewish law, the rabbi or wedding officiate, if he is not related to the bride or groom, may also be counted as one of the witnesses.

Divar Torah: Words of Holiness and Reflection

The Talmud teaches that no meal or celebration is complete without words of Torah spoken to focus and sanctify the proceedings. Thus there is a longstanding custom for the groom to offer words of Torah at the *tish*. Some commentaries, notably the Shulchan HaEzer, note that on the day of their wedding bride and groom are like royalty and so it is fitting for them to hold forth with their own declarations and teachings. Certainly if the bride is a woman of Torah learning and she wishes to share a *divar torah*, a word of Torah, she may. If the groom does not wish to speak words of Torah or insight, that is fine since his comfort level and the bride's comfort is certainly more important.

In most circles today, if the groom or bride are going to share words of Torah they are interrupted after a few sentences with shouts of mazel tov and a round of wedding song. The purpose of this custom is twofold. First, even if the groom is learned he may not be in any state to concentrate on the lecture he is about to give, and so by beginning a speech it is assumed he is wise but he does not need to be well prepared. Second, he is interrupted so as not to embarrass grooms who are not learned and would not be able to share words of Torah. Thus all grooms or brides are interrupted and all are viewed on their wedding day as men and women of wisdom.

Bedekin: Veiling of the Bride

The *bedekin* is a very joyous moment and a wonderful way to prepare for the more solemn ceremony that is about to come. When the *tish* is finished, the band is notified and they strike up a lively wedding tune. If there is no band in the room, people can sing a Jewish wedding tune. If the bride and groom are in separate rooms, the groom—with his father, the bride's father, and the rabbi at his side—walks into the bride's room in the center of a very lively parade of guests. Some dance in front of the groom, leading the way, and some follow. The groom walks with full retinue like the king he is on this day.

When the groom reaches the bride, especially if they have not seen each other for a period of time, it is a very auspicious moment. The groom approaches the bride who is seated upon her "throne," lifts her veil, exchanges words with her, and places her veil back down.

The idea of the *bedekin* is rooted in several ancient biblical episodes. In the book of *Birashit*, Genesis, when Eliezer brought Rebecca to meet Isaac they came across Isaac in a field mediating and praying. As Rebecca approached on her camel she saw Isaac from afar, was so moved that she fell off her camel, and then covered her face with a veil. The rabbis explain that Rebecca wanted to be loved not for her outside appearance, which was very beautiful, but for her inner depth. Perhaps seeing Isaac in the midst of his meditations prompted Rebecca to focus on the deeper side of marriage at that moment.

FACT

Some traditional brides, wanting their *bedekin* to be more than checking to see if it is the right bride, choose to present the *chatan* with a gift after he lifts her veil. This gift is often his *kittel* or *talit* that he will wear under the chuppah at the approaching ceremony.

The other biblical episode from which the *bedekin* ceremony is derived is the story of Jacob and Rachel. Jacob went to the house of his uncle Laban and fell in love with Rachel, Laban's youngest daughter. Laban agreed to let Jacob and Rachel marry, but only on the condition that Jacob work for Laban for seven years. Jacob does this easily out if his love for Rachel, but on their wedding night Jacob realized he had not been given Rachel in marriage but Leah, her older sister.

Indignant, Jacob approached Laban and asked why he fooled him. Laban replied that their custom is for the oldest daughter to be given in marriage first and if Jacob would like to marry his true love, Rachel, he would have to work an additional seven years for her. Jacob accepted out of his deep love for Rachel, despite having been fooled. In remembrance of this, the groom lifts up the veil and checks to make sure he is about to marry the right woman.

Blessings from Parents

As the *bedekin* comes to a close, just after the groom sees the bride and puts down her veil, there is a beautiful custom for the parents of bride and groom to bless the couple. Some use the traditional Jewish blessing that many parents give to their children each Friday night after the *kiddush*. It consists of the biblical priestly blessing that the *kohanim*, the priestly tribe, bestows upon the Jewish people, as recorded in the Book of Numbers: "May the Lord bless you and keep you. May the Lord let His face shine upon you and be gracious to you. May the Lord look kindly upon you and give you peace." Or in Hebrew, "*Yivarechicha Adonay V'yishmarecha, Yaer Adonay Panav Aylecha V'iyichuneka, Yisa Adonay Panav Aylechcha V'yasem Licha Shalom.*"

FACT

Some have the custom of the groom also blessing his bride using the words that Rebecca's brother and mother blessed her with just before she left to be married to Isaac: "Our sister, may you become the mother of tens of thousands."

Some parents put their hands on the head of the bride and groom at the *bedekin* when they give them this blessing, just as many parents do on Friday night at the Shabbat table. The custom of putting one's hands on another as they are blessed is an old practice, perhaps going back as far as Moses and Joshua. When it was time for Moses to transfer the leadership of the Jewish people to Joshua, who would guide the Jewish people into the Land of Israel, Moses puts his hands on Joshua's head, symbolically transferring the mantle of leadership to him.

This sense of transference and blessing through the placing of hands on someone's head is reflected also in the blessing Jacob gives to his grandchildren before he dies, in the book of Genesis. Jacob blesses Ephraim and Manasseh, the two sons of Joseph, and transfers the mantle of being a tribe of the Jewish people onto them through the resting of his hands on their heads.

The Torah writes that in the future the Jewish people should bless their children in the same way that Jacob blessed his children and grandchildren, so we not only place hands on their heads as we give them a blessing, but before reciting the priestly blessing parents often recite the following phrase when blessing a son: "God make you as Ephraim and Minashe." This is a reference to Jacob's blessings to his children as recorded in the Torah, "In you shall Israel bless, saying, God make you as Ephraim and as Manasseh." For the bride, as for any daughter on Friday night, the blessing preceding the priestly blessing is, "God make you like Sara, Rebecca, Rachel, and Leah," followed by the priestly blessing.

Of course, the blessing that parents give to their children at the *bedekin* by no means must be the priestly blessing. It can be fully their own personal words of blessing to their child, or a combination of the two. The blessing that a parent gives a child at the *bedekin* can be silent, just between them and their child, or between them and the couple, or it can be said out loud for friends and relatives to hear, or a combination of the two. This moment of blessing just before one's child marries is a powerful moment that should be taken advantage of, sharing words of blessing, love, and encouragement for the future.

Weddings are a particularly appropriate time to give blessings. In Genesis, after Adam and Eve are created, the biblical verse states: "And God blessed them and said to them be fruitful and multiply." According to the Midrash Rabbah on Genesis 8:15, God, as it were, acted as the *misader kiddushin*, the wedding officiate, for Eve and Adam and also was their "parent," and so it was as part of this original "wedding" that God blessed them.

CHAPTER 17

The Ceremony

The wedding ceremony is called *kiddushin*, which is the Hebrew word for holiness. Holy in Judaism also has the connotation of separateness, and indeed the wedding ceremony serves to separate the husband and wife as a couple from the rest of the world. They will now only have each other as full life partners. The *kidusha*, or holiness, of the ceremony also reminds us of the Sabbath *kiddush* ceremony, which separates the Sabbath from the weekday, and also of the *kidusha*, the sanctity of the ancient temple that separated it from all other space.

The Processional

Though the actual wedding ceremony will take place under the chuppah, as in most weddings the bride, groom, and any members of the wedding party usually walk down an aisle from the back of the room. If the chuppah is to take place outside, the wedding party walks out from behind the audience. There are no requirements for the order in which the wedding party walks down the aisle except that the bride should walk to the chuppah last.

Walking Down the Aisle as a Queen and King

When the groom, and especially the bride, walk down the aisle, the custom is for everyone to stand. This is because on their wedding day we consider the bride and groom to be as honored as a queen and king. Further reflecting this formality, there is a Jewish custom among some people that those who accompany the bride and groom down the aisle carry candles or torches. Candles and fire evoke the moments at Mount Sinai during which, amid lightning and thunder, the Jewish people accepted the Torah and thereby became "married" to the Torah and to God.

FACT

In past centuries some communities had a custom to wave or toss lit lamps as the bride and groom walked to their chuppah as a kind of primitive fireworks display. Given this range of customs, if you do not plan to have candles but want fireworks or sparklers at your wedding, this would be highly appropriate.

An additional reason for candles at a wedding is that the bride and groom themselves are compared to fire. The Hebrew word for husband is composed of three Hebrew letters—*alef*, *yod*, and *shin*—and the Hebrew word for wife is also composed of three letters—*alef*, *shin*, and *heh*. The two letters both words have in common are *alef* and *shin*, spelling the word *aish*, which means fire in Hebrew. The two letters each word brings to the mix are *yod* and *heh*, which spells one of the Hebrew names of God. The Talmud teaches that if the divine name is not present in a relationship it will be as disharmonious as an unbridled fire, which consumes. But if God is present in a relationship, it will embody a fire that can facilitate warmth, closeness, and love. Of course, according to many customs no candles are carried down the aisle at all. If your family has a particular custom you may want to keep with that; if they do not, feel free to discuss, imagine, and experiment.

Approaching the Chuppah

As the groom approaches the chuppah, the cantor, rabbi, or another appointed individual with a good voice declares, "*Baruch habah*." ("Blessed is he that approaches.") Following these opening words is an additional sentence known as *mi adir*, which asks that God bless the *chatan* and *kalah*, the groom and bride.

The custom of the groom entering the chuppah first and the bride being brought to him is reminiscent of the second chapter of the book of Genesis in which God made Adam and then created Eve from his rib and "brought her to Adam."

When the bride approaches the chuppah the groom walks out in front of the chuppah to meet her and together they enter their house, which the chuppah represents. The cantor then declares, "*Birucha haba'ah*." ("Blessed is she that approaches.") This is followed often by a traditional chant in Hebrew declaring the beauty of the bride and the relationship of bride and groom to each other, and asks God to bless them.

Circles of Wholeness and Protection

When the bride and groom enter under their chuppah canopy, there is a custom among Ashkenazi Jews that the bride circles the groom three times. In some customs, the bride circles her groom seven times. The bride's mother and/or her mother-in-law will often walk behind her, accompanying her and helping to be sure she is steady on her feet, especially if she has a long train. Jewish thought gives many reasons for these circles. Some see them as the "walls" of the chuppah, which are formed by the couple themselves, or by the wife, who in Jewish tradition is considered the foundation of the family and the home.

As with much of the wedding ceremony, a distinction should be made between custom and law. While the giving of a ring, witnesses, and a *ketubah* are part of Jewish law, customs such as whether to have the bride circle the groom or not, and if so how many times, are much more flexible. Most Sephardic Jews do not have any circles and customs differ among Ashkenazi Jews.

Becoming familiar with the procedures of a Jewish wedding and getting to know the areas of flexibility within Jewish law and tradition can be helpful in making the ceremony meaningful and in personalizing it. You might choose not to circle at all or you might choose to circle each other (though not at the same time!) three or seven times. If you lean more toward the traditional, you may want to have the bride circle the groom seven times and the groom not circle the bride at all. On the other hand, if you wish to express a commitment to tradition but also want the groom to "revolve" around the bride, perhaps he could perform three or seven of his own circles around his bride after she circles him.

Additional Traditions and Customs

In addition to the circles with which many Jewish wedding ceremonies open, there are many optional traditions that can be incorporated into your wedding ceremony to make it fit you, your fiancé, and the style with which you plan to forge your Jewish life together.

Fragrant Spices

Sephardic Jews generally do not perform any circles or utilize a *yichud* room, but they have several other traditions that are unique to their communities that you might draw upon. For instance, many Sephardic weddings include a blessing on sweet smelling spices such as myrtle leaves, or an *etrog*, a citron, the fragrant fruit which is used on the holiday of Sukkot and shaken together with the *lulov*, the palm branch. After the blessing thanking God for the fragrant sweet spices, they are passed around for others to smell and enjoy.

The blessing that is made before smelling the sweet spices is the same blessing made on spices at the *havdalah* ceremony that closes the Shabbat, or anytime one smells fragrant spices: "*Baruch atah adownay elohaynu melech haolam borey miney bisamim.*" ("Blessed are you God Sovereign of the universe, who creates different kinds of fragrant smells.") Even if you are not Sephardic, there is no reason you could not include this tradition in personalizing your wedding ceremony if it is meaningful to you.

Blessings in Judaism are ubiquitous. Before deriving any pleasure from the universe, permission is asked of God through a blessing. A blessing recited before all foods and good smells serves to focus our awareness on the amazing and miraculous nature of the universe we live in.

Using your Prayerful Moment for Others

There is a temptation for the bride and groom to focus completely on the auspicious wedding moment and the relevance it has to them. After all, it is a moment of utter transformation in their lives. Jewish traditions teach that these moments under the chuppah are a time when one is particularly close to the divine presence. This being so, it has become popular for many brides and grooms to take a few moments under the chuppah to nudge their inner focus away from themselves and toward others who are in need. Under the chuppah, the gates of heaven are open, so it is a time when one's prayers can easily be accepted. Brides and grooms often opt to close their eyes and pray for friends and relatives who are in need of healing, or are in the process of trying to find their own *bashert* but have not had success.

One groom was standing under the chuppah in a state of great nervousness. He was focused on his bride and himself and the hundreds of people watching him make the biggest commitment of his life when his rabbi leaned over and whispered in his ear, "Pray now for the welfare of the Jewish people." At first he was taken aback, but then he realized how shifting the focus from himself to the bigger picture of his brethren and their needs was a meaningful and liberating experience.

Joining Bride and Groom in a Talit

The spreading of a *talit* over the bride and groom—or even wrapping them in one—was a custom that until recently was only prevalent in Sephardic communities. In recent years, some Ashkenazi Jews of Eastern European ancestry have begun to embrace the tradition as well. At the beginning of the *sheva berachot*, close relatives or the parents of the bride and groom spread a *talit* over them, covering them both. For some Sephardic Jews this joining together under a *talit* takes the place of the *yichud*, and for some it is used in addition to the *yichud*. Sometimes additional blessings are offered to them or appropriate biblical verses or poetry are recited. The *talit* is then removed prior to the breaking of the glass.

QUESTION?

Does prayer really work?
In Judaism it is taught that God hears the prayers of everyone, no matter how educated. As long as one is sincere, prayer is significant.

What to Have Under the Chuppah

Be sure to consult with your rabbi regarding which religious objects will be required under the chuppah, and appoint someone you trust to take them there before the ceremony. The *ketubah* must find its way from the *tish* to the chuppah, and you will also require wine and cups, a glass to break, printed versions of the blessings and any other prayers, and any poetry or vows that you will use at the ceremony. Making a list far in advance and appointing a friend to be sure it is all there at your chuppah will save you much stress at the time of the wedding itself.

How many of these traditional wedding ceremony items you require will depend on the type of ceremony you are having. If it is an Orthodox or Conservative ceremony, your rabbi will probably require most of them. If it is a Reform, Reconstructionist, or Humanist service, there may be more flexibility in the structure of the wedding service, and the ritual objects required will depend on how your ceremony is constructed and what you and your rabbi are comfortable with.

If you are having a liberal wedding ceremony, it may be up to you to decide on many things, including which ritual sections of the ceremony to have and how to contextualize them, since not everything required at a *halachic* ceremony would be necessarily utilized at a more liberal ceremony. Among the questions to think about will be whether you want to break a glass at the close of your ceremony. If so, how do you wish to contextualize it? Will it be preceded by words of the psalmist about the destruction of Jerusalem? Will it touch on other destructions that might be better known from current events? Will it be connected to personal sadness and mourning? Will you relate it to all of these? In addition, if your wedding is not fully traditional you will need to think about whether to have a *ketubah* and what it will say if you do have one.

Blessings and Drinking the Wine

In Judaism, Jewish law and tradition requires the recitation of a blessing before a mitzvah is performed. The blessing on a mitzvah usually mentions the specific commandment and blesses God, "who sanctifies us with commandments."

The wedding ceremony commences with a few words of introduction from the wedding officiate and then a blessing on a glass of wine or grape juice. The Talmud writes, based on a verse in Psalms, that when we bless God it should bring joy to us and, as it were, to God also. But how, the Talmud asks, could the act of blessing God give both joy to God and physical joy to us? The Talmud answers that we must bless God over wine so that the blessing "gives joy" to God, and the wine will give joy to us. In light of this, many blessings in Judaism are made over a cup of wine.

If it is a traditional ceremony, a second blessing will be recited after the rabbi blesses the wine. This blessing is a blessing on the actual commandment of marrying. It is a paragraph long and closes with the words, "Blessed are you God who sanctifies Israel through the chuppah and *kiddushin*, (the wedding canopy and the wedding ceremony)."

Following the blessings, the cup of wine is given to the bride and groom to drink. Some couples like to involve parents or close relatives, having them bring the wine cup to the lips of the bride and groom. This is especially convenient for the bride if she is wearing a veil because it can take more than two hands to lift a bridal veil and a cup of wine, especially if the bride is also holding flowers.

Ayrusin: The Ring Ceremony

In the Talmud and in Jewish law, the act that is considered the actual wedding is the giving of a ring or other thing of value to the bride from the groom in the presence of two witnesses. The rabbi will usually call up the witnesses for this procedure if they are not already under the chuppah. Since Jewish law requires that the ring be something of value, the rabbi may ask the witnesses to verify its value by looking at the ring to see that it is a real ring and of at least a minimal value. Different rabbis have varied methods of conducting the ring ceremony, some with more words and explanations and others with less.

The Meaning of the Ring

In the times of the Talmud, anything of value—even services rendered—could be used to create the marriage covenant. Today, almost all weddings are performed with a ring, and this has been so for longer than a millennium.

There are many reasons for the use of a ring. A circle is quite appropriate for a wedding since it has no end, just as we hope the couple's marriage will have no end. According to many traditions, the circle is the most perfect of shapes since it has no edges or corners. A circle reminds us of the ancient Jewish communal dances, which were performed in a circle. According to the Midrash, in the world to come it will be God who occupies the center of the proverbial dance circle. A circle is something that joins other things together and that envelops them, as we hope the couple's love will envelop their family and as God envelops and protects the universe.

The rabbi may then ask if the ring does indeed belong to the groom, since the Talmud writes that the groom must give the bride a ring that belongs to him. The rabbi may then ask the groom and bride if they are ready to be married in order to ascertain that she is entering into the marriage with sound mind and free will. Then the rabbi will ask the bride to put out her right index finger. Before the groom places the ring on the bride's finger he will be asked to repeat after the officiate the following words: "*Harey at mikudeshet li b'tabaat zoo kida'at Moshe v'Yisrael.*" ("Behold you are sanctified unto me with this ring according to the law of Moses and the people of Israel.")

There is a strong custom that brides not wear any jewelry under the chuppah except the wedding ring they receive from the groom. Another tradition stipulates that the groom is not to have anything in his pockets and no knots in his clothing. Even his shoelaces are untied; thus, the only "knot" is that which binds him to his bride.

How the Ring Is Given

Despite the fact that rings today are typically worn on the finger next to the pinky, the bride receives the ring from the groom on her right index finger. Many reasons are given for this long-standing tradition. The most straightforward reason is given by Rabbi Samuel Segal of Mezeritch, Poland, in the seventeenth century in his book *Nachalat Shivah.* He writes that since the index finger is the finger most commonly used to point to things, and therefore the finger most in the forefront and visible, this is the one we use for the giving of the ring before witnesses.

Why is the wedding ring placed on the right index finger?
The right index finger is the one that we point with, and the right side is considered one of love in Jewish mysticism.

The index finger of the right hand is utilized because the right hand is seen as having precedence in Judaism since a majority of people use their right hand dominantly. The right is also appropriate because in the Kabbalah, the right "side" of the divine is a reference to the characteristic of love. Additionally, many people suggest that in ancient times, rings, as is still the case in some eastern cultures, were worn on the index finger, and that this tradition may have just remained with us since that time.

Though at many Orthodox weddings the bride does not usually respond with any words, and there is technically no need for her to recite any words after receiving the ring, she may do so if she wishes, according to Jewish law. Though "thank you" might be a bit prosaic, if she wishes to respond with her own poetic words or those of the ancient Jewish writers, such as from the Song of Songs, that is perfectly appropriate.

According to Jewish law, weddings must not utilize a double ring ceremony in which rings are exchanged. The *kiddushin* is indeed a business deal, but it is not a purchase or exchange of one ring for another ring. The ring is a symbolic gift the groom gives the bride for her hand in marriage.

In addition, at traditional weddings in keeping with Jewish law and the Talmud's instruction, it is the groom who always gives the ring to the bride. The bride may give the groom a ring, but it should not be given to the groom in exchange for the ring he has given to her. Among liberal Jewish denominations it is quite common for the bride and groom to exchange rings, each reciting their own words or words from Jewish tradition.

Some groups of Orthodox men do not wear wedding rings for fear that this might violate the Bible's commandment that men not wear the clothing of woman. Others do wear wedding rings since in Western countries most married men wear a ring and it is therefore considered a unisex accoutrement.

If you would like the bride to give the groom a ring under the chuppah, be sure to discuss this with your rabbi. Your rabbi may have some rules as to exactly when during the ceremony it should be given. Though many Reform, Conservative, and Reconstructionist rabbis will allow an exchange of rings, no Orthodox or traditional rabbis will allow such a direct exchange of rings. Some will allow the bride to give the groom a ring under the chuppah at another point in the ceremony.

Depending on your rabbi, he may allow the bride to give the groom a ring under the chuppah after the *sheva berachot* or following the reading of the *ketubah*. This ensures that it is an act separate from the ring the groom gives the bride, thereby avoiding the *halachic* problem of an exchange of rings. Other Orthodox rabbis will ask that the bride wait to give her ring to the groom after the ceremony in the *yichud* room.

Reading the Ketubah

After the ring is given, the *ketubah* is usually read aloud. If your *ketubah* is in Aramaic or Hebrew, you will want to be sure to ask someone in advance to be prepared to read it. Though Aramaic utilizes Hebrew letters, even those who are fluent in Hebrew often have difficulty reading the Aramaic *ketubah*, since the Aramaic words are quite different from Hebrew. You may have the rabbi read the *ketubah* if you have no other person you wish to honor who is capable of doing so.

Anyone you wish may read the *ketubah* at a wedding if she is able. According to many Orthodox rabbis, a Jewish woman may be asked to read the *ketubah*. This is something that will differ depending on the individual Orthodox rabbi, and indeed some will probably require that a man read it. If your *ketubah* contains an English section, you may have the same person read both the Hebrew and the English, or you can honor two people by having one read the Hebrew or Aramaic and another read the English section.

After the *ketubah* is read, it should be given to the groom, who then gives it to the bride to cherish and keep. Since it is not convenient for the bride to be left holding the *ketubah* during the rest of the ceremony, especially if it is large and framed, she usually hands it to her maid of honor or another friend or relative under the chuppah to hold for her.

Chuppah Honors and Speeches

There are many opportunities to honor friends and relatives under the chuppah. You can offer to have friends or relatives recite the seven blessings, and if you will have these read in Hebrew and in English you may be able to honor up to fourteen people. Guests can also be asked to hold up the chuppah if it is on poles, and Jewish weddings require many witnesses—for the signing of the *ketubah*, the giving of the ring, the signing of the *tanaim*, and to stand guard outside the *yichud* room. All of these are good ways to honor people.

Different rabbis and different denominations will have varied requirements for who can be a witness. Orthodox rabbis will require observant Jewish males, Conservative rabbis will require Jewish men or women, and Reform and Reconstructionist rabbis may allow non-Jewish people to serve as witnesses or they may require no witnesses at all.

Following the reading of the *ketubah*, it is customary for the rabbi or wedding officiant to speak. It is advisable not to allow others to speak under the chuppah since it is a solemn moment and speeches of a less formal nature given by friends or relatives are more appropriate at the reception.

Rabbis should take care not to give long-winded sermons but to get to know the couple well prior to their wedding ceremony and use this speech to praise them and offer them words of encouragement and advice. If the rabbi has had conversations with the couple before their wedding about their relationship and what they love about each other, this may be a good time to relate some of those sentiments and to outline the bride and groom's commitments to each other and the uniqueness of their relationship. If the bride and groom both have a rabbi they are close to, they may ask both rabbis to speak under the chuppah. Alternately, one rabbi could conduct the ceremony and the other could deliver some words. In any case, the speeches given under the chuppah will be long remembered by the couple and should contain inspiring words for them to live by.

CHAPTER 18

Sheva Berachot: The Seven Blessings

18

The second half of the wedding ceremony that is performed under the chuppah is called *nisuin* in Hebrew and Aramaic. The *nisuin* happens automatically after the giving of the ring. While long ago this part of the ceremony was accomplished by building a house and living in it together, today we do the entire wedding ceremony under the chuppah, which stands in for the couple's home. The *shevah berachot* are a celebration of the *nisuin* and a completion of the marriage bond.

Spiritual Significance of the Seven Blessings

Seven is a very significant number in Judaism. The number seven hearkens back to the very creation of the universe, which God accomplished in seven days, culminating in the holy Sabbath on the seventh day. There were seven days in the first complete cycle, the week, in the history of the world, as recorded in the Torah. Following a Jewish wedding are seven days of feasting, during which these seven blessings are again recited. This double cycle of seven also reminds us of the seven-year agricultural cycle that the Jewish people were commanded to observe after they entered the land of Israel. The seventh year of each cycle was the sabbatical year during which no land could be cultivated.

This seven-year agricultural cycle was also part of a double seven-year cycle of forty-nine years. After the seventh seven-year cycle, the forty-ninth year, the Jewish people would celebrate a fiftieth year, a jubilee year, during which all land in Israel would return to its original owners. In each Jewish calendar year, we also experience a double cycle of seven days. From the holiday of Passover until the holiday of Shavuot fifty days later, we formally count seven weeks—seven cycles of seven.

FACT

Many reasons are given for the number seven and its connection to marriage. In his book *Made in Heaven*, Rabbi Aryeh Kaplan suggests a most unique idea: that the number seven alludes to the numerical value of the Hebrew word *echad*, which means "one." This, of course, is the moment at which the bride and groom become one entity, a reflection also, perhaps, of the great and ultimate unity of the divine.

The Sabbath, which is the seventh day of each week, is the moment of ultimate unity between God and the world. On the Sabbath a song called "*Licha Dodi*" ("Come My Beloved"), is sung. This song describes the Sabbath as a marriage between the part of the divine that resides within the physical universe, the *shechinah*, and the more infinite divine. These aspects of God seem separate, but ultimately God is pure unity. Thus, seven is also the number representing the ultimate spiritual unity of the universe.

The number seven may also refer to the seven lower *sefirot*, the seven mystical realms through which the infinite divine flows to the finite world. Though there are ten *sefirot* all together, these "lower" seven *sefirot* are much closer to merging with the universe than the three *sefirot* above them, which are more removed. Thus, the number seven in reference to the *sefirot* represents bonding and unification between the divine and the world. Perhaps it is this ultimate unity of the divine, this merging, that is reflected in the unification of two people under their chuppah.

The Meaning of the Seven Blessings

The *sheva berachot* contain several themes, ranging from the creation of the world to Adam and Eve in the Garden of Eden to the bride and groom. They end with a description of the joy of bride and groom that will be heard in the streets of Jerusalem at the time of messianic redemption. This links the couple under the chuppah to all of history—to the past and to the ultimate future.

The *hagafen* blessing is the first of the seven blessings recited under the chuppah, but it is the last blessing recited during the seven blessings that are part of the grace after meals following the reception. Take care to assign the *hagafen* to the first person reciting a blessing under the chuppah and not the last.

The first of the seven blessings blesses God, "who creates the fruit of the vine." This blessing, the *hagafen*, is the same blessing that is recited anytime wine is drunk. Since it is a well-known blessing, you may want to give the honor of reading it to someone who is less familiar with the Hebrew language but may know this blessing from hearing it recited each Sabbath.

The second of the seven blessings is, "Blessed are you God, Sovereign of the universe, Who created everything for your glory." This second blessing tells of God's creation of the universe and focuses us on its purpose. By extension, it focuses our attention on what our own intentions should be in everything we do, including marriage.

We begin the seven blessings by stating that God created everything for the divine glory because this moment of marriage is not just a spiritual or legal process by which to link two people forever, but also is a part of the bigger Godly purpose of the universe. Everything was created to reveal and bring glory to God, and this wedding, too, must serve that purpose by invoking God's name and the Jewish spiritual rituals we perform within the wedding. Indeed, a Jewish wedding, which enables the building of a Jewish family, is considered one of the highest ways of bringing glory to God.

The third of the *sheva berachot* is "Blessed are You God, Sovereign of the universe, Who formed the human being." Here we move from God creating the world to the creation of humans, since humans are the purpose of the creation, the bridge between the physical created world and the infinite divine.

QUESTION?

Why are the first and second blessings often recited by the same person?

The blessing of the wine is said every time wine is consumed. It is not part of the seven blessings in the way that the next six are, so the second blessing is often combined with it.

The fourth blessing is related to the third but takes it one step further; it states that we are created in God's image. "Blessed are You God Who created the human being in your image, and in your likeness, and prepared for him, from himself, a structure for eternity. Blessed are You God who forms the human being."

This blessing declares that we are made in the image of God and are also God's partners in the creation. Humans are most Godlike, according to this, in marrying and creating a family, thus bringing new people into the world as God did. The gift of having such deep, unifying relationships that can result in the creation of new people makes us not only higher than animals but higher than angels also. The gift of marriage is part of the eternal purpose of the creation.

The fifth blessing introduces a new theme, that of Zion, the Land of Israel. "May the barren one rejoice when her children are gathered to her in joy. Blessed are You God, Who makes Zion rejoice with her children." The Land of Israel is barren since the people have been exiled, but we hope, just as marriage unites two disparate individuals in a lasting bond, so too the people of Israel will be united with the land once again.

The sixth blessing refocuses on the couple under the chuppah and relates them to Adam and Eve at their wedding in the Garden of Eden: "Bring abundant joy to these friends who are lovers, as You brought joy to the ones you created in ancient Eden. Blessed are You God Who brings joy to the groom and bride." We have gone from the creation of the world to the creation of humans to the people of Israel, and now we have refocused on the couple themselves, to see them as the culmination of it all. Just as Adam and Eve were the only people in the universe, the true purpose and focus on the universe, so, too, the couple that stands under the chuppah together today is the purpose of it all. They should feel that great honor and responsibility.

Each entire blessing should be heard by the audience as said by the honoree who is holding the wine cup. If many people join in to sing parts of the seventh blessing, the one reciting the blessing should repeat those words so that everyone hears the whole blessing as recited.

The seventh blessing is the longest and usually has sections that are sung. You may want to have this blessing recited by whomever you wish to honor that is most familiar with the Hebrew language and the tunes of wedding blessings. There are recordings and websites that are easily accessed to help with learning the words and tune. You could also ask your wedding officiant to make a recording of the blessing to give to whomever you wish to read it.

This seventh blessing links the bride and groom not only to the past but also to the future: "Blessed are You God, Sovereign of the universe, Who created gladness and joy, groom and bride, rejoicing and song, delight and cheer, love and harmony, peace and friendship. Quickly, God, may there be heard in the cities of Judah and in the streets of Jerusalem, the voice of gladness and the voice of joy, the voice of the groom and the voice of the bride, the voice of bridegrooms rejoicing at their weddings, and young people from their feasts of song. Blessed are You God Who gives joy to the groom with the bride."

Since their exile from the land of Israel in the year 70 C.E., the Jewish people have looked forward to retuning and prayed about the return to Zion three times a day. It is the greatest, most central hope of our people. Here we imagine the joy of this bride and groom spreading and becoming part of the messianic joy, love, and peace that will ultimately be heard in the streets of Jerusalem.

Who Should Chant Them and How?

A second glass of wine is poured and the *sheva berachot* are recited in Hebrew and optionally translated into English. One person may recite all of the blessings or you may choose to ask up to seven different people to recite one blessing each. Each person who recites a blessing should hold the cup of wine during their blessing.

According to Jewish law, the *sheva berachot*, except for the *hagafen* blessing on the wine and the longer seventh blessing, are only recited in the presence of a *minyan*, a quorum of ten that are considered a public gathering.

Traditionally, this meant ten Jewish males who are over the age of thirteen. Since the 1970s, many Conservative congregations have begun to count women in the *minyan* as well, although the determination of whether to do so is left to the individual congregation and rabbi. Reform and Reconstructionist congregations that consider a *minyan* mandatory for communal prayer count both men and women. Among Orthodox communities, according to some authorities, women can count in a *minyan* for certain prayers and events, but not usually for the *sheva berachot*. If your wedding will be a small one, speak to your rabbi to ascertain who may be included.

The *sheva berachot*, when recited in Hebrew, are usually chanted with a tune. Any tune may be used, but there are one or two traditional tunes that are most common. If the people you wish to honor with reciting the seven blessings are unfamiliar with the seven blessings, give them a copy of the blessings in Hebrew and transliteration and also in translation so they know what they are reciting. This can be found in Appendix B. Inform them that there are traditional tunes to which the blessings are usually chanted and help them locate a recording of the tune so no one feels embarrassed when it is his turn.

If you are asking various people to say one of the seven blessings under the chuppah, be sure to supply them with a copy of the blessing to review beforehand, and have a copy of the blessings under the chuppah as well. Be careful because the order of *sheva berachot* after the wedding meal is slightly different from those under the chuppah.

In Jewish law, anyone who is Jewish may recite the seven blessings, whether they are related to the bride and groom or not. Most liberal Jewish denominations will allow an adult woman to recite the *sheva berachot* under the chuppah and after the meal, and some may permit a non-Jewish individual also. Among Orthodox Jews, while many Orthodox rabbis will only allow men to recite the *sheva berachot*, some may allow women to do so. Additionally, some Orthodox rabbis will allow women to recite the *sheva berachot* after the meal but not under the chuppah.

The Groom's Ring: What the Bride Should Say

Traditionally, the bride did not give the groom a ring under the chuppah, and according to the Talmud and Jewish law an exchange of rings was never considered effective in generating a Jewish legal marriage bond. Non-Orthodox rabbis, depending on their denomination, will often permit an exchange of rings. If they do, most will allow the bride to recite the same words that the groom has recited when he gave her a ring, or she may utilize other words from traditional sources or of her own composition.

Some Orthodox rabbis do permit the bride to give the groom a ring under the chuppah, though not in exchange for the ring he gives to her. Orthodox rabbis who permit the bride to give the groom a ring under the chuppah will usually only permit it at the end of the ceremony just before or just after the seven blessings. This way, it is clear that this is not a trade of one ring for another. Instead, it is a ring given from the groom to the bride to effect the *kiddushin* and a ring given from the bride to the groom as a symbol of her love and his commitment. When the bride does give a ring to the groom at an Orthodox or traditional wedding, she may recite words she has authored or she may use words of love and commitment from traditional Jewish sources such as King Solomon's love poem, *Shir Hashirim*, the Song of Songs.

In Jewish tradition, the Song of Songs, which is part of the Jewish Bible, is viewed not just as a love poem between two lovers, describing their feelings of intimacy and distance, their love, their fears, and their praise for each other, but as a metaphorical depiction of the relationship and love between God and the Jewish people. *Shir Hashirim*, the Song of Songs, is one of the most popular sources for phrases expressing the love of bride and groom.

Some phrases in the Song of Songs with which the lovers describe each other, though resonant for the day in which it was written, may be culturally strange today. For instance, Chapter 7, Verse 3: "Your belly is like a heap of wheat."

The Song of Songs is a vast and holy treasure trove of statements about love from which to draw many aspects of a wedding. As a couple you can read the book together, finding phrases for the header of your invitation, for the bride's words to the goom when she gives him a ring, and for the cover of your *bencher* or wedding booklet. Some of the most common phrases are listed in Chapter 9.

Breaking the Glass

The last part of a Jewish wedding ceremony is the tradition of breaking a glass in memory of the destruction of Jerusalem. Breaking something at the moment of our greatest joy is a profound statement that though for us personally we may feel all is whole and joyous, for the larger world in general and for our people in particular, all is not wholeness and peace.

The Jews are a people whose history has been one of myriad ups and downs, with moments of terrible persecution on the one hand and grand success on the other. The great Rabbi Abraham Magence once said that, due to this unique history and trust in God even in the dark times, for Jewish people no moment of joy is so overwhelming that it does not contain a tinge of sadness and no moment of sadness is so complete that there is not within it some joy and hope in the Almighty.

It is precisely at this moment of marraige, which can easily be one of abandon and one that is completely self-centered on our personal fortune that we remain cognizant of the fact that others may be in a place of suffering, and for us, too, we are not in our land dwelling in peace as we should be. In addition, the breaking of the glass can also be a way to remember those who are not with us. Relatives who have passed away and people who we would have liked to have included at our wedding but could not come may be remembered and honored.

When breaking the glass, use the heel of your shoe and be sure the glass is wrapped well in a napkin or towel. If this is an art glass and you are planning to keep the pieces, ask someone specifically to retrieve it for you or else it may be thrown away.

The breaking of the glass is often introduced with a song from psalm 137, "*im eshkachech yirushalayim, tishkach yimini*" ("If I forget thee o Jerusalem let my right hand wither"). Sometimes a moment of silence is taken to remember anyone whom the bride and groom would like to remember, or to focus on current destructions in the world that the bride and groom would like to call attention to.

Some couples are turned off by this focus on the imperfect in the midst of their ultimate joy, but it needs to be seen in the right light. It is a tribute to living a life and relationship that will be grounded in reality. Things will not always be joyous, and there will be difficult times as there are in every life and relationship. The trick, of course, is to weather those difficult times with trust in each other and in God, and to find some redemption and something deeper within oneself even in times of difficulty and pain. This can help a relationship to not only endure the rocky times but to become even more powerful from having gone through them.

The glass that is broken does not have any requirements in Jewish law and tradition. Some people even use a burned-out light bulb so as not to waste a good glass. You can use an ordinary glass or even one of the glasses you used for the seven blessings; or you can purchase fancy glasses that can be made into artistic mosaics after they are broken. Whatever you choose to break, be sure to wrap it well and use your heel to do the deed. The sound of the glass breaking is a classic one at Jewish weddings and usually results in shouts of mazel tov and sometimes spontaneous wedding songs for the recessional.

Yichud: Time with Each Other

Following the breaking of the glass, the bride and groom leave the chuppah first, followed by family, the wedding party, and the rabbi. The bride and groom go to the *yichud* room, the room where they will be alone with each other for about ten minutes.

The bride and groom should proceed directly to the *yichud* room since their time spent together there is, at least in most Ashkenazi traditions, actually part of the wedding ceremony itself. If the bride and groom wish to participate in a receiving line with their families before they go to the *yichud* room, this is acceptable, but the preferred path would be to go directly to the *yichud* room to spend their first few minutes of married life alone with each other.

The minutes in the *yichud* room are truly magical. While there is bustling outside, the bride and groom are safely locked away from the crowd. Spending quiet moments just with each other in the middle of your wedding is so meaningful, yet so rare. At most weddings, the bride and groom are constantly busy interacting with guests and accepting people's good wishes. While this is important, the main goal of a wedding is to join the bride and groom together in a life of intimacy with each other.

The time spent in the *yichud* room together truly begins this ideal sense of the marriage relationship for the couple. It is a moment when they can look into each others' eyes and realize that for the first time they are spiritually and legally bound to each other forever. It is at this time that the bride can give the groom a ring if she has not already, and the bride and groom, in addition to sharing a profound, intimate moment of time together, can also break their fast if they are fasting.

Be sure to have the caterer put food in the *yichud* room for you. The food will usually be hors d'oeuvres or whatever the guests will be eating while you are in *yichud* and they are mingling. Especially if you have fasted, you will be very grateful to have a quiet moment to eat together before everyone vies for your attention.

In Jewish law, the minimum time spent in *yichud* is based on the time it would minimally take for the couple to consummate their marriage. A Jewish wedding is a ceremony that brings two people together not just spiritually, but physically and sexually. Though most couples do not actually have sexual intercourse in the *yichud* room, the potential for intimacy, emerging from their new marriage, must exist. Indeed, Judaism sees a couple's sexual life as something holy and powerful as well as private and bounded by modesty.

CHAPTER 19

The Reception

The reception that follows a wedding ceremony is known in Hebrew as a *seudat mitzvah*, a meal that is a holy command. In Judaism, the wedding meal is not just a celebration to let go, but a religious ceremony of sorts. It has several blessings and customs unique to it that can help ensure the meal is a joyous and meaningful one.

Simcha: *Jewish Wedding Joy Through Dancing*

If you have never been to a traditional Jewish wedding, the concept of wedding *simcha*, the amazing all-out joy at such a wedding, is hard to describe. It can, in fact, be quite wild, with people juggling fire, dancing in big hora circles, the bride and groom up on chairs in the middle, and so much more. The entire atmosphere is one of extreme joy, all done in fulfillment of the mitzvah of giving joy to the bride and groom.

FACT

The Talmud describes some of the extreme *simcha* at Jewish weddings in its era. It relates that the rabbis used to dance before the bride, with some juggling fire, some juggling myrtle branches, and some with wine glasses.

If you want to capture some of this *simcha*, contagious Jewish wedding joy, at your wedding, it will require a bit of advance planning. You should start by hiring a band that knows something about Jewish wedding music and can play it well and with energy. If you are unsure of their capabilities in this area, ask to see a video of a wedding they have played or seek a recommendation from a couple whose wedding they played that had *simcha* dancing. In addition to the band, you will want to let friends and relatives know in advance that you wish to achieve this *simcha* atmosphere.

One way to set a tone of *simcha* is to begin the dancing immediately when you enter the reception hall for the meal. To achieve *simcha*, this first set of dancing should be in big traditional Jewish dancing circles to fast Jewish wedding music. Songs such as "*Od Yishamah*" and "*Siman Tov*" can work well. If your band is familiar with traditional Jewish wedding music, they can recommend some energetic and joyous tunes to start the dancing off with. If they are not, purchase a CD of Jewish wedding music from one of the many online Jewish bookstores for them.

You and your fiancé may want a variety of different kinds of music to be played at your wedding. Beginning with traditional Jewish wedding music will set the tone of your wedding as one that is all-out Jewish fun and joy.

Remember, there will be lots of time at your reception, during and between courses, for various types of other music.

Jewish wedding dancing has some variations. The Jewish dancing at a wedding can often look like one circle going around and around. In truth, though, there are usually many variations. Inside the center of the circle, people often take turns doing their own personalized dances to entertain the bride and groom. Some of the dances from the annals of Jewish history are quite elaborate and difficult.

The *kitzatzke*, for instance, is a Russian dance in which one or several people cross their hands, squat and kick out their heels from under them. The spinning helicopter dance requires four people, two of heavier weight and two of lighter weight, to huddle in a circle. They spin the circle, quickly levitating the two lighter members of the circle. Another common Jewish wedding dance is performed by two people who face each other, hold hands crossed at the wrists, lean back, and spin as fast as they can. Sometimes this dance can get a bit out of control. Often, if the bride and groom are sitting on chairs in the dancing circles, two people will crouch at the bride and groom's sides with their hands joined together in front of the couple, protecting them from any dancers who might lose control. Of course, the bride and groom also join the circles when they are not too tired.

Make sure the *yichud* room locks and that the guards who are the witnesses and traditionally stand outside know not to disturb you. Toward this end, take care in choosing the *yichud* witnesses. They should be people who will not be inclined toward loud or improper conduct that may disturb you.

Another popular two-person dance was made popular in the film *Fiddler on the Roof*. Two people interlock arms at the elbows and turn in a circle opposite each other, switching directions every few turns. The bullfight dance is a popular Jewish wedding dance; one partner holds a suit jacket or cloth and the other partner is the "bull," trying to gore him. The bull fighter waves the cloth and the bull charges the cloth, their feet moving in a dance step. With the right dancers, this dance can become dramatic and seem well choreographed.

In recent years, many line dances and circle dances that fit the classic Jewish wedding tunes have emerged and can be seen on video-sharing sites on the Internet. Most of these classic Jewish wedding dances are very simple and require almost no practice—just a desire to give joy to the bride and groom.

What to Serve: Meeting Kashrut Requirements

One of the things that makes Judaism spiritually fulfilling is that its laws and customs apply to our regular everyday lives, not only in religious ceremonies or in the synagogue. *Kashrut*, the dietary laws that regulate and guide Jewish eating are a very important part of Jewish life, religion, and peoplehood.

What Is Kosher

The laws of *kashrut*, or kosher, are found in the Torah, the Bible itself. For the most part, the only foods subject to kosher laws are animals that are eaten. Though all fruits, vegetables, and growing things are considered kosher, only certain kinds of animals are considered kosher. According to the Bible and Jewish law, animals that chew their cud, called ruminants, and have split hoofs are kosher. The kosher animals include cows, sheep, deer, lamb, buffalo, and others. The only kosher fish are those from species that have fins and scales. These include salmon, tilapia, mahi mahi, trout, and many others. A full list can be found on the kosher websites in Appendix D. Only certain birds are kosher. These are all birds that are not birds of prey and conform to the biblical list of kosher birds, such as chicken, turkey, and duck.

If you would like your wedding to be up to the highest standards of kosher, you will need to find a wedding hall and caterer that does kosher events. These caterers are supervised by rabbis and kosher organizations to be sure everything is done according to the Jewish laws of *kashrut*. Asking a caterer or wedding hall to cook kosher if they are not supervised by a kosher certification organization does not guarantee the kosher standards of the event. In fact, the caterer may have little idea of how to make your wedding food kosher if she has not been properly trained. Even if she does know how to prepare kosher food, she will not be considered strictly trustworthy unless there is sufficient outside supervision.

There are more than 500 kosher supervisory organizations. However, not all supervision agencies are acceptable to all kosher-keeping Jews. Check with a local rabbi or kosher organization to determine which are recommended.

The meat of a fully kosher animal, such as a cow, is not kosher at all if the animal is not slaughtered correctly according to the Jewish laws of *shechitah*. To be kosher, a *shochet* must slaughter the kosher animal according to the Jewish laws with a particular kind of knife and using a special kosher method of slaughter. The *shochet* must then check to be sure the animal is healthy, since even kosher animals are not considered kosher if they are not healthy enough to live a year on their own. The meat must subsequently be salted to remove any blood, since the blood of the animal and certain parts of its body are not considered kosher.

The term "kosher-style" has nothing to do with kosher. Kosher-style has come to mean different things in different instances—everything from serving unkosher pastrami and pickles to food that is not kosher but simply does not mix meat and dairy.

Meat and Dairy

The mixing of meat and dairy products is strictly forbidden in Jewish law even if both are kosher. Not only can one not make a food of meat and dairy cooked together, but according to Jewish tradition dairy cannot be eaten immediately after one has eaten meat. This means that a dairy dessert is not acceptable if you are serving meat as your entrée. Most kosher-keeping Jewish people wait several hours after eating meat until they eat dairy. It is permissible to eat meat after eating dairy, though not at the same meal.

Given all the complexities of kosher standards, if you wish your wedding to be kosher you will need to talk to a local rabbi about which caterers are kosher and what kosher facilities are available. Kosher food is sometimes a bit more expensive, but many couples find it is well worth the money to accommodate all their guests equally and start off their marriage on a kosher foundation.

If you have guests who only eat kosher meat that is designated *glatt*, you will need to inquire of the kosher caterer if he can fulfill this standard. Today much of the meat on the kosher market is *glatt*, so accommodating your guests, especially in a large city with kosher resources, should not be difficult.

Additional Kosher Standards

There are different customs, even within the strict guidelines of *kashrut*. There are those who will only eat meat that is known as *glatt* kosher. *Glatt* is not more kosher; indeed, if something is kosher, it's kosher. All kosher animals must be healthy. The words *glatt* kosher just indicate that there were no questions about the health of the animal at all. Regular kosher meat comes from healthy animals, but in some instances there are certain lesions on the lung of the animal that are quite common and often form in reaction to a hole in the animal's lung, which would render it unkosher.

The law is that if these lesions come off easily then they are assumed to be benign and are not hiding a more severe lung injury. Such meat is kosher. *Glatt* (which means "smooth" in Yiddish) is meat from an animal that had no lesions on its lung at all, and thus no questions about the health of the animal's lung at all. In addition, other organs are checked to be sure the animal is healthy all around.

If you or your family does not keep kosher and you are not planning to have the food at your wedding be certified as kosher, there are several ways in which you might still achieve a modicum of *kashrut* at your reception. For instance, you may still be able to ask your caterer to cook with kosher ingredients. Perhaps she would be willing to order the meat for your reception from one of the many kosher meat packers and suppliers, some of which are listed in Appendix D. You could also skip meat or fish altogether and opt for a vegetarian wedding in recognition of the environmental concerns of our age. You might also consider asking a non-kosher caterer to refrain from serving dairy and meat together. For observant Jews, these kosher options will not suffice, but they may be acceptable for some Jewish people who are less observant.

If you and your fiancé or your families have different religious standards, the question of kosher at your wedding can be a great source of tension. Though some religious Jews may be able to compromise on things such as having mixed dancing, they may not be able to compromise on kosher.

Kosher Wine

Some beverages are also subject to the rules of *kashrut* in Judaism. Though almost all beer is considered kosher if it is not flavored, and most liquor, excluding those that are wine-based, are kosher, it is important to check that the items you will serve to drink are indeed under kosher supervision if you will have a kosher wedding. A list of kosher liquors and beverages can be found online at the websites of several national kosher organizations. For some specific references, see Appendix D.

Wine or wine-based liquor has some *kashrut* concerns. Though grapes are a fruit and are not subject to *kashrut* laws per se, there is a specific *kashrut* concern associated with wine. The Bible, in its commands to stay far from the worship of idols, forbids the use of things that were used in any idolatrous practice.

In Jewish history, there were times when idolaters would use wine as a libation in pagan religious services. Since wine in ancient days was sold in large barrels, wine would sometimes be used for idolatrous worship and then poured back into the wine barrel and resold as new wine. Thus in the Talmudic period, the rabbis made a *halachic*, a Jewish legal decree that wine manufactured by or handled after opening by non-Jewish people had to be treated as if it were not kosher and could not be consumed.

Be sure the wine you order is *mivushal* and says so on the label. Sometimes the word is printed in English on the bottle, but sometimes it is only in Hebrew. If you cannot find it on the label, call a kosher supervision organization to check if the brand you plan to use is *mivushal*.

The one exception to this rule was wine that had been pasteurized, since it was considered lower in quality and was not, therefore, used in such idolatrous services. As a result of this law pertaining to kosher wine, many kosher wines are pasteurized. This means that it is still considered kosher even if they are opened by non-Jewish waiters. Such wines are known by the term *mivushal*, "boiled." If your wedding will be kosher, it is advisable to buy not only kosher wine but kosher wine that says *mivushal* on the label, to be sure that it retains its kosher status even after it has been opened.

Nitilat Yadayim *and* Hamotzie

The Jewish view of the world is that almost everything—eating, drinking, celebrating, experiencing joy or sadness—can be holy. Awareness of what is holy is achieved through the use of blessings. In Jewish tradition, almost everything in life has a blessing associated with it. For instance, a blessing is recited before eating anything.

The Blessing on Bread

Eating food is truly a miraculous thing. According to the Talmud, since we do not make the rain fall or the sun shine, the food really belongs to God, the Creator. Through a blessing, the food we are about to eat becomes ours to consume. In blessing the food, we stop and become aware of the amazing food and of God, who created it and gave it to us as a gift. Since this constant awareness of the divine is such an essential part of Jewish life, everything from taking a trip to wearing a new piece of clothing to hearing good news to seeing wonders of nature is considered an opportunity for one of the myriad blessings in Judaism. For a list of blessings you can look online or in most Jewish prayer books.

Though there are various blessings to be made on foods depending on their source, only the blessing of bread is required if bread is eaten at a meal. Bread is uniquely seen as the staff of life. In fact, a meal in Jewish law is only a true meal if it contains bread. Thus, when eating bread as part of a meal, the blessing that is made on the bread covers almost all other foods that will be eaten at the meal. The full grace after meals is only recited after eating a meal containing bread. Therefore, most formal meals in Judaism begin with the *hamotzie*, the blessing on bread, which opens the meal and sanctifies it by thanking God.

Though many people could say the *hamotzie* for themselves, you may want to honor someone by asking her to make this blessing out loud on behalf of everyone present. A wedding usually has a large loaf of bread or challah that is prepared especially for a Jewish wedding. The *hamotzie* is said over this.

FACT

Bread is in a class by itself, so it has a unique blessing. The blessing thanks God, who "brings out bread from the ground," in recognition of the fact that without the knowledge God gives to humans they would not be able to process the grain and make the bread.

To make the *hamotzie* blessing on the bread or challah, the loaf is lifted in both hands and the following blessing recited, "*Baruch ata adonai elohaynu melech ha'olam, ha'motzie lechem min ha'aretz.*" ("Blessed are You God, Sovereign of the universe, Who brings bread from the ground.") The bread is then cut and some salt sprinkled upon it. After the one who makes the blessing eats the bread, she can cut it up for anyone who would like to partake in it.

Hand Washing for Bread

Prior to the blessing of the *hamotzie* and the eating of bread, Jewish tradition dictates the ritual washing of the hands in preparation for this holy moment. The ritual washing of the hands is performed in a special way with a special "washing cup." This ritual washing for the *hamotzie* is not for physical cleansing but spiritual preparation.

To wash the hands for the *hamotzie*, use a cup, preferably with one or two handles. Most Judaica stores sell washing cups especially for this purpose, and since no Jewish home should be without one you could keep it after your wedding.

If you do not have a ritual washing cup at the wedding reception and there are people who plan to ritually wash their hands for the bread, you can use any glass or cup, even one that is plastic. It is preferable for the cup to have one or two handles, but it is not required.

The cup is grasped by the right hand and filled with water, then is transferred to the left hand and poured twice over the right hand. The cup is then transferred to the right hand and poured twice over the left hand. Before drying the hands, the following blessing is recited: "*Baruch atah adonai, elohaynu melech ha'olam, asher kidishanu b'mitzvotav vi'tzivanu al nitilat yadayim.*" ("Blessed are You God, Sovereign of the universe, Who has sanctified us with your commandments and commanded us on the washing of the hands.")

Shtick: Rejoicing with the Bride and Groom

The Yiddish word shtick refers to the crazy stuff people will do to entertain you and your new spouse at your wedding. Entertaining the bride and groom is a mitzvah, and it's no holds barred when it come to creating this joy. Many kinds of shtick are popular today. Some guests do it by dancing with all their might, some bring their juggling balls, and some do cartwheels. Usually, the more traditional the Jewish wedding, the crazier the shtick.

It is not uncommon at traditional Jewish weddings to see people who were dressed in a tuxedo or suit for the ceremony to be decked out in a full-body gorilla costume or clown costume during the Jewish dancing. Some guests have been known to begin jumping rope in the center of the circle in front of the bride and groom, or all of a sudden for the wedding party to appear in basketball uniforms and begin a game on the dance floor, moveable hoop and all. Funny hats, noses, and colored wigs are de rigeur when it comes to wedding shtick.

If you wish to have shtick at your wedding but are not sure anyone knows what it is, tell some of your guests about it in advance. They can watch Jewish wedding videos on the Internet and get a sense of what is involved. They can prepare costumes and shtick in advance.

If you have never been to a traditional Jewish wedding complete with shtick, having some may take you or your family by surprise. Weddings, which are often seen as so formal an affair, can suddenly seem like a comedy show—and sometimes a wacky one at that. But the feelings of sincere mirth and joyful abandon set a truly amazing tone for the joyful life it is hoped the bride and groom will share. If your friends plan to bring some shtick to your wedding and your family or your fiancé's family is unfamiliar with the custom, you may want to have a conversation about it in advance so everyone is prepared.

Bircat Hamazon: A Special Grace after Meals

In Deuteronomy, the Torah states, "And you shall eat, and be satisfied, and bless the Lord your God on the good land which God has given you." This commandment is fulfilled after each meal though the recital of the *bircat hamazon*, the grace after meals. Though different Jewish denominations might say different versions of this grace after meals the sentiment is the same—giving thanks to God for the food. The Talmud suggests it is more intuitive to thank God for food before eating when one is hungry than after one is full, but the Torah goes out of its way to command blessing God when we are full because that is usually when it is easiest to think only of ourselves.

The *bircat hamazon* that is recited after a wedding meal is unique and auspicious. In addition to the regular grace after meals blessing, it also contains a repetition of the *sheva berachot*.

The Process

Before the *bircat hamazon* the guests are asked to take a *bencher* booklet and, if they wish, to bring their chairs closer to the bride and groom's table. Two cups of wine are filled. The *bircat hamazon* will be said over the first cup, and the *sheva berachot* will be chanted over the second.

You may want to choose someone who is familiar with the *bircat hamazon* to lead it. If you don't have anyone who knows Hebrew or have many guests who do not, be sure to buy *benchers* that contain a translation and transliteration of the Hebrew text.

The first cup of wine is given to the leader of the *bircat hamazon*, who will hold it in his hand as he leads everyone. The *bircat hamazon* opens with several sentences that are read responsively, blessing God, "from Whose food we have eaten." At the end of the *bircat hamazon*—but before the leader drinks any of the wine—the second cup is passed to those whom the bride and groom have chosen to honor with reciting one of the seven blessings. Each person in turn holds the cup and recites their blessing.

After the cup has been passed to each person to hold as they recite the blessing they have been given, the cup is passed back to the leader of the *bircat hamazon*. He makes the *hagafen*, the blessing over the wine, on the cup that was used for the grace after meals. Then the two cups of wine are mixed.

The method of mixing is quite specific. The two cups must produce three cups, each of which contains wine from the grace after meals cup and from the seven blessings cup. First pour from the cup upon which the grace after meals was recited into an empty third cup, and then pour some wine from the cup upon which the seven blessings were said into that same third cup. Now pour some of the mixture from the third cup back into the first two, and thus all three will contain wine from both cups mixed together. Some people like to use one cup of red and one of white for a more dramatic effect. One cup is then given to the leader of the *bircat hamazon* to drink, another is given to the bride to drink, and the third is given to the groom to drink.

The seven blessings recited after the meal will end with a blessing on the wine. This is in contrast to the ceremony under the chuppah, where the *sheva berachot* began with the blessing of the wine.

Do not be surprised if some of your unmarried friends come to ask for a sip of wine from your cup after you have drunk. There is a belief among some Jewish people that drinking from the cup of the bride or groom will help to bring those who are looking for a spouse good luck. While some might consider this superstitious, drinking from a cup of blessing is considered a source of blessing itself.

Tzedaka: *Making Giving Part of Your Celebration*

Charity is an important part of Jewish life. To celebrate one's own joy without thinking of those who do not have as much would be anathema in Judaism. The Bible itself commands that when one harvests food for oneself, one tenth of the crops must be given to the needy in addition to the various other parts of the field that must also be left for those less fortunate. In keeping with this it is very appropriate—in fact many might say, required—to give to the needy as part of one's wedding celebration.

In past times, when a wedding was celebrated in a town, special tables would be set up for the needy so they could come to the wedding and partake, whether they had been invited or not. This is in fact still the custom in larger cities with heavy Jewish concentrations, such as New York or Jerusalem. Outside of these strong and large Jewish communities it may be difficult and fruitless to expect the needy to come and partake.

Instead of giving a set sum to charity in honor of the wedding, some couples give a percentage of what they spent on the celebration. This method sometimes makes it easier to keep in perspective how much you spent on the wedding, and extreme extravagance will be curtailed. Even if it is not, it will at least result in the mitzvah of charity.

There are other ways to share one's *simcha*, one's joyous celebration, with those who are hungry. Many couples make it a point of donating a percentage of the cost of the wedding to organizations that provides food and support to those in need. You can donate food or money to a local food pantry or Jewish direct service charitable organization in your city, or you can choose to donate to a national organization whose mission is the alleviation of hunger.

One well-known organization to which many couples donate funds in honor of their wedding is Mazon, a Jewish organization whose mission is to feed the hungry of the world and to provide for those who are less fortunate. See Appendix D for their website. It is not uncommon for the bride and groom to declare in their wedding booklet the charitable organization to which funds have been donated in honor of the wedding. In this way, everyone knows that the couple has thought about those less fortunate, and this also encourages others to do likewise at their weddings.

Seven Days of Feasting

Instead of leaving town for a honeymoon, the Jewish practice is to invite the couple to attend seven days of parties with friends and family. These celebrations that usually take place one, several, or all seven nights following the wedding day are hosted by family and friends. They may take place in a home, restaurant, or other venue. These celebrations are known as *sheva berachot* after the seven blessings that are recited at the end of each party's grace after meals.

If you want to leave on a honeymoon right away and your fiancé would like to stay and attend *shevah berachot* parties in your honor, think about compromising. Though the seven days after your wedding are all joyous, you need not have a party all seven nights. The first few might do.

There are several laws regarding *sheva berachot* to be aware of and with which to inform those who are hosting or throwing *sheva berachot* parties in your honor. Any celebratory meal at which the newly married couple is present may be deemed *sheva berachot*. There could in theory be two in one day or none on a particular day; as long as they take place within the first seven days after the wedding they are *sheva berachot*–worthy.

The *sheva berachot* meals should include bread so that they will be followed with the *bircat hamazon*, the grace after meals. At the beginning of the grace after meals, two cups of wine are filled and the procedure for the blessings and the mixing and drinking of these cups is identical to the *sheva berachot* procedure at your wedding reception.

The person who is a "new face" need not be at the *sheva berachot* for the entire meal. As long as he sat with you for a few minutes and ate something he can be included in the *sheva berachot* as *panim chadashot*. Even a Jewish neighbor whom you do not know will do fine.

In addition to the requirement of a *minyan*, a quorum of ten, to recite the *sheva berachot*, in Jewish law there is an additional requirement of *panim chadashot*, "new faces." This means that in order to recite the *sheva berachot* after the grace after meals there must be at least one person who is new and was not in attendance at a previous *sheva berachot*. In the absence of a *minyan* or *panim chadashot* the sixth and seventh blessings may still be recited.

This week after the wedding has been one of joy and celebration going back as far as biblical times when Jacob married Leah and celebrated with her for seven days. Even if you are not going to have big parties or do not want to have *bircat hamazon* and *sheva berachot*, schedule a celebratory meal or two with friends and family. Your wedding is a very personal thing, but it is also a celebration for the community and the Jewish people at large, not all of whom could be at your wedding.

CHAPTER 20

A Jewish Wedding, a Jewish Home

The traditional greeting and blessing given to a new couple on the occasion of their wedding is, "May you merit to build a *bayit ne'eman b'yisrael* (a trustworthy home among the Jewish people)." The purpose of a Jewish wedding is not just for the thrill or even the moving moments of the wedding day; rather, it is the first day of the building of a new home together "among the Jewish people." What, though, is meant by a "Jewish home?"

What Makes a Jewish Home?

A Jewish home is not necessarily the same as a home in which Jewish people live. A Jewish home takes on a certain character and atmosphere. This unique ambiance is achieved in many ways—through the books and objects that are present in the home, by the way in which the home's residents conduct themselves, and perhaps even through the conversation and the music in a Jewish home.

The amazing thing about a home is that it is enclosed. It is a semiprivate space that can be, to some extent, controlled, influenced, and tweaked to reflect specific ideas and feelings. These ideas and feelings will be communicated to those who live there and to others who enter, not because they are told, but because of the very air of the home.

Judaism has a particular way of perceiving things. The aspects of our everyday lives, even in our homes, such as our time, space, food, languages, and the objects that comfort and surround us, all become part of our Jewish vision and our outlook on life. All the aspects of our lives—our home, family, and way of speaking—are a symphony of living. You can often sense the tune of a particular home and life just by entering a family's space.

Jewish Time: The Shabbat

Judaism's take on spirituality and holiness is that it exists primarily in our everyday lives and actions—at home, at work, in our leisure time, and in every room of the house, from the bathroom to the kitchen to the bedroom. Jewish mysticism teaches that God is infinite and everywhere, but that we must live in a universe in which the Divine—for reasons only God completely knows—is almost fully hidden.

Sacred Time

The Torah has many commandments that guide and dictate two major realms of life, two relationships—that between us and God and that between us and other people. Jewish time helps to cultivate both of these relationships. In his famous book, *The Shabbat*, Rabbi Abraham Joshua Heschel states that many ancient religions had concepts of sacred space, whether in a temple, the place of a particular idol, or a sacred city. But Judaism was the first to teach the centrality of sacred time.

Sometimes we see time as completely linear. It moves on into the future as one flat line with no particular texture of its own. There are only minor variations in the weather, the seasons, or the ways in which we experience time differently at different ages of our life. In contrast, Judaism views time as a kind of spiral, akin to a giant stretched-out slinky. Time, of course, does move on into the future. Our lives begin in one spot and end in another when a new generation takes over. But at the same time, Judaism believes that the many subcycles built into time are highly significant and have a reality of their own. The Jewish year has holidays that not only commemorate historic events, but that are seen as being able to tap into the very texture, feeling, and root nature of a particular time.

For instance, the Torah tells us that the holiday of Passover must be celebrated each year in the springtime; thus for Jews spring is the "season" of freedom. The Jewish mystics, however, have a slightly different understanding. Spring is not the season of freedom because the Jewish people simply happened to leave Egypt in the spring. Instead, they say the Jewish people left Egypt in the spring because that time of the calendar is conducive to understanding and experiencing freedom. Time itself has spiritual qualities, aspects, and real textures.

Cultivating holiness in our everyday lives is the mission of Jewish people. We are supposed to help reveal the hidden divine even within the very physical and sometimes seemingly mundane world of our everyday lives. Judaism teaches that the Torah, the written and oral tradition, is the handbook for this enormous undertaking.

Accordingly, time in Jewish life is both personal and universal. Each moment of cyclical time affects us as a nation, but if we can tune into the spiritual nature of time, it affects us personally in our own inner lives as well.

The Shabbat

The Shabbat is probably the most central pillar upon which Jewish time and, consequently, Jewish homes are built. Abraham Joshua Heschel is famous for coining the adage, "More than the Jews have kept the Shabbat, the Shabbat has kept the Jews." The Shabbat comes each week on Friday night for twenty-five hours, from sundown on Friday until darkness on Saturday.

FACT

It is written in the Mishna that there are actually four New Years. One for the counting of years begins when the world was created, but the New Year from which we count months and holidays begins in the month of Nisan. That's when we left Egypt and became a people.

The Shabbat is referred to as a queen in Jewish literature and is ushered in by the lighting of two candles, typically by the woman of the house along with her children and husband. The image of the Shabbat as a queen is a telling one. It is very special, like royalty, but it is also feminine and maternal, a source of comfort and nurturing. Jewish mysticism teaches that the Shabbat brings the ultimate unity of the divine and the world. God is infinite but hidden in the universe. On Sabbath the curtain is parted and we can glimpse, even while engaging in the very physical pleasures of Shabbat, the ultimate unity of God. This is known in Jewish thought as a "taste of the world to come."

Friday night songs and meals are an especially beautiful time for families to gather together after a busy week and interact. The Friday night meal has specific songs in Hebrew that can be found in books and on the Internet. Some songs welcome the Sabbath, and there are also tunes for the *kiddush*, the prayer over wine or grape juice that welcomes and sanctifies the Shabbat and the Shabbat meal.

Following the wine, challah, special bread for the Shabbat, is eaten with some salt sprinkled upon it. The wine, bread, and salt are reminiscent of the services in the Holy Temple of old. The Jewish home now is the temple, and we have to re-create the temple in Jerusalem where God's presence rested.

The table in our home is an altar, and the wine, bread, and food we eat—especially on the Sabbath—are like a holy service, reflecting the services of the pouring of wine, the baking of bread, and the offering of sacrifices in the Temple in ancient Jerusalem.

A good way to involve children in the ceremony of the Shabbat candle lighting at the onset of Shabbat each week is to have them light a candle of their own and make the blessing together with you. In addition, some children receive Shabbat treats after the lighting, ensuring that Shabbat is associated with sweetness.

A traditionally celebrated Sabbath is an amazing thing, quite unique in our society. Jews who observe the Sabbath traditionally do not use electricity, drive cars, or do business on the Sabbath. They don't go to soccer games on the Sabbath or to the mall or even answer the phone. This may sound overly restrictive, but in truth the restrictions of the Sabbath help to create its miraculous atmosphere. After a week that over time has become busier and busier, Shabbat forces us into quality time. Indeed, if they were not commanded to rest on the Sabbath, few people would.

Sex between a husband and wife is a mitzvah, but on Shabbat it is considered an especially holy mitzvah. It adds to the pleasure we are supposed to feel on Shabbat and the unity of two people mirrors the ultimate unity of God.

The Sabbath is a day of space, a day of not doing and finding within that the deeper things we overlooked all week. In traditional communities the twenty-five hours of the Sabbath are spent with community, with family, and with friends, eating meals together, talking, studying, praying, and playing games. There is no television or shopping to draw one away from the things in life that can be truly meaningful.

Jewish Spaces: The Holidays

Each holiday has its own unique feeling and atmosphere. There are three major Jewish holidays and several smaller ones throughout the cycle of the Jewish year. The major festivals listed in the Torah are Passover, Shavuot, and Sukkot. All three were harvest celebrations in ancient times, but they also commemorate historical events and contain rituals through which we live these holidays in their powerful present.

In Israel, the first and last days of Passover and Sukkot and the one day of Shavuot are like the Sabbath, since the Bible commands that no work be done on these days. Outside of Israel, an extra day is added to each of these holy days, though some Reform communities even outside of Israel celebrate only one day. The middle days of Passover and Sukkot are semi-weekdays on which most work may be done but the festival is still celebrated.

Passover

Passover is a seven-day biblical holiday that begins on the full moon, the fifteenth day of the Hebrew month of Nisan, and commemorates the day the Jewish people were redeemed from Egypt. This seminal act of freedom from Egyptian bondage is the moment in Jewish history that is commemorated more than any other. Twice a day, the exodus is remembered in the *shemah* prayer, and each week Shabbat is celebrated in memory of this exodus. Much more than the powerful revelation at Mount Sinai or the people entering the land of Israel forty years later, it is this moment of leaving Egypt that is remembered and relived.

The primary reliving of the exodus—or as the Midrash sees it, the birth process of the Jewish people from the womb of Egypt—is at the Passover Seder meal. In Israel on the first night of Passover and outside of Israel on the first and second nights of Passover, Jews sit together as a family and tell the story of leaving Egypt. Questions are asked at the meal to spur discussion and the foods of slavery and freedom are consumed in an attempt to truly relive the moment of transition form slavery to freedom.

Questions are such an integral part of the Passover Seder experience that, according to the Talmud, even if it is just you as a couple with no other family or guests, you must ask the four questions or other questions about the exodus to each other. In fact, if one person celebrates the Seder alone, they must ask questions of themselves, showing how essential dialogue is to this night.

Why are questions such an important part of the Passover Seder? Why not just tell the story of redemption?
Much more than telling the story, it is important that the Seder be an interactive—and preferably intergenerational—dialogue, since this moment of freedom was one of transition from slavery to free community.

Before Passover, we rid our houses of *chometz*, leavened bread. Instead of bread, we eat matzah, unleavened bread, for these seven days. Though the Bible says we eat matzah and not *chometz* to remember the bread that did not have time to rise as our ancestors were chased from Egypt, the Jewish mystics tell us that matzah and *chometz* represent much more. Matzah is flat and humble in contrast to *chometz*. Passover is not just a time of commemorating the past but of personally living the present and preparing for the future. We must search not only our homes to rid them of *chometz* but also our hearts to be sure ego and haughtiness are removed and replaced with matzah—with humility and an opening of our hearts to the divine and the Torah, which will be received fifty days later on the holiday of Shavuot.

Children should be engaged at the Seder. Giving out stickers or prizes for asking good questions is a custom many find helpful. In ancient times children's attention was kept by doing things out of the ordinary, such as dipping foods. Think of new things to do at your Seder that are unusual, so the children will ask and stay awake.

If the Seder consists only of adults it is important to remember that this is not a holiday for children but primarily for adults. Adults should engage in dialogue and try to discover new insights of their own and deeper messages for each of us today in the story of Egypt. Many *hagadas*, the book used on the Seder night, have been recently reprinted with explanations in English, and some also make the story of the Seder night applicable to issues of slavery and freedom we may face in our own lives and world.

Shavuot

Shavuot is a holiday many Jewish people are not very familiar with but can be a great opportunity for inspiring Jewish family and home celebrations. Shavuot perhaps does not get as much press as Passover because it does not have any symbols like Passover (matzah) and *Sukkot* (the *sukkah*, *lulav*, and *etrog*). Shavuot commemorates both thanking God for the wheat harvest and the day the Jewish people stood at Mount Sinai to receive the Torah, fifty days after leaving their Egyptian bondage.

The open-ended nature of the holiday of Shavuot can create great opportunities to shape your own traditions and celebration. It is a time of rededication to the study of Torah, and in many communities people stay up all night studying Torah in celebration of Shavuot. Even if you do not plan to do this, taking some time on the night of Shavuot to study and discuss something Jewish with your spouse or family can make this day a special one dedicated to the beauty of Torah study itself.

There is a tradition that Mount Sinai bloomed with flowers on the day the Jewish people stood to receive the Torah, so you might want to take advantage of the opportunity to buy a special bunch of flowers for your spouse and share memories of your wedding, since Shavuot is also considered a wedding day between God and the Jewish people. Indeed, many of the Jewish traditions from your recent wedding were based on the experience the Jewish people had at Sinai at their "wedding."

Sukkot

The holiday of Sukkot is the only one on which we enter entirely, with our whole body, into the symbol of the holiday—a *sukkah*, the quintessence of Jewish holy space. We build a *sukkah*, a temporary hut, and, as the Bible commands, live in it for seven days beginning on the fifteenth day of the seventh month of the year, the month of Tishrey.

Dwelling in a temporary hut can make us feel vulnerable, especially when it rains and we must run out so we don't get soaked. Ironically, though, it is the holiday of Sukkot that is termed "the holiday of joy," and it is in the *sukkah* that we feel most joyous. During Sukkot we can gain the realization that we do not need all the material possessions we usually perceive as so essential—our televisions, solid roofs, and heat and air conditioning. On this holiday it is just us, other people, and God, but it is pure joy. The level we reach on Sukkot reflects the utopian time of the messiah during which we will have unity without walls separating us and yet we will feel joy and experience peace. In the words of the prophet Isaiah, we will see even "the lion lying down with the lamb."

FACT

Sukkot falls only four days after Yom Kippur, the day on which we return to God and our true divine selves and became spiritually whole for another year. Thus, on Sukkot, we are intimately connected to God. The *sukkah* is often seen as a chuppah or even a *yichud* room in which we live in great closeness to the spiritual. Sukkot is truly a lover's holiday.

Hanukah

On its most basic level, Hanukah celebrates a miracle at the time of the second temple in the first century B.C.E. A small band of Jews defeated a large Greek army. After entering the desecrated temple in Jerusalem to rededicate it, the Jews found only one pure jar of olive oil—enough for one day. Miraculously, this oil lasted for eight days, the time it would take to produce new pure holy oil.

On a deeper level, Hanukah brings light at the darkest time of year since it falls on or about the winter solstice, teaching us that by taking this temple ritual of lighting the menorah into our own homes and families, we affirm that as Jews we believe we are commanded to constantly strive to bring light into a dark world. Each night we increase the number of candles lit until on the eighth night we have a full *chanukiah* (candelabra) of eight candles. If you can find a menorah that holds olive oil, this is a great way to light the Hanukah candles since it mirrors the beautiful light in the temple of burning pure olive oil.

Purim

Purim is a one-day holiday that falls a month before Passover and commemorates a time during the first exile of the Jews from Israel in the year 586 B.C.E in the Persian Empire. A wicked king and his advisor wished to perpetuate genocide of the Jewish people. We were miraculously saved, and in memory of this and in thanks to God we read this story from an ancient parchment scroll, the scroll of Esther, named after the Jewish queen of Persia who risked her life to save her people.

This scroll dictates a one-day holiday on which the story is read, charity is given to the needy, and gifts of food are exchanged, creating a feeling of great unity among the Jewish people. We would have died as one unified people and so we must live as one. The *megiliah*, the scroll of Esther, also commands that on this day big parties are held. According to the Talmud we are commanded to get drunk, further bringing people together, no matter their class, intellect, or lineage. On Purim we learn what it truly means to be one people and one family.

Sometimes we see the Jewish holidays as just small slivers of what they really are. We sometimes see them as holidays for children when in truth their messages are much deeper. The system of Jewish holidays is one that helps to unite a Jewish family and to condition, through its underlying messages, holy and inspirational ways to see our lives together.

Jewish Thoughts: Ritual Objects

The character of a Jewish home is to some extent cultivated by the objects and symbols in it. From many of these, the home's occupants absorb a certain spiritual sensation. When entering a home with a *mezuzah* on the door, its occupants are made, even if unconsciously, to think for a moment of the holiness of a home. This is a Jewish home in which God colors its entryway. The *shemah*, the most essential Jewish declaration of belief, on a handwritten parchment, is rolled up and placed inside its decorative cover. To live in a home with a small "Torah" scroll affixed to its door is to feel the divine presence watching over it.

The *mezuzah*, along with Jewish books and objects such as charity boxes, menorahs, Sabbath *kiddush* cups, and Shabbat candles, help create a space for you as a couple and the family you may one day have that always focuses on what is truly important. Here is a list of some Jewish items you may want to have to facilitate your home's Jewish awareness:

- Mezuzahs
- Pushka (charity box)
- Shabbat candlesticks
- Shofar
- Mizrach (a sign with the Hebrew word for east indicating which direction to pray)
- Havdalah set
- Etrog holder (for the fruit we wave with a palm branch on the holiday of Sukkot)
- Hanukah menorah

The danger exists that a home may have Jewish holy things that the people living there see only as *objets d'art* and not things to live with and use. Be sure to pick these objects up. If you have a menorah, light it; if you have a shofar, blow it; if you have Shabbat candles, light them. In this way they can all come alive as virtual occupants of your home along with you; they can be teachers of the tradition and Jewish spiritual depth.

Jewish Food: Keeping Kosher

Eating is a big part of life, and cumulatively every human spends about seven full years of his life doing it. Judaism believes that all things have a place. If things are done right, they can be sanctified, made more meaningful, and ultimately become a way of connecting with the infinite. The laws of kosher govern eating in Judaism. What may be eaten and when and how it is to be prepared are the subjects of many Jewish laws and traditions. If you have ever considered kashrut, read a book on kosher with your partner and discuss how you would like your Jewish home to relate to food. Some books and websites on kosher are included in Appendix D.

In Judaism, eating is a holy act preceded by a blessing. The preparation of food has rules, such as not mixing milk and meat products. Milk represents life while meat represents death. How we eat and what awareness we bring to the preparation and consumption of food deeply colors our Jewish homes. In a Jewish home where food is not just consumed but thought about and blessed, the food itself and the process of eating become a kind of teaching and learning process.

Blessings on food are very specific, and they reflect where each item grows from—the ground, a tree, or an animal. Planting a garden is a great way to teach children blessings and to help them make the connection between the food, its origin, and the miraculous way in which it grows.

There is a story of a couple who went to a rabbi and asked him how to bring up their first child, who was due in several months. The rabbi said, "I'm sorry but you have come too late." "What?" the couple exclaimed. "But the baby has not even been born yet." "I know," the rabbi replied, "but the baby will learn from you. Who you are, how you act, and how you grow will condition the way in which your child grows."

This story reflects Judaism's most basic approach to teaching. Children learn through their parents' actions much more than their words. The best way, perhaps, to teach the blessings and their purpose is to learn them yourself and say them before eating with *kavanah*, with concentration, meaning, and intent. Seeing this, children not only learn what the blessings are and their importance, but also that such blessings can serve as a vehicle to a deeper spiritual awareness of their food, their world, and a relationship with God.

Jewish Family: Children and Nachas, Real Jewish Joy

The word *nachas* is difficult to translate. On the surface it means joy, but in Hebrew there are ten or so words for joy. *Nachas* is the kind of joy that comes from children. Usually it refers to the joy parents have in watching children not merely grow bigger, but also grow into people who know what is valuable and important. To see a child go outside of themselves and help someone else gives a parent *nachas*. To see a child make a blessing without prompting because they realize the importance of recognizing the good that God has given us is true *nachas*.

In Judaism, having children is not just something parents do to be fulfilled or to comply with our genetic drive to make a new generation. Children are most precious because they are the future of our people. It is through subsequent generations that the world can be brought to its ultimate purpose and a holier destiny.

The main mitzvah that Jewish parents are constantly engaged in with their children is that of *chinuch*, teaching children religious practices and life lessons. We all want to teach children to navigate life and to give them the tools to live a meaningful life. In Judaism this process is built into the interactions between parents and children. For that reason, model the making of a blessing and the appreciation of what God has given us. Blow the shofar on Rosh Hashanah morning before attending synagogue so your children can blow it and can see it as something personal and not just something in the synagogue.

When we practice Judaism with children, to a greater or lesser extent, each time we do so we teach them that that their real everyday life is the place of spiritual fulfillment. God, community, and a greater meaning are not just relegated to the walls of the synagogue or temple but can be present in our everyday lives.

One of the greatest and most ancient sources of *nachas* is taking a few moments to say the *shema* prayer with children before their bedtime; this prayer goes back more than 3,000 years to its source in the Hebrew Bible. In addition, to read a child a Jewish story, to give charity with them—not just as something good to do, but as a mitzvah—these are things that will stay with them forever and cultivate their Jewish self.

Jewish Talk: Torah and Family

For Jewish people, the Torah is not just a book of instruction but a vast sea of learning and speaking about Jewish ideas, values, and laws. Torah study and discussion are not just a tool to use to know how to observe Judaism. They are considered mitzvahs themselves. Just speaking words of Torah is a holy act.

Talking Torah with each other and with children raises the level of conversation to something much larger. When parents speak with children about ancient and spiritual ideas, it colors the relationship between them and transmits a message about what is truly important.

The Talmud says that no meal should be eaten without words of Torah spoken at it. When we engage in conversation about Torah over a meal, it elevates the entire meal to a level at which it is considered to be eaten in the presence of God and a holy service.

Even if you know little about Torah, today there are many books and websites that are very accessible. For instance, the weekly Torah portion, the section of the Bible read in the synagogue each week, is not just for the synagogue but for our everyday lives that week. The Jewish week is colored by the Torah portion during which it falls. Utilize the websites in Appendix D to learn about the weekly Torah portion and use some of the child-oriented websites to have a discussion with the whole family.

To facilitate Torah discussion, read a summary of the Torah portion and the thought questions that follow it each week online. Summarize one part of the portion, then ask children or another family member a discussion question. This will often lead to a great family Torah discussion.

If you do not have a Jewish copy of the Torah, it is worth having one with a commentary, many of which are available in English. Each Saturday on the Shabbat, many couples and families have the ritual of reading the Torah portion together. Everyone takes a turn reading a few paragraphs and then asking a question that can be discussed. Learning and discussion are a deep-rooted and essential part of forging a Jewish home and an empowered Jewish life together.

CHAPTER 21

Staying Married

Mazel tov! You're married! It's a relief to be done with all that wedding planning, but now it's time to think about how to keep a good marriage going great. Marriages, like anything worth having, need nurturing. It takes some knowledge and forethought to keep a marriage fulfilling and joyous even during difficult times, but it can be done.

The Work and the Joy of a Good Relationship

Sometimes we imagine that marriage does not take work, and instead that it will be pure bliss because we have found our true love. Judaism understands that just as a relationship with God takes constant nurturing, vigilance, and the initiative to capitalize upon opportunities for growth, so, too, do human relationships. Like a muscle, if they are not cultivated and used they will atrophy. The reason you married your *bashert* was that you love them and love spending time with them. Remember this even after the initial bliss wears off.

Get into the habit of making a date night once a week. If you do not have children, it will feel like every day is date night, but this will get more difficult as you get back into your jobs, real life, and especially after you have children. Even if it's just going out for coffee, studying a piece of Torah together, taking a walk, or discussing a book, setting aside time on the calendar is important.

The sacred bond between husband and wife always binds you even though you are not together every minute. This bond does not magically stay with you; you must be smart and considerate about your relationship. Just because you love someone does not mean it is going to work, and just because you have a great relationship does not mean it will stay that way forever. Relationships, like children, require attention and feeding.

Appreciating Strengths and Weaknesses

Often people's strengths are also their weaknesses. For instance, if your spouse is a philosopher and not very good at paying attention to detail, you might get annoyed that he was going to do something, pick something up, or get the oil changed in the car and did not. On the other hand, you may have married him precisely because of who he is.

Evaluating Weaknesses as Strengths

Remember you like the philosophical side of him because he brings a bigger picture—perhaps a more spiritual vision to you, your life, and your relationship. When the other side of his personality makes you frustrated, it is of course important to talk together and negotiate how what needs to get done will get done, but at the same time it is important to keep in mind that no one can be everything. Your husband's inattention to detail might be the other side of what you love about him—his focus on the big picture.

FACT

Sometimes women who complain that their husbands are not emotional or vulnerable enough admit it was this strength and independence that attracted them to their husbands in the first place when they are asked to explore their feelings about why they married their husbands.

Your spouse might be a procrastinator and you see this as a weakness because it's time to get the taxes done and she has waited until the last minute. The other side of this "weakness" might be her ability to put tasks aside to focus on you or to have fun with your children. When you feel your spouse's weaknesses, ask yourself what you love about her, why you married her, and how she complements you by being different. No doubt, this strength may also be part of what you see as a weakness and annoys you. So talk together about what irks you, but also focus on what you have always loved about your partner.

Don't sacrifice yourself or your relationship for your kids. When partners lose their own interests and become only about their children, they are left with little of themselves and it can be difficult for them to find what they originally loved in each other. You must cultivate intimacy, adult interactions, and learning, even when you have children in your lives.

Working on a relationship, considering what you love about each other, and talking about what bothers you is a lot of work, but can bring great joy. The Torah tells us that it is forbidden to harbor hatred in one's heart; we are commanded instead to confront others with what is bothering us. There is no need to tell your spouse everything that annoyed you at work each day, but when he does say something that bothers you and you have a hard time seeing it as endearing, talk to him about it. Of course, finding the right way to phrase such a conversation is of the utmost importance. Talk about his strengths and how he also has something, the flip side of one of his strengths, that annoys you. Be specific, and don't simply launch into general complaints; that usually leads to an argument.

Making It Work

Remember, you can be the ultimate trusting couple to each other, the only people in the world with whom you both can be completely open about your challenges. This is because you really know and appreciate each other better than anyone else in the world can.

Some couples find that going out on a date, even just for coffee, and making a ground rule to ban certain topics of conversation, such as work, money, and kids, can be very productive. It creates space to allow you to focus on your relationship and each other even in a hectic life.

One of the important prerequisites to having a good relationship and marriage is having become fully "you" first. For many people, psychotherapy is effective because understanding what makes each of us tick then enables us to go outside ourselves and truly be there for someone else. Way before you have any problems in your relationship, think about counseling, therapy, couples therapy, or a retreat for couples where you can talk about how you communicate and what you love about each other and what is hard for each of you about being in your relationship. Couples that do not stay together often have waited too long before finding help.

Spouses must learn to hear each other even when things are not clearly spelled out, while at the same time working toward being able to say what they need. For instance, if one's wife says she is stressed because there is a lot of laundry to do, a husband should not think that he just worked a long day and she does not appreciate it; rather, he should realize that loving means wanting to help, and this is her way of telling him she needs partnership. When two people love each other they are complete partners, and everything involved in building a marriage and a family should be seen as the responsibility of both partners. When both feel they are doing more than their share, the odds are that things are closer to equal. The Talmud says that people who are married to each other are like one person and that—perhaps to equalize the amount of influence spouses have in a relationship—a husband must honor his wife more than he does himself.

Partners in Building the Future

Judaism can be very helpful in keeping a good marriage going. You and your spouse are on a mission together—it is your job to raise a Jewish family, cultivate your religious life, and make the world a better place. If you view your marriage from this perspective, you will see it as much more than just the love of two people; it is indispensable because it makes a difference to the world.

FACT

Some of the signs that a relationship needs immediate help are feelings of resentment, seeing coming home as a chore, seeing your spouse's quirks as an irritant, and cessation of sexual intimacy. In such cases a couple will need to air their feelings to each other in a safe space such as a therapist's office.

Get into the habit of making positive statements about your relationship and go back to the things you said you loved about each other before your wedding. Make a list of what you love about your spouse and review it periodically. There will always be things you don't like. He may have bad habits or do things that annoy you. He might be the complete opposite of you in some ways, and this might frustrate you. It is important to remember that it is the whole person you love.

One of the great things about being married is the time you have together as a couple, not just on dates or weekends, but living a life that is intertwined and having the sense that you are always together. In good relationships, people still feel excited to see their spouse each day even after many years of marriage, though obviously couples become more accustomed to each other and the level of immediacy of desire may not be like it was.

Though it is a cliché, the notion of never going to bed angry is a good one. It is not a hard and fast rule, but it is true that issues that cause anger will result in resentment if they are left to fester. Things that bother you about your spouse or issues between you that create tension should not be swept under the rug. Bring them into the open and deal with them.

Most people's tendency is to try to discuss the issue and air their grievances in the heat of argument. This is the worst time for it. Wait until there is a calm moment and tell your spouse how you value your relationship with her. Tell her you always want your relationship to be completely honest, and you have an issue you would like to discuss. Then bring up the issue that is bothering you. Don't blame her. Phrase the issue in terms of yourself. For instance, "I find that I feel 'x' when you do (or say) 'y.'"

Growing Together

From a Jewish perspective, personal growth is vital. For your relationship to be a great one, you must be fulfilled as individuals. This happens through constant growth, whether it is intellectual, personal, or religious. If one member of the couple is engaged in growth and the other is not they may find they are in different places. Not everything must be done together—you and your spouse may have different interests—but you must both be engaged in growth so you can share your experiences with each other.

Some people feel that their spouse must be everything to them. The reality is that usually spouses are very different; not only do they often have different interests, but people marry each other because they appreciate how different and sometimes opposite their spouses are from them. Your spouse is your life partner, your most trusted lover.

Just as in business and sales, a good attitude goes a long way. Always remember what you love about your spouse and their strengths and make time for happiness and joy together. However, this does not mean you can avoid talking about problems in your relationship.

However, this does not mean that your entire life's fulfillment will come from your spouse. If you like to have deeply intellectual discussions of philosophy or are interested in politics and your spouse is not, that is fine. It is okay to have close friendships and relationships with other people. A spouse is the relationship that will always be there, that is not based on a certain thing or commonality, but on just love and partnership. A spouse is the only one we are physically intimate with, but this does not mean our entire fulfillment must come from him.

The longer people are married, the more often they have friends who are couple friends. Sometimes spouses must encourage each other to have friends that are just theirs to study with or talk with. This should not be seen as threatening but as a necessary part of helping each other to grow as individuals.

Keeping the Passion

In Judaism very powerful things are usually seen as having much potential for holiness and, conversely, a lack thereof. Jewish law governs the powerful aspects of life very strictly. Food and sex, for instance, are elemental passions, and they have the most rules in the Torah. They have the most potential to be a vehicle for the holy. Sex and passion are among the most important aspects in a Jewish marriage. Keeping the passion alive is considered a holy undertaking and is an important part of living a holy Jewish life.

The Talmud relates the story about two great rabbis: Rabbi Kahana and his great teacher Rav. One day, the Talmud says, Rabbi Kahana went and hid under his teacher's bed and heard his teacher Rav engaged in conversation and passionate foreplay with Mrs. Rav. Hearing their passionate interaction, Rabbi Kahana forgot his cover and exclaimed, "It seems like your first time together!" Rav realized someone was under the bed and asked, "Kahana, is that you? It is not good manners to hide under your teacher's bed." Rabbi Kahana answered from under the bed, "It is Torah and I have to learn it."

At first glace, the story may be shocking. Was Rav's student just being a voyeur? What did he mean when he said "it is Torah"? Everything in this world is subject to Torah and all things have the potential to be holy. When in the right context, everything—sex included—can be a mitzvah. One must know how to do it well since it is an essential part of a couple's relationship, and the relationship of a husband and wife is so important that the rabbis teach that God allows His name to be erased to facilitate peace between husband and wife. Little in Judaism is considered more important than *shalom bayit*, peace and love in a home.

It's no secret that communication is part of the key to a passionate sexual life. Sexual intimacy does not begin and end in the bedroom; rather, it is a reflection of two people's lives together. Sexual passion is a climactic representation of the intimacy between two people that functions in their life every day. The trust, the sharing of self, everything that happens in every moment of living life is a part of a couple's sex life. So, too, their sexual life resonates between them throughout their daily life outside the bedroom, because sex is a reflection of their relationship. Indeed love, intimacy, sadness, and joy—all the ups and downs and complexities of sharing life with each other—are all intertwined.

APPENDIX A

Glossary

Agunah
A "chained women" who has no divorce and therefore cannot remarry

Aliyah
Being called to the Torah

Amidah
The silent prayer recited thrice daily

Ashkenazi
Jewish communities of Eastern European heritage

Bashert
A soul mate

Bedekin
Veiling of the bride

Birkat Hamazon
Grace after meals

Chalitzah
Ceremony performed after death of husband if couple had no children, permitting wife to remarry

Chanukiah
Candelabra lit on Hanukah

Chatan
Groom

Chinuch
Jewish education for children

Chometz
Leaven or bread

Chuppah
Wedding canopy

Ezer Kinegdo
The biblical term for a spouse; literally, "a helper opposite you"

Get
Jewish divorce

Gililah
Tying and covering the Torah scroll

Hachnasat Kallah
Welcoming the bride; charity given to a couple to help pay for their wedding

Hagbah
Lifting up the Torah scroll

Haftorah
Section of the prophets read after the Torah portion on the Sabbath and holidays

Halacha
Jewish law

Hora
Traditional Jewish circle dance

Kabbala
Jewish mysticism

Kabalat Panim
Pre-ceremony reception

Kallah
Bride

Kiddush
Blessing recited over a cup of wine to sanctify the Sabbath

Kiddushin
Jewish wedding ceremony

Kittel
White robe worn by groom at wedding and by Jewish men on Passover and Yom Kippur

Ketubah
Jewish marriage contract

L'chaim
"To life!"—the toast that is said when drinking a Jewish toast; the first celebration of an engagement

Lebedic
With joyous abandon

Maftir
The last person called to the Torah on the Sabbath

Matzah
Unleavened bread eaten on Passover

Mazel tov
Congratulations; good luck

Mechitza
Divider

Mechutonim
In-laws

Mezuzah
Hebrew parchment scroll of the Shemah affixed to doorposts in a Jewish home

Midrash
First century commentary on the Torah

Mikvah
Ritual bath of rainwater

Misader Kiddushin
The wedding officiant

Mitzvah
Commandment

Mivushal
Boiled wine

Panim Chadashot
New people who were not at the wedding reception or previous sheva berachot party

Pareve
Food that is neither dairy nor meat

Sefirot
Ten mystical realms

Sephardic
Jewish communities of Spanish, North African, and Asian heritage

Shabbat
The Jewish Sabbath

Shadchan
Matchmaker

Shalom Bayit
Peace in the home

Shechitah
Ritual kosher slaughter

Shemah
Hebrew biblical passage recited twice daily by Jewish people affirming their faith in one God

Sheva Berachot
The seven blessings recited under the chuppah, following the reception meal, or following the meals during the seven days of feasting; also the name given to a party during the seven days of feasting

Shofar
Ram's horn blown on Rosh Hashanah, the Jewish New Year

Shtick
Short, madcap performances at a wedding to entertain the bride and groom

Shulchan Aruch
Code of Jewish law

Siddur
Prayer book

Sifirat Ha'Omer
Counting of the fifty days from Passover to Shavuot

Sukkah
Temporary hut with natural roof to celebrate the holiday of Sukkot

Talit
Prayer shawl

Talmud
Judaism's most basic book of law and tradition

Tanaim
Terms of engagement

Tish
The word for table in Yiddish; the pre-ceremony room in which the ketubah is signed

Tisha B'av
Ninth day of the Hebrew month of Av, a day of mourning

Tzedakah
Charity

Tzniut
Traditional Jewish standards of modesty, usually in dress

Ufruf
Calling up to the Torah on Shabbat prior to a wedding

Vort
"A word"; a short speech about Torah; an engagement party

Yichud
Post-ceremony seclusion of bride and groom together

Yiddish
Language spoken by the Jewish people of Eastern Europe combining German and Hebrew

Zuz
Ancient coin referred to in the ketubah

APPENDIX B

Seven Blessings in Hebrew, English, and Transliteration

✡ First Blessing

ברוך אתה ה" אלהינו מלך העולם בורא פרי הגפן

Baruch Ata Adoni Elohainu Melech HaOlam, Boreh Pri HaGafen

You are Blessed, Lord our God, the Sovereign of the world,
Who created the fruit of the vine.

✡ Second Blessing

ברוך אתה ה" אלהינו מלך העולם ודובכל ארב לכהש

Baruch Ata Adoni Elohainu Melech HaOlam, SheHakol Barah Lichvodo

You are Blessed, Lord our God, the Sovereign of the world,
Who created everything for Your glory.

✡ Third Blessing

ברוך אתה ה' אלהינו מלך העולם יוצר האדם

Baruch Ata Adoni Elohainu Melech HaOlam, Yotzer Ha'Adam

You are Blessed, Lord our God, the Sovereign of the world, creator of human kind.

✡ Fourth Blessing

ברוך אתה ה' אלהינו מלך העולם אשר יצר את האדם בצלמו בצלם
דמות תבניתו והתקין לו ממנו בנין עדי עד ברוך אתה ה' יוצר האדם

Baruch Ata Adoni Elohainu Melech HaOlam, Asher Yatzar Et Ha'Adam Betzalmo, b'Tzelem Dmut Tavnito, VeHitkon Lo Mimenu Binyan Adei Ad. Baruch Ata Adoni Yotzer Ha'Adam

You are Blessed, Lord our God, the Sovereign of the world, who created the human in Your image, in the image of Your own likeness, and prepared for him a building for eternity, Blessed are You Who fashioned the human.

✡ Fifth Blessing

שוש תשיש ותגל העקרה בקבוץ בניה
לתוכה בשמחה ברוך אתה ה' משמח ציון בבניה

Sos Tasis VeTagel HaAkarah, BeKibbutz Bane'ha Letocha BeSimchaa. Baruch Ata Adoni, Mesame'ach Tzion BeVaneha

Let the barren city be jubilantly happy, when her children are gathered within her in joy, You are Blessed, Lord, Who rejoices Jerusalem with her children.

✡ Sixth Blessing

שמח תשמח רעים האהובים כשמחך יצירך
בגן עדן מקדם ברוך אתה ה' משמח חתן וכלה

Sameach TeSamach Re'im Ha'Ahuvim, KeSamechacha Yetzircha BeGan Eden MiKedem. Baruch Ata Adoni, MeSame'ach Chatan VeKalah

Gladden the beloved companions as You gladdened Your creations in the Garden of Eden in ancient time. You are Blessed, Lord, Who gladdens groom and bride.

✡ Seventh Blessing

ברוך אתה ה' אלהינו מלך העולם אשר ברא
ששון ושמחה חתן וכלה גילה רינה דיצה חדוה אהבה ואחוה ושלום
וריעות מהרה ה' אלהינו ישמע בערי יהודה ובחוצות ירושלים קול
ששון וקול שמחה קול חתן וקול כלה קול מצהלות חתנים מחופתם
ונערים ממשתה נגינתם ברוך אתה ה' משמח חתן עם הכלה

Baruch Ata Adoni Elohainu Melech HaOlam, Asher Barah Sasson VeSimcha, Chatan VeKalah, Gila Rina, Ditza VeChedva, Ahava VeAchava, VeShalom VeRe'ut. MeHera HaShem Elokeinu Yishama BeArei Yehudah U'Vchutzot Yerushalayim, Kol Sasson V'eKol Simcha, Kol Chatan V'eKol Kalah, Kol

Mitzhalot Chatanim MeChupatam, U'Nearim Mimishte Neginatam. Baruch Ata Adoni MeSame'ach Chatan Im Hakalah

You are Blessed, Lord our God, the Sovereign of the world, Who created joy and gladness, groom and bride, mirth, glad song, pleasure, delight, love, brotherhood, peace, and companionship. May there soon be heard, Lord, our God, in the cities of Judah and the streets of Jerusalem the sound of joy and the sound of gladness, the voice of the groom and the voice of the bride, the sound of the grooms' jubilance from their wedding canopies and of the youths from their song-filled feasts. Blessed are You Who makes the groom and the bride rejoice together.

APPENDIX C

Sample Wedding Booklets

Wedding Ceremony of

Dalia Nechama
and
Jeffrey Matthew

August 5, 2007

21 Av, 5767

"Man is incomplete without woman.
And woman is incomplete without man.
And both are incomplete without the Divine presence"
(Medrash Rabbah—Genesis 8:9)

Wedding Procession

(List of participants)

Welcome

Welcome to our wedding! We are honored that our families and friends are here to share in our simcha.

A traditional Jewish wedding is rich with meaningful customs and traditions. We have prepared the following explanation of this joyous occasion so our guests may join in our celebration with fuller understanding and happiness. Thank you for sharing this special day with us!

Love,

Dalia and Jeffrey

Kabalat Panim

In Jewish tradition, a bride and groom are compared to royalty, and as such, they both "hold court" at separate receptions before the actual wedding ceremony. All of the guests greet Dalia in one room, where she is surrounded by her female relatives and friends. At a men's reception, Jeffrey sits at the *Chatan's Tish*, the Groom's Table, where the *tanaim* (betrothal agreement) and *ketubah* (marriage agreement) are signed.

The tanaim is a contract in which the two families agree to the imminent marriage of their children. After it is signed, the mothers of the bride and groom break a plate to symbolize the seriousness of this agreement.

The *ketubah* is a traditional document that has symbolized Jewish marriage for more than 2,000 years. It outlines the moral and financial obligations of a husband to his wife. Two designated witnesses sign the *ketubah*, which is subsequently read under the chuppah. Dalia and Jeffrey have also signed a traditional civil license, witnessed by two friends.

Bedekin

Once the *ketubah* is signed, the *chatan* (the groom), escorted by family and friends to the accompaniment of joyous music, is led to where his *kallah* (the bride) is seated and lowers the veil over her face. The custom of *bedekin*, or veiling the bride, originates with our matriarch, Rebecca, who veiled herself upon seeing Isaac, her husband-to-be, for the first time. The *bedekin* also has roots in our patriarch, Jacob, who was tricked into marrying Leah instead of Rachel. This is why Jeffrey places the veil over Dalia himself during the *bedekin*. This emotional moment is further enhanced by the personal blessings bestowed on the *chatan* and *kallah* by both sets of parents.

Chuppah

The marriage ceremony takes place under a chuppah (wedding canopy), symbolizing the new home that Dalia and Jeffrey will build together. Like the tent of Abraham and Sarah, which was always open to welcome guests, the chuppah is open on all four sides.

Because the *chatan* and *kallah* are compared to royalty, many have adopted the custom of rising as they walk down the aisle. *Bruchim Ha'Baim*, a song of welcome, is sung to both Dalia and Jeffrey as they each arrive at the chuppah.

In accordance with his family's tradition, Jeff will don a *talit*, prayer shawl, under the chuppah. The *talit* symbolizes the "marriage" between God and Israel at Sinai. It is a sign of deep commitment.

Upon her parents escorting her to the chuppah, Dalia, together with Jackie and Darlene, will circle Jeffrey seven times. A *kallah* encircles her *chatan* to symbolize unity as they start their life together. She encircles him seven times because the number seven signifies a completion. Just as the seventh day (Shabbat) completes the creation of the world, the seven circles around the *chatan* complete their search for one another.

The Jewish Wedding Ceremony has two basic parts: *Kiddushin* (betrothal) and *Nisuin* (marriage). Both parts are introduced with the blessing over wine, the traditional symbol of joy.

During *Kiddushin*, Jeffrey will place a simple ring (without stones) upon the forefinger of Dalia's right hand and recite in Hebrew, "Behold, you are consecrated to me with this ring according to the law of Moses and Israel."

To separate the blessings of *Kiddushin* from the blessings of *Nisuin*, the *Ketubah* is then read aloud in its original Aramaic.

During *Nisuin*, the reciting of the *Sheva Berachot*, seven wedding blessings, takes place. It is customary for seven people—family members, friends, or Rabbis—to be called to the chuppah to bestow these seven blessings upon the couple. These blessings are chanted over another cup of wine.

In Jewish families of German descent, as is Dalia's, there is a custom to sing Psalm 128 from the Book of Psalms. This Psalm expresses our prayer that the bride and groom create a family together with happiness and contentment.

Even in moments of our greatest joy, we are obligated to remember our still incomplete national existence as symbolized by the destroyed Beit *Hamikdash* (Holy Temple) in Jerusalem. In commemoration of this reality, everyone sings together "*Im Eshkacheich Yerushalayim*" ("If I forget thee, Jerusalem"), a passage from Psalms.

In the same spirit, Jeffrey then breaks a glass with his right foot to commemorate the Temple's destruction. Symbolically embedded in this custom is the hope that, just as glass can be reblown and reshaped, so too the *Beit Hamikdash* will be restored and rebuilt.

At the conclusion of the ceremony, it is customary to clap joyously and to sing "*Od Yishama*" to the couple as they walk up the aisle. The lyrics, "*Od Yeshama, B'Arei Yehuda, U'Vechutzot Yerushalayim, Kol Sason V'Kol Simcha, Kol Chatan V'Kol Kallah*," translate to "Again may these be heard in the cities of Judah and in the streets of Jerusalem, the voice of gladness and the voice of happiness, the voice of groom and bride." This song, also sung at the Bedekin, will be sung again as the first dance at the reception.

While singing "*Od Yeshama*," friends and family escort Dalia and Jeffrey to a room where they spend a few private moments alone for the first time as husband and wife. This *Yichud*, time alone, completes the wedding ceremony.

"Many waters cannot quench love; neither can floods drown it."
Song of Songs 8:7

Wedding Ceremony of

Suzanne Ruth

and

Andrew Dudley

Sunday, October 14, 2007

2 Cheshvan, 5768

Welcome . . .

Welcome to our wedding! We are so excited that our family and friends are here to share this simcha *(happy celebration) with us. We know that for many of our guests the traditions and customs in our wedding may be unfamiliar, so we have designed this guide to enable our guests to share fully in the meaning and excitement of this day.*

. . . and Thank You

We want to take this opportunity to thank our family and friends for all the love and support shown to both of us throughout our lives, both separately and together. We also want to express particular gratitude to our many friends at Bais Abraham Congregation for being so open and welcoming to us and for their support in helping to make this wedding a reality.

Much Love,

Suzanne and Andy

On the day of their wedding, Jewish tradition treats the bride and groom literally like royalty. Royal symbolism is present throughout the day, including the bride and groom each "holding court" in separate receptions and guests rising as both the groom and bride walk down the aisle.

The wedding day is also in many ways like a Yom Kippur (Day of Atonement) for the bride and groom. The bride and groom fast from sunrise until the ceremony and pray special prayers of atonement. During the ceremony, both the bride and the groom wear white, as a symbol of spiritual purity and of the clean slate with which we begin our life together as a married couple.

Kabalat Panim (Receiving Faces)

The bride and groom hold separate receptions before the ceremony begins. During the *kallah's* (bride) reception, Suzanne sits in a throne-like chair, surrounded by female relatives. It is customary for guests to greet the bride and family. During this reception, Suzanne and Andy have chosen to have civil wedding documents signed and witnessed by friends.

Andy, meanwhile, is upstairs at the *Chatan's Tish* (Groom's Table).

During his reception, Andy will begin to give a *D'Var Torah* (speak a few words of Torah), which is customarily interrupted with songs and jokes. This is not meant to be rude; actually it is a long-standing tradition designed to level the playing field among men. All grooms are to be interrupted on the day of their wedding, thus reducing possible feelings of competition or insecurity on the part of the groom.

Two important Jewish contractual documents are signed and witnessed during the Groom's *Tish*: the *Tanaim* (engagement agreement) and the *Ketubah* (marriage agreement). The *Tanaim* is a contract signed by both Andy and Suzanne's families, agreeing to the marriage of their children. Following the signing of the *Tanaim*, Andy and Suzanne's mothers will break a plate jointly to symbolize the seriousness of the contract. The breaking of the plate is also said to symbolize the breaking of any acrimony that may have arisen between the two families in order to now join the two families together.

The *Ketubah*

The *Ketubah* is an essential component of a Jewish wedding, signifying the husband's moral and financial obligations to his wife. For thousands of years, the *Ketubah* has been executed between brides and grooms, in order to protect the interests of the Jewish wife. The

Ketubah is written in Aramaic, and is signed by two designated witnesses at the chatan's *Tish*.

Suzanne and Andy's beautiful *Ketubah* was designed by a close friend, Chasiah Haberman. In addition to the traditional Aramaic text, Suzanne and Andy have written in English their own commitments to each other regarding their marriage and the home they will create together. The traditional Aramaic text and the English adaptation will be read aloud during the wedding ceremony.

Jewish law requires that the *Ketubah* be physically present in the couple's home, and it is often hung in a special location. The *Baal Shem Tov*, the founder of Hasidism and an eighteenth-century mystic, suggested that couples re-read their *Ketubah* whenever they fight, as a reminder of how they felt as a bride and groom, surrounded by their family, friends, and abundant love.

Bedekin **(Veiling)**

The *Bedekin* is one of the most beautiful and emotional parts of a Jewish wedding. Andy is escorted from the *Chatan's Tish* by a large group of men, dancing and singing a song called "*Od Yishama*." (This song will be sung throughout the festivities, and is transliterated at the end of this program so that all guests can join in.)

Andy is led to where Suzanne is seated on her "throne;" this is the first time Andy and Suzanne see each other on the day of the wedding. When Andy is brought to Suzanne, we exchange a brief, intimate moment and then Andy lowers Suzanne's veil.

The tradition of lowering the veil derives from the tricking of our patriarch Jacob into marrying Leah. Because he did not see his bride's face, Jacob married Leah instead of Rachel, the sister he loved. To ensure that it is Suzanne he will be marrying, Andy himself covers Suzanne's face with a veil. When the veil has been lowered, our parents may bestow on us personal blessings and kind words.

Chuppah (Wedding Canopy)

The marriage ceremony takes place under a chuppah, symbolizing the home Suzanne and Andy will build together (not literally—we've done enough home building for a while!). The chuppah is open on all four sides, like Abraham and Sarah's tent, a symbol that our home will always be open to guests. The fabric of our chuppah was made by two friends and members of Bais Abraham, Phyllis Shapiro and Lyla Puro. This chuppah has been part of many weddings, and we are honored to share in its long and meaningful history.

We have chosen to both walk down the aisle to a "*niggun*" (wordless song) sung by all of our guests. In some Jewish communities, a *niggun* is believed to be a way to lift the soul to higher levels of spirituality. We have chosen this somewhat atraditional processional so that all of our friends and family can be an active part of our wedding ceremony. We hope that each of our guests will join in and sing along as we walk down the aisle.

In Jewish weddings, it is customary for both the bride and groom to be escorted by their parents. Andy is first escorted to the chuppah by his parents, Alison and George, and then Suzanne is escorted to the chuppah by her parents, Charlene and David. Suzanne and Andy also are accompanied by their siblings: Andy's brother, Robert, and Suzanne's brother and sister, Steven and Erica. Because the bride and the groom are like royalty on this day, it is traditional to rise for the processionals both of the groom and bride.

When Andy is brought to the chuppah, he is welcomed with a song of welcome, Bruchim Ha'Baim. He then leaves the chuppah to greet

Suzanne as she walks down the aisle. Together as a couple, they enter their new home, symbolized by the chuppah.

Upon entering the chuppah, as a song of welcome also is sung to her, Suzanne will circle Andy seven times. This represents the binding of the bride and groom together, creating a space unique to the two of them. Seven is a particularly significant number in Judaism and is integrated throughout the wedding day. Here, seven signifies the completion of the creation of the couple.

Andy will put on a "*kittel*" (a white ceremonial robe) before Suzanne arrives. Both the bride and the groom will be dressed in white (or ivory) under the chuppah and will wear no jewelry and have no possessions in their pockets. This symbolizes that Suzanne and Andy accept each other as who they are, without regard to material possessions.

Kiddushin **(Betrothal)**

The Jewish wedding ceremony itself is composed of two parts. The first part, represents the betrothal of the bride and groom. Our rabbi, Rabbi Hyim Shafner, who has been an incredible influence and support for us over the past two years, recites a special blessing over a cup of wine. Both Andy and Suzanne drink from this cup.

Then, Andy places a simple ring on Suzanne's index finger, reciting a declaration that makes the betrothal official. The English translation of this declaration is: "Behold, you are consecrated to me with this ring according to the Law of Moses and Israel." According to Jewish law, the ring must be a simple ring, pure metal without stones or carvings.

The *Ketubah* now is read aloud in the language in which it is written, Aramaic. Following the Aramaic reading, our personal English adaptation of the *Ketubah* also is read aloud. The reading of the *Ketubah* separates the *Kiddushin* from the *Nisiun*, the second part of the wedding ceremony.

Nisuin (Marriage)

During *Nisiun*, the *Sheva Berachot* (seven wedding blessings) are recited. These blessings are chanted over a cup of wine. Friends and family members are called to the chuppah to bestow these seven blessings on the couple, both in Hebrew and in English, after which Andy and Suzanne drink from the cup of wine. The seven blessings, which will also be recited at the end of the wedding meal, are translated at the end of this guide.

According to Jewish law, the groom gives the bride a ring during the *Kiddushin* as a gift to her, and an exchange of rings at that time may be seen as negating this act of marriage. Therefore it is not customary for the bride and groom to exchange rings at the *Kiddushin*. However, Suzanne and Andy both feel that it is important to both wear wedding rings as a sign of their commitment to each other. Therefore, in a separate act during the *Nisuin*, Suzanne will give Andy a wedding ring as a sign of her love for him.

Even in our most joyous moments, it is incumbent upon us to remember the suffering that has been experienced in the world and our responsibility to "*Tikun Olam*," repairing the world where we find it to be broken." In engaging in celebration and joy for the newly married couple, we first take a minute to sing "*Im Eshacheich Yerushalayim*" ("If I forget you, oh Jerusalem"). This is followed by the final part of the wedding ceremony, the well-known breaking of the glass, remembering the destruction of the Holy Temple in Jerusalem in

70 C.E. After Andy crushes the glass with his foot, it is customary to shout "Mazel Tov!" ("congratulations, good luck").

After the breaking of the glass, guests joyously sing "*Od Yishama*" to the couple as they walk up the aisle. This is a ubiquitous wedding song, sung earlier at the Bedekin and likely sung again during the wedding day.

Yichud (Seclusion)

At the conclusion of the ceremony, Suzanne and Andy are escorted to a private room, where they spend a few moments alone for the first time as husband and wife. Two witnesses guard the door to make sure that this private time is not interrupted, enabling the couple time to take in the moment together and to reflect on the significance of the day. Also at this point, the couple is able to break the fast that they have kept all day.

Celebration

It is a particular mitzvah (commandment) in Judaism to rejoice with the bride and groom at their wedding through song and dance. The dancing at our wedding is in the form of group circle dancing. We hope that you will join us and be a part of the unique and joyous sense of community and celebration created by this group dancing. In keeping with the tradition at Bais Abraham Congregation, we ask that men and women dance separately during the reception.

The dancing may be interrupted for "shtick," random merry-making for the enjoyment of the bride and groom. Feel free to share your own jokes and funny dancing moves! It is also typical during the dancing to lift the bride and groom up in chairs accompanied by much singing and dancing.

Wedding *Seudah* (The Wedding Meal)

The wedding meal also carries special significance and incorporates specific traditions. This is a festive meal, which begins with a *hamotzie* (blessing over bread). This is preceded by a ritual washing of hands, which guests are welcome to join in if it is their custom. When the meal is complete, we will recite the *Birkat Hamazon* (a grace after meals). A grace after meals is commonly recited after every meal, but at a wedding, a special grace is recited that concludes with the *Sheva Berachot*, the same seven blessings recited under the chuppah. The text for the *hamotzie*, *Birkat Hamazon*, and *Sheva Berachot* can be found in the small books at each place setting during the meal. At the end of the wedding, guests are welcome to take these books (known as "benchers") home with them.

Wedding Songs and Blessings

Sheva Berachot *(Seven Blessings)*
Blessed are You, Lord our God, King of the Universe, Creator of the fruit of the vine.

Blessed are You, Lord our God, King of the Universe, Who created everything for His glory.

Blessed are You, Lord our God, King of the Universe, Creator of man.

Blessed are You, Lord our God, King of the Universe, Who created man in His image, in the image of His likeness, and provided for perpetuation of His kind. Blessed are You, Who formed man.

Let the barren city (Jerusalem) be jubilantly happy and joyful at her joyous reunion with her children. Blessed are You, Who fills Zion with the joy of her children.

May You gladden the loving couple as You gladdened Your creations in the Garden of Eden of old. Blessed are You, Who fills the groom and bride with joy.

Blessed are You, Lord our God, King of the Universe, Who created joy and celebration, groom and bride, rejoicing, jubilation, pleasure and delight, love and brotherhood, peace and friendship. May there soon be heard, Lord our God, in the cities of Judah and in the streets of Jerusalem, the sound of joy and the sound of celebration, the voice of a groom and the voice of a bride, the happy shouting of grooms from bridal canopies, and of young men from their feasts of song. Blessed are You Who makes the groom and bride rejoice together.

Od Yishama
Hebrew transliteration:

"Od yishama, b'arei Yehuda, u'vechutzot Yerushalayim, kol sason v'kol simcha, kol chatan v'kol kallah"

Translation:

"Again may these be heard in the cities of Judah and in the streets of Jerusalem, the voice of gladness and the voice of happiness, the voice of groom and the voice of the bride"

Siman Tov
Hebrew transliteration:

"Siman tov u'mazel tov, mazel tov u'siman tov, yehei lanu, yehei lanu, u'lechol Yisroel"

Translation:

"It is a good sign and good luck for us and for all of Israel"

Hebrew transliteration of Blessing #7

"Baruch Ata Hashem, Eloheinu Melech haolam, Asher barah sason v'simcha, chatan v'kallah, gila rina, ditza v'chedva, ahavah v'achava, v'shalom v're'ut. Mehera Hashem Eloheinu yishama b'arei Yehudah u'vechutzot Yerushalayim, kol sason v' kol simcha, kol chatan v'kol kallah, kol mitzhalot chatanim mechupatam, u'nearim mimishte neginatam. Baruch Ata Hashem mesame'ach chatan im hakalah."

APPENDIX D

Books and Websites

Resources on Jewish Weddings

Books

Adler, Rachel. *Engendering Judaism.* Contains a chapter on Brit Ahuvim, a liberal Jewish wedding ceremony.

Diamant, Anita. *The New Jewish Wedding.* A book on less traditional Jewish weddings.

Kaplan, Aryeh. *Made in Heaven.* A very detailed book on the halachot of Jewish weddings.

Lamm, Maurice. *The Jewish Way in Love and Marriage.* A classic traditional book on the halacha, Jewish laws and customs, of love and marriage.

Websites

Chabad.org

Contains a Jewish calendar for wedding planning and lots of other Jewish wedding and life information.

www.chabad.org

Jofa.org

The website of the Jewish Orthodox Feminist Alliance. Contains articles on women's roles within traditional halachic weddings as well as general information about Jewish family life and family purity laws.

www.jofa.org

Mazon.org

Website through which to donate part of your wedding budget to battle hunger.

www.mazon.org

Mazornet

Website with information about Jewish genetic diseases and testing.

www.mazornet.com

Rabbis.org

Website of the Orthodox Rabbinical Council of America; contains copies of the halachic prenuptial agreement and classical ketubah text. Resource for obtaining a get, a religious divorce.

www.rabbis.org

Resources on Building a Jewish home

Books

Greenberg, Blu. *How to Run a Jewish Household*. Contains a chapter on Jewish weddings as well as all other lifecycles and holidays, traditional and accessible.

Greenberg, Irving. *The Jewish Way: Living the Holidays*. A deeper view of the Jewish holidays.

Zion, Noam, and David D. Shon. *A Different Night*. A very accessible family hagadah for Passover.

Websites

Aish.com

Lots of information about Jewish laws and customs

www.aish.com

Resources for Kosher Information

Books

Apisdorf, Shimon. *Kosher for the Curious but Clueless*. An accurate and accessible handbook on keeping kosher.

Websites

Star-k.org

A kashrut website with much information about kosher products

www.star-k.org

crcweb.org

Website of the Chicago Rabbinical Council on kosher products and caterers

www.crcweb.org

Kosherwine.com

Website for ordering hard-to-get kosher wine

www.kosherwine.com

OU.org

Website of the Orthodox Union one of the nations largest kosher supervisors

www.ou.org

Resources on the Laws of Mikvah and Family Purity

Books

Kaplan, Aryeh. *Waters of Eden: The Mystery of the Mikvah*. An overview of the laws and meaning behind the mikvah, purity and impurity.

Zimmerman, Deena. *A Lifetime Companion to the Laws of Jewish Family Life*. Guide to laws of family purity with an eye to its medical and psychological sides.

Websites

Yoatzot.org

A website for questions regarding the details of family purity laws

www.yoatzot.org

Mikvah.org

A website of *mikvah* information and essays that includes a worldwide *mikvah* directory

www.mikvah.org

Resources on the Torah Portions and Divar Torahs

Books

Ben David, Aryeh. *Around the Shabbat Table.* Divar Torahs and thought questions on each of the Torah portions.

Websites

Artscroll.com

A publisher of Jewish books and Torahs with commentary

www.artscroll.com

Tanach.org

Lectures on the weekly Torah portion

www.tanach.org

Torah.org

A website containing summaries of Divar Torahs on each weekly portion

www.torah.org

Carpool Curriculum

A website containing thoughtful questions about the weekly Torah portion for discussion with children

www.jewishcurrentevents.com

Index

THE EVERYTHING® SERIES!

BUSINESS & PERSONAL FINANCE

Everything® Accounting Book
Everything® Budgeting Book, 2nd Ed.
Everything® Business Planning Book
Everything® Coaching and Mentoring Book, 2nd Ed.
Everything® Fundraising Book
Everything® Get Out of Debt Book
Everything® Grant Writing Book, 2nd Ed.
Everything® Guide to Buying Foreclosures
Everything® Guide to Fundraising, $15.95
Everything® Guide to Mortgages
Everything® Guide to Personal Finance for Single Mothers
Everything® Home-Based Business Book, 2nd Ed.
Everything® Homebuying Book, 3rd Ed., $15.95
Everything® Homeselling Book, 2nd Ed.
Everything® Human Resource Management Book
Everything® Improve Your Credit Book
Everything® Investing Book, 2nd Ed.
Everything® Landlording Book
Everything® Leadership Book, 2nd Ed.
Everything® Managing People Book, 2nd Ed.
Everything® Negotiating Book
Everything® Online Auctions Book
Everything® Online Business Book
Everything® Personal Finance Book
Everything® Personal Finance in Your 20s & 30s Book, 2nd Ed.
Everything® Personal Finance in Your 40s & 50s Book, $15.95
Everything® Project Management Book, 2nd Ed.
Everything® Real Estate Investing Book
Everything® Retirement Planning Book
Everything® Robert's Rules Book, $7.95
Everything® Selling Book
Everything® Start Your Own Business Book, 2nd Ed.
Everything® Wills & Estate Planning Book

COOKING

Everything® Barbecue Cookbook
Everything® Bartender's Book, 2nd Ed., $9.95
Everything® Calorie Counting Cookbook
Everything® Cheese Book
Everything® Chinese Cookbook
Everything® Classic Recipes Book
Everything® Cocktail Parties & Drinks Book
Everything® College Cookbook
Everything® Cooking for Baby and Toddler Book
Everything® Diabetes Cookbook
Everything® Easy Gourmet Cookbook
Everything® Fondue Cookbook
Everything® Food Allergy Cookbook, $15.95
Everything® Fondue Party Book
Everything® Gluten-Free Cookbook
Everything® Glycemic Index Cookbook
Everything® Grilling Cookbook
Everything® Healthy Cooking for Parties Book, $15.95
Everything® Holiday Cookbook
Everything® Indian Cookbook
Everything® Lactose-Free Cookbook
Everything® Low-Cholesterol Cookbook
Everything® Low-Fat High-Flavor Cookbook, 2nd Ed., $15.95
Everything® Low-Salt Cookbook
Everything® Meals for a Month Cookbook
Everything® Meals on a Budget Cookbook
Everything® Mediterranean Cookbook
Everything® Mexican Cookbook
Everything® No Trans Fat Cookbook
Everything® One-Pot Cookbook, 2nd Ed., $15.95
Everything® Organic Cooking for Baby & Toddler Book, $15.95
Everything® Pizza Cookbook
Everything® Quick Meals Cookbook, 2nd Ed., $15.95
Everything® Slow Cooker Cookbook
Everything® Slow Cooking for a Crowd Cookbook
Everything® Soup Cookbook
Everything® Stir-Fry Cookbook
Everything® Sugar-Free Cookbook
Everything® Tapas and Small Plates Cookbook
Everything® Tex-Mex Cookbook
Everything® Thai Cookbook
Everything® Vegetarian Cookbook
Everything® Whole-Grain, High-Fiber Cookbook
Everything® Wild Game Cookbook
Everything® Wine Book, 2nd Ed.

GAMES

Everything® 15-Minute Sudoku Book, $9.95
Everything® 30-Minute Sudoku Book, $9.95
Everything® Bible Crosswords Book, $9.95
Everything® Blackjack Strategy Book
Everything® Brain Strain Book, $9.95
Everything® Bridge Book
Everything® Card Games Book
Everything® Card Tricks Book, $9.95
Everything® Casino Gambling Book, 2nd Ed.
Everything® Chess Basics Book
Everything® Christmas Crosswords Book, $9.95
Everything® Craps Strategy Book
Everything® Crossword and Puzzle Book
Everything® Crosswords and Puzzles for Quote Lovers Book, $9.95
Everything® Crossword Challenge Book
Everything® Crosswords for the Beach Book, $9.95
Everything® Cryptic Crosswords Book, $9.95
Everything® Cryptograms Book, $9.95
Everything® Easy Crosswords Book
Everything® Easy Kakuro Book, $9.95
Everything® Easy Large-Print Crosswords Book
Everything® Games Book, 2nd Ed.
Everything® Giant Book of Crosswords
Everything® Giant Sudoku Book, $9.95
Everything® Giant Word Search Book
Everything® Kakuro Challenge Book, $9.95
Everything® Large-Print Crossword Challenge Book
Everything® Large-Print Crosswords Book
Everything® Large-Print Travel Crosswords Book
Everything® Lateral Thinking Puzzles Book, $9.95
Everything® Literary Crosswords Book, $9.95
Everything® Mazes Book
Everything® Memory Booster Puzzles Book, $9.95
Everything® Movie Crosswords Book, $9.95
Everything® Music Crosswords Book, $9.95
Everything® Online Poker Book
Everything® Pencil Puzzles Book, $9.95
Everything® Poker Strategy Book
Everything® Pool & Billiards Book
Everything® Puzzles for Commuters Book, $9.95
Everything® Puzzles for Dog Lovers Book, $9.95
Everything® Sports Crosswords Book, $9.95
Everything® Test Your IQ Book, $9.95
Everything® Texas Hold 'Em Book, $9.95
Everything® Travel Crosswords Book, $9.95
Everything® Travel Mazes Book, $9.95
Everything® Travel Word Search Book, $9.95
Everything® TV Crosswords Book, $9.95
Everything® Word Games Challenge Book
Everything® Word Scramble Book
Everything® Word Search Book

HEALTH

Everything® Alzheimer's Book
Everything® Diabetes Book
Everything® First Aid Book, $9.95
Everything® Green Living Book
Everything® Health Guide to Addiction and Recovery
Everything® Health Guide to Adult Bipolar Disorder
Everything® Health Guide to Arthritis
Everything® Health Guide to Controlling Anxiety
Everything® Health Guide to Depression
Everything® Health Guide to Diabetes, 2nd Ed.
Everything® Health Guide to Fibromyalgia
Everything® Health Guide to Menopause, 2nd Ed.
Everything® Health Guide to Migraines
Everything® Health Guide to Multiple Sclerosis
Everything® Health Guide to OCD
Everything® Health Guide to PMS
Everything® Health Guide to Postpartum Care
Everything® Health Guide to Thyroid Disease
Everything® Hypnosis Book
Everything® Low Cholesterol Book
Everything® Menopause Book
Everything® Nutrition Book
Everything® Reflexology Book
Everything® Stress Management Book
Everything® Superfoods Book, $15.95

HISTORY

Everything® American Government Book
Everything® American History Book, 2nd Ed.
Everything® American Revolution Book, $15.95
Everything® Civil War Book
Everything® Freemasons Book
Everything® Irish History & Heritage Book
Everything® World War II Book, 2nd Ed.

HOBBIES

Everything® Candlemaking Book
Everything® Cartooning Book
Everything® Coin Collecting Book
Everything® Digital Photography Book, 2nd Ed.

Everything® Drawing Book
Everything® Family Tree Book, 2nd Ed.
Everything® Guide to Online Genealogy, $15.95
Everything® Knitting Book
Everything® Knots Book
Everything® Photography Book
Everything® Quilting Book
Everything® Sewing Book
Everything® Soapmaking Book, 2nd Ed.
Everything® Woodworking Book

HOME IMPROVEMENT

Everything® Feng Shui Book
Everything® Feng Shui Decluttering Book, $9.95
Everything® Fix-It Book
Everything® Green Living Book
Everything® Home Decorating Book
Everything® Home Storage Solutions Book
Everything® Homebuilding Book
Everything® Organize Your Home Book, 2nd Ed.

KIDS' BOOKS

All titles are $7.95

Everything® Fairy Tales Book, $14.95
Everything® Kids' Animal Puzzle & Activity Book
Everything® Kids' Astronomy Book
Everything® Kids' Baseball Book, 5th Ed.
Everything® Kids' Bible Trivia Book
Everything® Kids' Bugs Book
Everything® Kids' Cars and Trucks Puzzle and Activity Book
Everything® Kids' Christmas Puzzle & Activity Book
Everything® Kids' Connect the Dots Puzzle and Activity Book
Everything® Kids' Cookbook, 2nd Ed.
Everything® Kids' Crazy Puzzles Book
Everything® Kids' Dinosaurs Book
Everything® Kids' Dragons Puzzle and Activity Book
Everything® Kids' Environment Book $7.95
Everything® Kids' Fairies Puzzle and Activity Book
Everything® Kids' First Spanish Puzzle and Activity Book
Everything® Kids' Football Book
Everything® Kids' Geography Book
Everything® Kids' Gross Cookbook
Everything® Kids' Gross Hidden Pictures Book
Everything® Kids' Gross Jokes Book
Everything® Kids' Gross Mazes Book
Everything® Kids' Gross Puzzle & Activity Book
Everything® Kids' Halloween Puzzle & Activity Book
Everything® Kids' Hanukkah Puzzle and Activity Book
Everything® Kids' Hidden Pictures Book
Everything® Kids' Horses Book
Everything® Kids' Joke Book
Everything® Kids' Knock Knock Book
Everything® Kids' Learning French Book
Everything® Kids' Learning Spanish Book
Everything® Kids' Magical Science Experiments Book
Everything® Kids' Math Puzzles Book
Everything® Kids' Mazes Book
Everything® Kids' Money Book, 2nd Ed.
Everything® Kids' Mummies, Pharaoh's, and Pyramids Puzzle and Activity Book
Everything® Kids' Nature Book
Everything® Kids' Pirates Puzzle and Activity Book
Everything® Kids' Presidents Book
Everything® Kids' Princess Puzzle and Activity Book
Everything® Kids' Puzzle Book
Everything® Kids' Racecars Puzzle and Activity Book
Everything® Kids' Riddles & Brain Teasers Book
Everything® Kids' Science Experiments Book
Everything® Kids' Sharks Book
Everything® Kids' Soccer Book
Everything® Kids' Spelling Book
Everything® Kids' Spies Puzzle and Activity Book
Everything® Kids' States Book
Everything® Kids' Travel Activity Book
Everything® Kids' Word Search Puzzle and Activity Book

LANGUAGE

Everything® Conversational Japanese Book with CD, $19.95
Everything® French Grammar Book
Everything® French Phrase Book, $9.95
Everything® French Verb Book, $9.95
Everything® German Phrase Book, $9.95
Everything® German Practice Book with CD, $19.95
Everything® Inglés Book
Everything® Intermediate Spanish Book with CD, $19.95
Everything® Italian Phrase Book, $9.95
Everything® Italian Practice Book with CD, $19.95
Everything® Learning Brazilian Portuguese Book with CD, $19.95
Everything® Learning French Book with CD, 2nd Ed., $19.95
Everything® Learning German Book
Everything® Learning Italian Book
Everything® Learning Latin Book
Everything® Learning Russian Book with CD, $19.95
Everything® Learning Spanish Book
Everything® Learning Spanish Book with CD, 2nd Ed., $19.95
Everything® Russian Practice Book with CD, $19.95
Everything® Sign Language Book, $15.95
Everything® Spanish Grammar Book
Everything® Spanish Phrase Book, $9.95
Everything® Spanish Practice Book with CD, $19.95
Everything® Spanish Verb Book, $9.95
Everything® Speaking Mandarin Chinese Book with CD, $19.95

MUSIC

Everything® Bass Guitar Book with CD, $19.95
Everything® Drums Book with CD, $19.95
Everything® Guitar Book with CD, 2nd Ed., $19.95
Everything® Guitar Chords Book with CD, $19.95
Everything® Guitar Scales Book with CD, $19.95
Everything® Harmonica Book with CD, $15.95
Everything® Home Recording Book
Everything® Music Theory Book with CD, $19.95
Everything® Reading Music Book with CD, $19.95
Everything® Rock & Blues Guitar Book with CD, $19.95
Everything® Rock & Blues Piano Book with CD, $19.95
Everything® Rock Drums Book with CD, $19.95
Everything® Singing Book with CD, $19.95
Everything® Songwriting Book

NEW AGE

Everything® Astrology Book, 2nd Ed.
Everything® Birthday Personology Book
Everything® Celtic Wisdom Book, $15.95
Everything® Dreams Book, 2nd Ed.
Everything® Law of Attraction Book, $15.95
Everything® Love Signs Book, $9.95
Everything® Love Spells Book, $9.95
Everything® Palmistry Book
Everything® Psychic Book
Everything® Reiki Book
Everything® Sex Signs Book, $9.95
Everything® Spells & Charms Book, 2nd Ed.
Everything® Tarot Book, 2nd Ed.
Everything® Toltec Wisdom Book
Everything® Wicca & Witchcraft Book, 2nd Ed.

PARENTING

Everything® Baby Names Book, 2nd Ed.
Everything® Baby Shower Book, 2nd Ed.
Everything® Baby Sign Language Book with DVD
Everything® Baby's First Year Book
Everything® Birthing Book
Everything® Breastfeeding Book
Everything® Father-to-Be Book
Everything® Father's First Year Book
Everything® Get Ready for Baby Book, 2nd Ed.
Everything® Get Your Baby to Sleep Book, $9.95
Everything® Getting Pregnant Book
Everything® Guide to Pregnancy Over 35
Everything® Guide to Raising a One-Year-Old
Everything® Guide to Raising a Two-Year-Old
Everything® Guide to Raising Adolescent Boys
Everything® Guide to Raising Adolescent Girls
Everything® Mother's First Year Book
Everything® Parent's Guide to Childhood Illnesses
Everything® Parent's Guide to Children and Divorce
Everything® Parent's Guide to Children with ADD/ADHD
Everything® Parent's Guide to Children with Asperger's Syndrome
Everything® Parent's Guide to Children with Anxiety
Everything® Parent's Guide to Children with Asthma
Everything® Parent's Guide to Children with Autism
Everything® Parent's Guide to Children with Bipolar Disorder
Everything® Parent's Guide to Children with Depression
Everything® Parent's Guide to Children with Dyslexia
Everything® Parent's Guide to Children with Juvenile Diabetes
Everything® Parent's Guide to Children with OCD
Everything® Parent's Guide to Positive Discipline
Everything® Parent's Guide to Raising Boys
Everything® Parent's Guide to Raising Girls
Everything® Parent's Guide to Raising Siblings
Everything® Parent's Guide to Raising Your Adopted Child
Everything® Parent's Guide to Sensory Integration Disorder
Everything® Parent's Guide to Tantrums
Everything® Parent's Guide to the Strong-Willed Child
Everything® Parenting a Teenager Book
Everything® Potty Training Book, $9.95
Everything® Pregnancy Book, 3rd Ed.
Everything® Pregnancy Fitness Book
Everything® Pregnancy Nutrition Book
Everything® Pregnancy Organizer, 2nd Ed., $16.95
Everything® Toddler Activities Book
Everything® Toddler Book
Everything® Tween Book
Everything® Twins, Triplets, and More Book

PETS

Everything® Aquarium Book
Everything® Boxer Book
Everything® Cat Book, 2nd Ed.
Everything® Chihuahua Book
Everything® Cooking for Dogs Book
Everything® Dachshund Book
Everything® Dog Book, 2nd Ed.
Everything® Dog Grooming Book

- Everything® Dog Obedience Book
- Everything® Dog Owner's Organizer, $16.95
- Everything® Dog Training and Tricks Book
- Everything® German Shepherd Book
- Everything® Golden Retriever Book
- **Everything® Horse Book, 2nd Ed., $15.95**
- Everything® Horse Care Book
- Everything® Horseback Riding Book
- Everything® Labrador Retriever Book
- Everything® Poodle Book
- Everything® Pug Book
- Everything® Puppy Book
- Everything® Small Dogs Book
- Everything® Tropical Fish Book
- Everything® Yorkshire Terrier Book

REFERENCE

- Everything® American Presidents Book
- Everything® Blogging Book
- Everything® Build Your Vocabulary Book, $9.95
- Everything® Car Care Book
- Everything® Classical Mythology Book
- Everything® Da Vinci Book
- Everything® Einstein Book
- Everything® Enneagram Book
- Everything® Etiquette Book, 2nd Ed.
- **Everything® Family Christmas Book, $15.95**
- Everything® Guide to C. S. Lewis & Narnia
- **Everything® Guide to Divorce, 2nd Ed., $15.95**
- Everything® Guide to Edgar Allan Poe
- Everything® Guide to Understanding Philosophy
- Everything® Inventions and Patents Book
- Everything® Jacqueline Kennedy Onassis Book
- Everything® John F. Kennedy Book
- Everything® Mafia Book
- Everything® Martin Luther King Jr. Book
- Everything® Pirates Book
- Everything® Private Investigation Book
- Everything® Psychology Book
- Everything® Public Speaking Book, $9.95
- Everything® Shakespeare Book, 2nd Ed.

RELIGION

- Everything® Angels Book
- Everything® Bible Book
- Everything® Bible Study Book with CD, $19.95
- Everything® Buddhism Book
- Everything® Catholicism Book
- Everything® Christianity Book
- Everything® Gnostic Gospels Book
- **Everything® Hinduism Book, $15.95**
- Everything® History of the Bible Book
- Everything® Jesus Book
- Everything® Jewish History & Heritage Book
- Everything® Judaism Book
- Everything® Kabbalah Book
- Everything® Koran Book
- Everything® Mary Book
- Everything® Mary Magdalene Book
- Everything® Prayer Book
- Everything® Saints Book, 2nd Ed.
- Everything® Torah Book
- Everything® Understanding Islam Book
- Everything® Women of the Bible Book
- Everything® World's Religions Book

SCHOOL & CAREERS

- Everything® Career Tests Book
- Everything® College Major Test Book
- Everything® College Survival Book, 2nd Ed.
- Everything® Cover Letter Book, 2nd Ed.
- Everything® Filmmaking Book
- Everything® Get-a-Job Book, 2nd Ed.
- Everything® Guide to Being a Paralegal
- Everything® Guide to Being a Personal Trainer
- Everything® Guide to Being a Real Estate Agent
- Everything® Guide to Being a Sales Rep
- Everything® Guide to Being an Event Planner
- Everything® Guide to Careers in Health Care
- Everything® Guide to Careers in Law Enforcement
- Everything® Guide to Government Jobs
- Everything® Guide to Starting and Running a Catering Business
- Everything® Guide to Starting and Running a Restaurant
- **Everything® Guide to Starting and Running a Retail Store**
- Everything® Job Interview Book, 2nd Ed.
- Everything® New Nurse Book
- Everything® New Teacher Book
- Everything® Paying for College Book
- Everything® Practice Interview Book
- Everything® Resume Book, 3rd Ed.
- Everything® Study Book

SELF-HELP

- Everything® Body Language Book
- Everything® Dating Book, 2nd Ed.
- Everything® Great Sex Book
- **Everything® Guide to Caring for Aging Parents, $15.95**
- Everything® Self-Esteem Book
- **Everything® Self-Hypnosis Book, $9.95**
- Everything® Tantric Sex Book

SPORTS & FITNESS

- Everything® Easy Fitness Book
- Everything® Fishing Book
- **Everything® Guide to Weight Training, $15.95**
- Everything® Krav Maga for Fitness Book
- Everything® Running Book, 2nd Ed.
- **Everything® Triathlon Training Book, $15.95**

TRAVEL

- Everything® Family Guide to Coastal Florida
- Everything® Family Guide to Cruise Vacations
- Everything® Family Guide to Hawaii
- Everything® Family Guide to Las Vegas, 2nd Ed.
- Everything® Family Guide to Mexico
- Everything® Family Guide to New England, 2nd Ed.
- Everything® Family Guide to New York City, 3rd Ed.
- **Everything® Family Guide to Northern California and Lake Tahoe**
- Everything® Family Guide to RV Travel & Campgrounds
- Everything® Family Guide to the Caribbean
- Everything® Family Guide to the Disneyland® Resort, California Adventure®, Universal Studios®, and the Anaheim Area, 2nd Ed.
- Everything® Family Guide to the Walt Disney World Resort®, Universal Studios®, and Greater Orlando, 5th Ed.
- Everything® Family Guide to Timeshares
- Everything® Family Guide to Washington D.C., 2nd Ed.

WEDDINGS

- Everything® Bachelorette Party Book, $9.95
- Everything® Bridesmaid Book, $9.95
- Everything® Destination Wedding Book
- Everything® Father of the Bride Book, $9.95
- **Everything® Green Wedding Book, $15.95**
- Everything® Groom Book, $9.95
- **Everything® Jewish Wedding Book, 2nd Ed., $15.95**
- Everything® Mother of the Bride Book, $9.95
- Everything® Outdoor Wedding Book
- Everything® Wedding Book, 3rd Ed.
- Everything® Wedding Checklist, $9.95
- Everything® Wedding Etiquette Book, $9.95
- Everything® Wedding Organizer, 2nd Ed., $16.95
- Everything® Wedding Shower Book, $9.95
- **Everything® Wedding Vows Book,3rd Ed., $9.95**
- Everything® Wedding Workout Book
- Everything® Weddings on a Budget Book, 2nd Ed., $9.95

WRITING

- Everything® Creative Writing Book
- Everything® Get Published Book, 2nd Ed.
- Everything® Grammar and Style Book, 2nd Ed.
- Everything® Guide to Magazine Writing
- Everything® Guide to Writing a Book Proposal
- Everything® Guide to Writing a Novel
- Everything® Guide to Writing Children's Books
- Everything® Guide to Writing Copy
- Everything® Guide to Writing Graphic Novels
- Everything® Guide to Writing Research Papers
- **Everything® Guide to Writing a Romance Novel, $15.95**
- Everything® Improve Your Writing Book, 2nd Ed.
- Everything® Writing Poetry Book

Available wherever books are sold! To order, call 800-258-0929, or visit us at ***www.adamsmedia.com.***

Bolded titles are new additions to the series.
All Everything® books are priced at $12.95 or $14.95, unless otherwise stated. Prices subject to change without notice.